Rick has been a journalist and writer for over fifteen years. He is the winner of the 2013 Kennedy Award for Young Journalist of the Year and the 2017 Kennedy Award for Outstanding Columnist. In 2019, Rick left *The Australian* where he worked as the social affairs writer with a particular focus on social policy and is now a senior reporter for the *Saturday Paper*. Rick regularly appears on television, radio and panels across both the ABC and commercial networks discussing politics, the media, writing and social policy.

MY YEAR OF LIVING VULNERABLY

RICK MORTON

Fourth Estate

Fourth Estate
An imprint of HarperCollins*Publishers*

HarperCollins*Publishers*
Australia • Brazil • Canada • France • Germany • Holland • Hungary
India • Italy • Japan • Mexico • New Zealand • Poland • Spain • Sweden
Switzerland • United Kingdom • United States of America

First published in Australia in 2021
by HarperCollins*Publishers* Australia Pty Limited
Level 13, 201 Elizabeth Street, Sydney NSW 2000
ABN 36 009 913 517
harpercollins.com.au

A catalogue record for this book is available from the National Library of Australia.

ISBN 978 1 4607 5911 0 (paperback)
ISBN 978 1 4607 1285 6 (ebook)
ISBN 978 1 4607 8654 3 (audiobook)

Cover design by George Saad
Author photograph by Dany Weus
Typeset in Adobe Garamond Pro by Kirby Jones
Printed and bound in Australia by McPherson's Printing Group
The papers used by HarperCollins in the manufacture of this book are a natural, recyclable product made from wood grown in sustainable plantation forests. The fibre source and manufacturing processes meet recognised international environmental standards, and carry certification.

To my sister, Lauryn
I wrote this for us

Here I understand what they call glory:
the right to love without limits.

– Albert Camus, 'Nuptials at Tipasa', *Nuptials*, 1938

Contents

Introduction

When I phoned my mum, Deb, to tell her I was writing a book about love she was overcome immediately with wheezing laughter.

'What, *you*?' she managed to ask, although the emphasis on 'you' was long and made it sound like it had been shouted by a ghost on a passing skateboard.

She had a point.

Since late childhood, love and I had been on poor terms.

Of all the gauntlets high school asked us to run, Valentine's Day was the one that challenged me the most. I wasn't smart enough then to latch on to the fact that it was an invention of marketing, and instead disliked it for how it made me an unwilling participant in love itself.

Of course, teenagers don't really understand what love is. The cruel stings of passion and jealousy do not match the grace and acceptance of true love any more than those first attempts at sex matched the elegant freestyle of later encounters.

As we neared graduation, most of the grade were engaged in figuring this stuff out. To attend any house party was a lot like trying to stack the glass display counter in a butcher's shop with the day's fresh cuts; just flesh and hands.

My fate, for what it's worth, was to avoid these embarrassing attempts at intimacy in favour of complete celibacy on account of being gay in a regional Queensland school. Gay and in the closet, moreover. Except for two occasions when secrecy demanded proactive misdirection, my lips remained sealed.

And though all I was really doing was deferring the awkward discovery tour until my mid-twenties (on the whole, not recommended), I was unable to escape the broader pursuits of the heart and, for all the desperate willing in the world, could not stop others from deciding that they loved me.

One year, on 14 February, I was handed a single yellow rose from a friend who had given it to me on behalf of another student, an anonymous admirer. Anonymous admirers are cowards who would absolutely give away your hiding location during a war if it meant they could better protect their own interests. In a sense, this is what this girl had done to me. I mean, who gives a rose in public, forcing the recipient to smuggle it back to the bag racks so that it can be hidden before people start gossiping about whether they have feelings? Monsters, that's who.

She may as well have given me a grenade with the pin released. Or anthrax.

This wasn't love. None of the rituals we practised as teenagers met the criteria for romantic love, but my reaction to this one act exposed the weakness in the scaffolding that would bring me down later in life.

The rose, with its delicate assemblage of yellow petals and disappointing thorns, was an admission of vulnerability because it signalled that perhaps its new owner was a vessel for human emotion.

Emotions. What a horrible word, I thought. It sounded like the accidental bowel movement one of my then classmates had during computer studies. In my extended family, we didn't love anything. It was a necessary precondition of survival in a world that punished vulnerability. Animals died, so we did not love them. Humans erred, so we did not love them. Friends, well, you only loved your friends if you were queer or dying.

Although I had, unfortunately, turned out to be gay, I was determined to uphold the rest of the Morton family legacy by turning my feelings into a misplaced work ethic – like in origami when you set out to make a swan and end up with a chest of drawers.

There were darker overtones here that my teenage self had not managed to recognise, largely because the work required to recognise them was intricate, substantial and largely beyond me.

Through a combination of knowing and subconscious necessity, I had grown afraid of exposing my emotional hinterland to the world because I knew, in my essence, that doing so would mark me for destruction.

This rose might have seemed innocent and entirely irrelevant to that bigger project of self-protection, but another thing I had learned was this: the smallest transgressions must be rigorously policed because the whole falls in parts.

There could be no leave passes, not even for telling my mum I loved her. I did – more than anything else in the world – but saying so out loud made my insides twist in uncomfortable ways. It was an opening. A small one, true, and one most people everywhere are willing to allow. Even the tough boys in gangs I saw on television loved their mothers and told them so, before opening fire in a drug deal gone wrong and going to prison.

Even them.

Where had I learned this shrinking behaviour?

My first pet was a blue budgerigar called Pretty Boy, a name I had been allowed to choose. On this evidence, my natural state must have been one of alarming openness and soft edges. I mean, really, what kind of a name is *Pretty Boy*?

Once, on a school holiday, we took him with us up the coast and decided to visit Steve Irwin's family zoo at Beerwah on the way home. We couldn't leave the bird in the car, obviously, so we asked the lovely people at the zoo if they could mind him for us in the office.

This was the home of *the* Crocodile Hunter – he was there that day, feeding the remnant dinosaurs with his mate Wes – and the place itself featured an assortment of other deadly reptiles and spiders. Even the tortoise, Harriet, had been alive at the time of Charles Darwin and in that small detail managed to take on the mantle of an interesting creature.

And here we were, the gall of it, asking predator wranglers to budgie-sit my tiny parrot with the weak name.

I knew the Welsh were fond of sending canaries down the mines but, given a few years, there was no way I would let Pretty Boy act as a sort of early warning system for the exposed flesh of my psyche.

The boy who named that bird grew into a young man who was alert to being found out; as gay, as loving, as vulnerable. I weep for that child because in his desire to hide himself he was forced to cut out every permutation of love, every last gorgeous edge of it. As if it were a tumour.

That's the crime of it, that excision of beauty.

We make mistakes of nomenclature if we think love is just one thing and not, say, the way the light makes little furnaces of the rusted leaves when it streaks through the sky at an angle in late autumn afternoons. Bring me the person who says love is just that spark of romantic desire between human beings and I will show them Maxwell's equations describing electromagnetism or the weight of grief at a funeral. We could also look, and I mean really look, at the face of a baby as it recognises you on a second visit, and study the dive of a peregrine falcon as it tucks its wings into the body and rockets to the ground.

Falcons used to do this on the cattle station where I grew up, hurtling through space until they aborted at the last moment. Mum hated how they did this because they landed next to the large cages where she housed her budgerigars and this death-tilt upset the other birds; there's no denying there was a certain chaos that filled the air afterwards, but I always found it beautiful. For any of us to make an object that aerodynamic we'd need formulas and a long testing tunnel, like aerospace and motorcar companies use, but falcons simply evolved that way.

So, yes, add the theory of evolution to the list of love and its humble merchants. Any system that takes tens of thousands and millions of years to form the wing can only be truly appreciated through the prism of love. Think of it this way: love is the common ancestor of beauty and the sublime. It is the first entry in the tree of our own existence because, without it, there isn't any life at all.

Of course, in such a radical act of appreciation, we are also asked to confront the fact that evolution gave female spotted hyenas completely fused-shut vaginas (forcing them to give birth in an even more dangerous fashion than other animals: through their clitoris), as well as depriving a whole number of other species of waste management functions we take for granted, which gave rise to one of my favourite news headlines: 'A huge mouth and no anus – this could be our earliest known ancestor.'

Don't be fooled though, this is beautiful, too. Precisely because it challenges us in our thinking.

In his 1963 bestseller, *The Fire Next Time*, the African-American writer James Baldwin offered what I have come to view as the most complete proof-of-concept for love.

> Love takes off the masks that we fear we cannot live without and know we cannot live within. I use the word 'love' here not merely in the personal sense but as a state of being, or a state of grace – not in the infantile American sense of being made happy but in the tough and universal sense of quest and daring and growth.

In early 2019, I was diagnosed with complex post-traumatic stress disorder (complex PTSD), which is just a fancy way of saying that one of the people who should have loved me the most during childhood didn't.

I was impressed by this determination, not only because I had long assumed I was a simple man with basic problems (it's *complex* now), but because this condition underscored a theory I had been working on independently.

You see, I was born into a family already beset by generations of violence and its terrifying aftershocks. The cruelty of my own father's upbringing – the scion of a powerful family that owned a string of outback sheep and cattle stations – had turned him to stone. Some people continue the damage in the same old ways, with fists and anger, but he was too broken even for that.

His was a wounded silence that shattered people all the same. I've written about my family before, in my debut book *One Hundred Years of Dirt*, but spent so much energy focused on everyone else's trauma that I never noticed my own.

More specifically, I didn't know there was a name for what I had. And knowing that coloured in so much of what I had

body and brain worked in tandem to tell the other that I was under attack.

It always happens the same way.

The moment I find out my friend is seeing someone it is as if the world goes blurry. I can feel myself leave my own body. There is ringing in my ears and a sensation that has no equal in daily life but what I can only describe as 100,000 ants marching up from my feet along the length of my nervous system, nesting in my chest. It is the most agonising type of fear where death itself feels imminent.

After the first shock the only thing I care about is modelling. I need data, as much as possible, to run every conceivable simulation of how events will unfold. I do this to convince myself that there might be a way he doesn't leave me and, in so doing, confirm my fundamental truth: that I am unloveable.

But, if I am honest, these simulations are cooked from the beginning because really what I hope to establish is proof. I know I cannot be loved and these moments of despair are arranged so as to push this beyond reasonable doubt. If only I could prove it, perhaps then I might move on with my life.

What interests me about these episodes is that they never last for more than a couple of months at a time. I mean, thank God, because they feel like a lifetime. But if these men, my friends, enter into a stable relationship with the women they have started seeing, my fear vanishes. Like it never happened.

As if those months of furious internal dying were a total scam.

This only became obvious to me after yet another debilitating onset late in 2020, while I was writing this book. It's in *uncertainty* that I face psychological ruin. And I don't just mean a generic form of the unknown but the specific kind of insecurity that forces me to search, just like my boyhood self, for an answer to an impossible question.

Is anybody coming to save me?

As a seven-year-old I wandered the halls and rooms of our two-storey homestead for clues to my own demise. The governess on my father's lap. Him kissing her in the kitchen. Her with the stained bedsheets. His emotional distance. Strange mannerisms. The shock adults wear on their faces when they realise a small child has not been deceived.

All of them, clues.

And that was what I was still doing as an adult: searching the corridors of my own relationships for an evidentiary burden that could establish the original hurt.

The saddest thing about all of this, even now, is that I know it in the evolved part of my head but am captive to the sensations all the same. Trauma is not a memory. It is a Broadway production of the first hurt, a leg-kicking, show-stopping conflagration of the mind and body that needs no remembering. It is the thing. Each and every time.

During one moment of flailing, before I had figured any of this out, my closest friend hugged me and apologised. It was 2015, the year my precious foothold on sanity was lost.

'I'm so sorry I never told you I love you,' she said.

It was true, she hadn't, but neither had I. And I had thought I'd liked it that way: this unspoken agreement, this tacit knowledge that bound us.

What I had relied on as my key virtue, this mass of unfeeling, was in fact the thing that corroded my circuits and siphoned so much joy from my life that the outcome was inevitable, even if it was unintelligible to me at the time: I was broken and completely spent.

After that conversation with my friend, I felt marginally better. Was it because I'd told her that I loved her and that she'd said the same to me? Surely it wasn't that easy, I thought. But it was worth a shot.

I began telling everyone I loved them. Indiscriminately, at first. I would have moved on to objects such as fence posts and lawnmowers but for whatever reason there were still a lot of people in my life who cared about me and there was no time.

It was as if the colour had begun to run back into my world from the top of the frame, pooling at the bottom around the moss-covered rocks on one of my infrequent bush walks.

Before scientific studies explored the way language works as a defining principle, Ludwig Wittgenstein said: 'The borders of my language are the borders of my world.' We can only understand the bits of the world we have chosen to name, in other words.

Speaking of other words, the Inuit have a label for that specific feeling, while waiting for a friend or loved one, when you check to see if they have arrived yet: *Iktsuarpok*. The Germans coined *Geworfenheit* to describe that state of existence that comes after a person has been thrown into circumstances not of their choosing. Spaniards have one of the most beautiful words – *duende* – to describe the heightened sensation of passion or spirit, especially when it is linked with dance or art. And the Finnish, bless them, have a word for 'bouncy cushion satisfaction' – *Hyppytyynytyydytys* – to detail the distinct pleasure of sitting down for the first time in a comfortable chair.

University of East London positive psychology lecturer Tim Lomas started a list of such words (he calls it a 'positive lexicography'), which includes 'party pig', a delightful entry from the Dutch, and 'underpants intoxication' from the consistently entertaining Finnish people.

It's a fun exercise in its own right, but it proves Wittgenstein's point. Sure, we English speakers might have roundabout ways of describing the same feelings, but without the direct word for 'bouncy cushion satisfaction', the chairs that have given us such delight in our own lives remain largely unremarked upon.

And where we limit the language of love and all its forms, we squander the chance to experience those same sensations.

Having opened the door just a crack, I began to let the light wash in.

After more than a decade of concerted emptiness, guarding always against feeling, this was a small but new routine. I told people I loved them and tried very hard to believe them when they said the same to me. How I adored this renaissance of tiny joy.

It's not a cure. I can't tell you the number of times I've wanted to slug someone who says my at times crippling anxiety and suicidal ideation exist because I'm thinking about it all wrong. You know, just, kind of, think nicer?

I want, also, to hold parades for them. Celebratory parades, with streamers and confetti, that announce the long sought-after solution for acute mental illness has been discovered by the Darren or Mary or Karl who's made such a pronouncement. And though they all approach a level of serenity that borders on suspicious, we know it emerges from the lived experience of never having been told the trauma wormed deep into the grey matter of their brain is just *bad juju*.

This is, sadly, not that book. And, yes, I still have complex PTSD and a tendency to dissociate when it is triggered. It feels a lot like I'm in one of those extended sequences in war movies, after the bomb has gone off and the sound disappears and the world around is blurred.

What my rediscovery of love did do, however, is give me permission to do the work required to get better. Not cured, nor fixed or entirely healed. Just better.

It is only fitting. The condition is caused by an extreme lack of love and it makes sense that we should counter it by the intense, rigorous and scattergun application of love.

I practised random acts of kindness and targeted, precision acts of forgiveness – in the understanding that such acts would help me love myself. I learned to say the words out loud, over and over again, as if the phrase *I love you* were an animal's name, and calling it again and again would stop it walking over the threshold of a door and out of my life for good.

When I was in Year 10, I saw a pigeon get sucked into an air-conditioning vent in a shopping centre. *Shoonk.* The air filled with a burst of white and grey feathers. I imagined being the protagonist now in that vignette but instead of a pigeon, I hurled good grace and the ability to be awestruck by life into that vent and watched it coat the room.

I was Oprah, bestowing surprise gifts to audience members, but instead of giving cars, I gave abiding affection. *And you get warmth and attachment! And you get warmth and attachment! And you!* People think they want cars – and they do, to get to jobs and appointments in cities and regions where public transport has failed them. But what gets them into those cars, out of the house, out of *bed* for God's sake, is love.

I've been a news reporter for more than fifteen years. In journalism, we are trained to be cynical and distrusting. This has its uses in the political arena where there is more spin than an orbiting lazy susan, but I find it is a tool that fundamentally fails when applied to real human beings. People, the ones who are going about their lives and sampling survival as if at a buffet, should not be handled as such.

In my reporting job, covering social affairs from all corners, I traverse the full range of human suffering. Addiction, mental illness, entrenched intergenerational poverty, the trauma of institutions on the old and disabled. Grief. Injustice. Homelessness. The staggering hurt of hope offered and snatched away.

The way these individual deprivations coalesced was slow, at first. I couldn't see the common theme for the various tributaries. But, gradually, the waters of my understanding began to flow together, surging on and into my consciousness with urgency.

All of these different people had a unity about them. Their suffering had a unity. Whether it was their own or foisted on them by parents, family, friends, caregivers or *the system*, what these people all lacked was love.

This isn't some new-age moment of epiphany. It's right there, written into all their lives. Trace the lines back far enough and you will find someone who should have loved them and couldn't, which begat the perpetuation of neglect and emotional abuse down the generations. Go back far enough in any direction and the evidence is knotted together through family breakdown, abandonment and the stories of a thousand people who all wanted to be loved in one thousand specific ways, but who never were.

I saw this in my own life, too. There was a man, my father, who I believe wanted to love his children but was never shown how and was too frightened to discover it for himself. That fear destroyed his life and the damage was cast outward in the radius of the explosion. The shrapnel of that great terror lodged in everyone he held dear.

And what was he afraid of? Weakness.

Just like his boy who would follow.

In deciding to try to change this one fact about myself, I realised it couldn't be done alone. My story is not singular and there are, just maybe, ways back for each of us. We are all due a resurrection of feeling and emotion.

First, however, I had a more pressing concern to deal with.

You see, it started with my skin.

Touch

I had never met Jasmina but she'd agreed to cuddle me for forty-five minutes, which would unfairly shoot her up the leaderboard of my top ten longest cuddles.

Unfairly, I say, because she was charging me $150 for the privilege.

Though I might ordinarily wonder what was wrong with me, I couldn't help thinking of her: what is wrong with *you*? Why would you subject yourself to this?

A younger version of myself would have been deeply cynical of this approach to therapeutic healing. I would have dismissed it as a sex thing, like those adults who wear nappies. Or a gateway to a full-service cult, where the cuddles morph into indefinite servitude in northern New South Wales, the lush subtropics from which I will be forced to launder money and traffic cocaine or geckos.

I'm too young to end up on *A Current Affair*, I would have thought.

Of course, I'm older now. Wiser. Less cynical. And certainly not too young to end up on tabloid television as a result of an ill-advised venture into the hug industry. In fact, it is exactly the kind of thing that would befall me.

But this sort of opposition to softer experience is what I was trying to poison, so I was going to hug Jasmina and let her hold me for precisely three-quarters of an hour and nobody, certainly not myself, could convince me otherwise.

Touch is the first madness, if you're counting.

By the time I entered a sort of permanent grief in my mid-twenties it felt too late to arrest the slide into isolation, even if I knew what was wrong with me. Namely: everything. But there was, I believe, something that tipped me over the edge into a nervous breakdown. It was an accumulation of absences.

I hadn't been touched for more than half my life.

Clearly, I had been 'handled' in the way you might push a friend down a stairwell as a joke, or briefly brush the arm of another during a conversation. I had been grabbed in moments of perfunctory celebration, usually at school sports carnivals, and released just as quickly. There were jabs and punches, the short illicit thrills of contact with other boys and men my age, always in jest; always under the banner of 'muck-around' time because we all knew leniency only applied to male-on-male touch during specific windows of physical interaction.

So, yes, I had been handled in the way a piece of salmon is handled at the seafood counter: passed through the hands with full knowledge there was no love in the contact; no love, just a process that would eventually consume me.

What I mean to say is that I had not been *held* in any deep and secure sense by man or woman for well over a decade. I had refused to entertain thoughts of such physical intimacy and had even begun withdrawing from the most administrative of hugs, the ones you make when you greet friends.

My skin was silent.

By the start of 2020 I had already put off making the booking with Jasmina twice. *There is always time to be held,* I told myself. It's not like there was any reason to suspect a great global event would force us all to withhold the most elemental thing about us as a species, togetherness. And besides I was heading to Japan and New York to do research for the book and it would all just have to fall into place on my return.

Reader, this did not happen.

By the time I returned home in March 2020 touching was banned on account of a deadly virus outbreak that had consumed the world. It was in Australia.

It felt personal, if I'm honest. And I couldn't help but wonder: *did … did I cause the pandemic?*

Before being brought into the world as an infant, it is touch that allows the child to feel against the only backdrop with which it is familiar: the mother's heartbeat. *Da-dum. Da-dum.* It is the first of the five senses to develop. And in households made right by good parents, a hug can soothe the sharpest of emotional stings. Physical pain, too, is within the remit of touch's balm. There is comfort in contact. It was ever so. Skin on skin, pulse to pulse, one vulnerable exterior offered to another.

Many have misattributed this quote to Michelangelo: 'To touch can be to give life.' Still, his fresco *Creation of Adam* is a ceiling-sized realisation of this truth: hands extended across the void in an act of animation. In sculpture, the Renaissance artist became a kind of mortal god who could give stone and marble the ability to breathe with his hands.

There isn't a civilisation on this planet that rejected the power of touch as a key feature in human affairs. What then, we must ask ourselves, is to become of the people who are denied it or who have denied it to themselves?

Madness.

Love is made real by touch, this much I know to be true. The sensation of contact is love's permanence; an avatar sent forth into the world to remind us of the stuff that lives beneath the surface. People can be dishonest, but touch is real.

Margaret Atwood said, 'Touch comes before sight, before speech. It is the first language, and the last, and it always tells the truth.'

Add to that the first medicine and the last over the span of a life; the held hand of a dying loved one is not just a ritual, it is pain relief.

Yes, it's true. The scientists have been at it again and they are here to tell you that study after study shows physical contact, especially the affectionate kind, has a documented analgesic effect.

Here I was woofing paracetamol for headaches and stomach pains as my anxiety worsened, when all I needed was a long, soothing embrace.

I think my body knew what my mind would not admit, however. Over time, the skin grows jealous. The magnetic field reverses and what suddenly was repulsed by another body, other skin, is now drawn in by an irresistible force. All in secret. It feels like pure biology; a force not even animated by the subconscious. After years of neglect the body wants what it wants, protocol be damned.

That is how I have come to see it, anyhow, when the dam wall of my inhibitions began to break in my mid-twenties. That decade of lonely flesh had taken its toll.

It happened with a single man, first. He could hug for Australia. Big, solid embraces that always lasted a second or two longer than an ordinary cuddle. Séamus is attractive and charming, a powerful combination in a hug merchant.

Back then, he was routinely told by women he dated that he was 'too affectionate' and liked cuddles too much. One of them broke up with him over it. When I first heard this I laughed but now all I want to do is go back in time and shake them. What are you looking for in a boyfriend? I want to ask them. Trade negotiations?

When Séamus and I were together we would say hello and goodbye with those big, shaking come-togethers, but then I started asking for more – just 'in-between' hugs. On many occasions my arms would fling out automatically, like oxygen masks in a jet cabin in the event of an emergency, and I would find myself in his warm hold, my body knowing what it had to do before my mind was invited to attend.

Sometimes when I'm driving I'll end up at my destination, apparently having just woken up there, guided by God-knows-what. This is how I came to get the hugs I needed, the same hugs I had shut out of my life for well over a decade.

I was a hug-seeking missile.

It is hard, I think, to overstate the importance of this corporeal miracle. There was a period of adjustment, certainly, but the pursuit of tactile contact dislodged something in me that had been jamming the gears. With touch, the luxurious kind that is allowed to linger and reassure, I rediscovered a lost world.

The self-imposed lock-in had dictated my mood for years. It governed how likely it was on any given day that I would cede territory to depression and anxiety and admit defeat over my most elemental of longings.

Séamus might have been the (thankfully enthusiastic) recipient of the initial experiment, but he was nowhere near its endpoint. I began hugging my friends as we met and as we left each other's company and often in between, apropos of nothing. I embraced strangers during interviews in my day job as a journalist and, on one occasion, accidentally hugged the editor of the newspaper I worked for when we came to the end of a seven-hour federal budget lockup and a few hours of drinking in a Canberra hotel bar.

He had meant only to offer his hand goodnight and, in my newly primed state, I mistook this for the initial stages of a hug, and by the time I had committed it was too late. But I didn't care.

When the elevator doors opened, I sprung off to my hotel room, confident that I had bestowed upon him, this strange man with peculiar notions regarding homosexuality, the gift of human affection. Yes, I thought, even he deserved it.

Of course, these things are a matter of degrees.

Though I'd had so much love from my beautiful mum in my life, I longed for the kind that I didn't get from my dad. Still, I had twice as much as others and even more than the worst cases of neglect and abandonment.

A few years ago, while doing a deep dive into some bigger policy questions in my day job as a social policy reporter, I came across the most harrowing example of this absence of love in the story of Romania's orphans.

In Romania's post-war Soviet years, for those willing to believe things could get better, there were some promising early signs that Nicolae Ceauşescu – who rose to become the general secretary of Romania's Communist Party in the 1960s – would be a more relaxed, inclusive leader of the nation.

At first, he eased press censorship rules and stood up to the orthodoxy of Soviet rule. But even as his popularity rose, the markings of a more sinister leader were already on display.

Ceauşescu had introduced some of the harshest anti-abortion laws in the world and became obsessed with the potential for economic rebirth through a concerted, abysmal tilt at social engineering that would haunt Romania for half a century.

His goal was to turn women into baby-making machines without the social apparatus to care for those same children. The state smashed the family unit when it was most needed, moving whole extended clans to the cities where men and women were scattered into jobs and worked to the bone.

The 'menstrual police' conducted random checks on women of child-bearing age by showing up at their workplaces and taking them out to be probed by gynaecologists. Women who were pregnant were frightened into giving birth and those who had no children were punished with a childlessness tax.

Women with many children were called 'heroine mothers' and those with seven or more were given the 'order of maternal glory' for their efforts. By all accounts, few women in Romania ever reached these stratospheric heights, but the birth rate skyrocketed nevertheless. With a population then of about nineteen million people, around 360,000 babies were born each year between 1970 and 1989, the year Ceauşescu was overthrown and executed by firing squad.

The blunt purpose of this system of control, in addition to supplying workers for the machinery of the nation state, was to turn the individual to dust through suffocating uniformity. Part of the equation was to convince mothers and fathers the state would do a better job of raising useful, functional citizens than them; and for reasons we will never truly understand – perhaps partly indoctrination, perhaps the crushing weight of the requirements of living and lack of childcare or any support – many families believed them.

The effects of this social fracture are hard to describe and even harder to stomach.

Most Romanians knew little about the state-run institutions that sorted abandoned children into those with productive potential and those with 'defects' who, in the convenient view of Soviet science at the time, could never be buffed into shape physically or intellectually.

The reality, of course, was that the institutions that deigned to sort these children – many as young as six months old – were the very reason many of them suffered so severely from illnesses of the mind, body and spirit.

Children were taken in by the state, certainly, but the plain truth was that they were never cared for while in state 'care'. They were rarely, if ever, held or soothed, comforted or reassured. The state had removed them from the very essence of love itself then scratched its head when these same children turned inward and stopped speaking. The Romanian state had penetrated so far into the lives of individuals that it had curled its wicked fingers around the psychic cord that allows babies and toddlers to learn and thrive and pulled the plug.

The world learned of these orphanages in early 1990 and the horror of them unfolded in the years that followed.

The world learned of these orphanages in early 1990 and the horror of them unfolded in the years that follows. Charles Nelson, a Harvard Medical School professor of paediatrics and neuroscience, wrote about his visit to a Bucharest facility in December 1998 in the 2014 book *Romania's Abandoned Children: Deprivation, Brain Development and the Struggle for Recovery*. He walked into a room containing twelve cribs in which babies aged six to eight months old were lying passively on their backs.

'Although we could make eye contact with them,' he wrote, 'it took considerable effort to get them to smile at us. With several, we never succeeded.'

The book, co-authored with professors Nathan Fox and Charles Zeanah from the University of Maryland and Tulane University respectively, charts the progression of one of the most ambitious child development research projects in the world.

As disturbing as these scenes were, they presented a rare opportunity to test long-held assumptions not just about whether children needed attentive and delicate care – this much seemed obvious – but how young people responded to the timing of such natural interventions.

Most pressing of all was this question: when do they need this care the most and what happens when they are robbed of it?

My life looks nothing like the deadening absence at the core of these institutions, and they are not alone in the world for the depths of horrors they harboured. Not even in recent memory are these Romanian orphanages unique.

I have never forgotten, for instance, the story of Peta Susan Doig, a woman whom I first wrote about in 2015.

Institutionalised in Western Australia's notorious Graylands Hospital at the age of eight with severe psychological, intellectual and, later, physical disabilities, she lived for decades locked away from society before her death at 12.21 pm on 4 January 2013.

For the last six years of her life, she had no contact with family whatsoever and was 'so severely institutionalised she had no meaningful relationships with anyone outside the hospital'.

Although Sam Connor, an advocate against the abuse of disabled people who has kept a running list of such cases, told me that wasn't quite true: she did have one other person interested in the content of her life, the minutiae of her existence, but it wasn't anyone who might have enriched it while she lived.

'Peta Doig had a biographer,' Sam told me. 'There's only one problem. Her biographer was the WA Coroner.'

In the coroner's report, it was noted that Doig lived in fear of those around her:

> The deceased had limited verbal expression and displayed stereotypical, repetitive movements and ritualistic, compulsive behaviours.
>
> She presented as withdrawn, with a lack of responsiveness to others, and gross deficits in language development. She would often become agitated, distressed and aggressive and would self-harm by cutting herself, picking her skin and banging her head.
>
> Her management was complicated by her behaviour in being aggressively resistant to staff and she was vulnerable to sexual exploitation by other patients.

Yes, Peta Doig had profound disabilities, but I can't help but notice how the coroner's description matches neatly the presentation of those orphans in Romania when they grew older. The children, especially compared with their peers in foster care or still living with their biological families, often displayed the hollow disposition of somebody who knew, at the deepest possible level, that they had been failed.

It was as if their hearts had been scooped out and replaced with lead. They avoided close contact and yet, at the precise same time, often displayed behaviour that was dangerously unregulated and bizarrely trusting of strangers.

Such programming, void of the love and care that should fine-tune it for our later lives, has a tendency to lead us further into pain, the kind we both run headlong into and inflict upon ourselves because the alternatives have never been properly sketched.

Who could draw that caring universe for these children, for Peta Doig?

Throughout a life, many of us take the most basic touch for granted. We kiss and hug our friends and our families and, further, experience the particular energy of romantic encounters. Some are luckier than others in this endeavour but even then, as the Divinyls succinctly put it, we touch ourselves.

That is the end of the story for most.

While I was writing this book, a landmark case involving the National Disability Insurance Scheme (NDIS) and an unidentified woman in her forties reached the Federal Court of Australia. The agency which runs the NDIS – a $25 billion disability support program – had already lost a tribunal appeal in its bid to reject funding for a sex worker to visit the woman a handful of times each year. The government, through the agency, had taken its case to the Federal Court.

'I am seeking funding for sexual services,' the woman, who has multiple sclerosis and other complex disabilities, told the tribunal. 'Without the assistance of a professional sex worker I am not able to achieve sexual release and am effectively denied the right to sexual health, pleasure and wellbeing.'

The case was intensely personal. Some details were so private and intimate that not even the court chose to air them publicly. It was fought at great cost to the woman, nonetheless, who had to convince round after round of legal inquiry that she had the right to be touched.

In May 2020, the Federal Court of Australia found in her favour. The judgement says:

> She was diagnosed with multiple sclerosis over 17 years ago and, relevantly, since that time has been single for reasons she attributes to her complex medical conditions.

> Prior to her illnesses the respondent had an active sex life, but her medical conditions are such that the prospect for her of sexual release of any kind without assistance is highly unlikely.

The decision sent some ministers within the Australian government into a tailspin of prudish alarm. Within weeks, the Minister for the NDIS, Stuart Robert, an evangelical Christian, announced plans to rewrite the legislation to ban sex therapy of any kind.

Once again, a government threatens to intervene and micromanage the lives of its citizens about which it knows precious little.

Touch, so vital, is the last frontier in our understanding of the senses.

Early in 2020, I flew to Japan, where I had arranged an interview with Dr Takanori Shibata, the inventor of Paro the robotic seal.

I had seen the white balls of fluff while researching the concept of touch and, because I have poor impulse control, decided I wanted to meet one where they were born. Paro is a robot covered in snow-white fur, modelled on a baby harp seal, and was first revealed to the public in 2001. Now in its ninth generation, the therapeutic seal has been used in aged-care homes and facilities around the world to simulate the bond between human beings, or them and their animals. In so many of these homes, the elderly residents spend most of their time without meaningful contact with people or pets they love. In Australia, for instance, almost half of the residents receive no visits from friends or family in any given year. And that was before Covid-19 closed the doors and tore families apart.

Dr Shibata wanted to change the score. Nothing beats a real animal, of course, but for reasons of infection control and allergies they are not always allowed or advised.

Five hours after I landed in Tokyo, I caught a taxi to the Shintomi Nursing Home in Chuo City to meet Dr Shibata. The home was in a nondescript tower, its entrance located in a dingy carpark and I was left in a waiting room with no apparent way of explaining why I was there.

I wasn't even sure if Dr Shibata had informed the front desk. They gave me cloth covers for my shoes nonetheless. The novel coronavirus had been stewing for weeks in the *Diamond Princess* petri-dish off the coast of Yokohama but it was still late January and Covid-19 hadn't made a significant jump into the local population. I was wearing a mask left over from the summer bushfires in Australia, which felt totally inadequate.

The nursing home was a forlorn place. Not because of the people who worked there or even the building itself. The idea of warehousing people makes me uneasy; that a robot might be necessary to ward off the worst of the loneliness even more so.

When Dr Shibata found me fifteen minutes later, we took the elevator to the fifth floor. And there they were. The Paro seals, stored in their pigeonholes like oversized slippers. They were pink and grey and white.

'I wondered what kind of robot would be accepted by people,' Shibata told me when we sat in an empty break room. 'Animals do not work for us but they can enrich our lives. People don't expect them to work for them so people just love them.'

It seemed obvious to make an animal, he explained, but what kind?

This question had been needling me too. Surely a cat or a dog would have been a more immediate option, I suggested. Why not those?

The people trialling the animal prototypes 'expected too much of dogs and cats', Shibata said, noting that he first tried these in the 1990s. 'They compared the robot to their real dogs and cats. But in the case of a seal robot, people don't have high expectations. People didn't know or they did not have experience with them. So I thought, as people do not know about seals, a seal robot is much more acceptable.'

And so it was. The latest-generation Paro is about as big as a mid-sized dog. It has ten computer processing units, seven little motors for movement – two in the neck, one in each front fin and one in the fused single back fin and in each eyelid – with twelve tactile surface sensors across the body and another in its whiskers. Paro also has three microphones to pick up audio cues, light sensors and voice recognition software that helps with bonding to its human.

Paro's eyes are big and its antibiotic fake fur plush. As I finally got the chance to hold it, it purred in a pleasing high-pitched whistle that sounded rather like a distant karate class.

Aiyaaaaaaa. Aiyoooooo.

I had held it for just seconds before deciding, in my very middle, that I would die for it. I would burn whole villages to the ground if it was wronged in any way, if we should be parted.

Takanori Shibata sensed this, I think, because he quickly moved to repatriate the seal to one of the elderly residents who had been staring at me.

The seals are funded under Australian aged-care legislation, but Shibata says they have also been used in children's hospitals where parents cannot stay with their child after visiting hours.

'At night, after seven o'clock, the parents have to leave,' Shibata told me. 'Some children cry or feel very sad, but Paro improves their mood. They can come to play and have fun with Paro.'

The robotic seal has become especially useful in wards where patients with low immune systems are treated because the fur is resistant to germs and easily cleaned.

There was something beautiful in the very practical design considerations for Paro. Such a functional baby seal had to be durable but also soft and cuddly. Strong but inviting.

In other words: *vulnerable.*

In the laboratory, Paro was tested for wear and tear in 100,000 drop and stroking simulations. I couldn't bear the thought of having to watch them in those machines, punted and pummelled, those round eyes repeatedly being sent to the floor.

A litany of other studies have been done on the animatronic baby seal and, to varying degrees, they have found its use can reduce stress, anxiety, depression, loneliness and even pain. Pain, as it turns out, is so often the cause of some of the more difficult behaviours that manifest in older people with dementia. When it isn't picked up or investigated, it leads to calling out, aggression or a compounding cycle of confusion that further masks the injury.

'Paro can improve quality of life,' Shibata said. 'Things like sleep, pleasure, engagement. And in the case of people with dementia or brain damage or post-traumatic stress disorder, they sometimes have negative behaviours. Using Paro can reduce the risk of falling.'

Such power in contact.

I mention these stories under the banner of a general love, a broad care, but in each case the least obvious sense – touch – is the one that holds the most power.

These children in the orphanages were never held or touched in the way most of us have come to experience it. Nor are the elderly in our institutions at the other end of life.

You know the kind of touch, the one that envelops you whole, even if it is a single point of contact on just a centimetre of skin and manages through the alchemy of this connection to melt everything else away.

A person is left, in this moment, as if they are suspended in time and space. As Atwood says, it is the truth of this coming-together that is so spellbinding. I have been in such embraces and, for the only times in my modest existence, felt the pervasive doubt in my body recede like the tide.

We know from decades of brain research that our genes provide a template for the people we will become but, as anyone who has tried to build an IKEA wall unit from the instructions will tell you, this is but a mere suggestion.

The rest of us get filled in by experience.

As Nelson and his colleagues write in their book on the Romanian orphans, a nurturing relationship formed from birth between an infant and their caregiver will be the foundation for all subsequent relationships.

The bonds help to strengthen a child's sense of self; teach them positive communication skills; help them form successful intimate relationships as adults; and establish a sophisticated emotional intelligence.

Something about seeing this list written out, though I knew it intellectually, was ruinous to me. I scored two out of the four, although the sense of self came much later and only after a lot of furious work that felt world-ending at the time. Now that I think of it, the jury is still out on my social skills, too. People seem surprised by this when I tell them I have always struggled with social settings.

I think the blazing fire of the neurons in my brain masks a lot of the effort. It is an internal first-generation steam engine, all chug and bluster and frightfully inefficient. But, it gets the work done, and the surface appears somewhat calm in comparison.

'You make it look so easy,' people tell me. To which I should like to respond: 'I do, but you should see my mind.' (Little joke about the apparent segregation of our consciousness, for those playing along at home.)

As the Harvard study, known as the Bucharest Early Intervention Project (BEIP), theorised before it was launched, there is no easy matrix for apportioning different influences on the unloved child to their final makeup. Brains start to develop not long after conception, Nelson and co write, and continue through to early adulthood.

The *timing* of any key influence, then, is just as important as whether it happens at all. A series of related but equally crucial levers must be pulled at all the right times for each individual, to give them the best shot at a loving, fulfilled life.

Of course, this almost never happens in the right way or the right order for any one person. We are all of us pockmarked by the scars of things that should have been otherwise, the way the moon bears the craters of collisions in space that it could do nothing to avoid. We exist on a continuum of people ranging from those who got the best at the most appropriate time to those who got little or nothing and never when they needed it the most.

This is how I relate to this big picture, as a boy who always had the love of his mother but lost the great love of his father, gradually at first from age three or four and then totally by age seven.

Like the moon, I'm still here, bright but blemished. I lost my atmosphere years ago and the grazes with objects in space have settled below the surface.

In many ways, the Romanian study reproduced the results of Harry Harlow's now famous experiments with rhesus monkeys in the 1950s. His work, focusing on attachments between infant monkeys and their mothers, was partly informed by a mirroring of natural hierarchies in monkey societies where women did the child-rearing. But it also reflected prevailing attitudes among people at the time that viewed the role of the mother in child-rearing as elevated above that of the father and therefore more important in the child's development.

I don't make this point to enforce the conservative view that bubbles up during same-sex marriage or parenting debates that children must have access to a mother and a father to truly be loved. That is, quite frankly, bullshit. But if you are born with two parents who are meant to love you – whether they are men, women, transexual or otherwise and in whatever combination – then a child must know she is loved by both of them.

The very thing that has given rise to my complex PTSD is the inescapable fact of my father, a man who was there at the beginning and then made an absence of himself.

I have traced the swirls of that sunken object in the waters of my life ever since.

Still, Harlow's monkey experiments are illuminating, if terribly difficult to watch. Baby rhesus monkeys were taken from their mothers, sometimes just one week after they were born and sometimes one month after, and they were raised with pale imitations of these key parental figures. Sometimes, too, the babies were raised with other monkeys, but often they were deprived entirely of social conditioning.

What we see in these experiments is deeply disturbing. For the baby monkeys, it is world-ending.

They skitter and cower, shake and tremble. They avoid eye contact and lash out in uncontrollable rages. Often in Harlow's experiments, the young monkeys are fed via a nozzle attached to a wire outline of an older monkey, meant to represent their mother. But they are also given access to the same wire body covered in terry-towelling, soft to the touch. This tactile model does not come with a feeding teat, however, so the babies must choose between food and comfort.

In the black-and-white videos of these scenarios, the baby primates will spend as little time as possible getting the bare minimum of food before racing back to grasp desperately at the terry-towelling figure.

Harlow even built a clattering, banging mechanical monster with a huge oblong head, headlights for eyes and oversized, gnashing and comically sharpened teeth. The apparatus has bent metal arms that extend beyond its body and move up and down, the noise of it all so intrusive and intimidating.

When the machine is introduced to the animals, they move like lightning to the terry-towelling mother and dig themselves into her soft covering. It is only after they have felt this embrace, a perversely simple approximation of the real thing, that they find the courage to fight back, making threatening gestures at the machine monster from the safety of their terry-towelling mother's clutch.

Surely any young animal would prefer a soft blanket to a hug with a wire alternative?

Harlow is posed the obvious question by CBS News correspondent Charles Collingwood in a documentary called *Mother Love*, produced by the network.

'Is this really love?'

Harlow is sure of himself in response. 'Well, what do you mean by saying that a baby loves its mother? Certainly one thing we mean is that it gets a great feeling of security in the presence of its mother. Now, Mr Collingwood, wouldn't you say that if you frightened a baby, that it went running to its mother, was comforted, and then all the fear disappeared and was replaced by a complete sense of security that that baby loved its mother?'

In the cloying actions of the scared little monkeys I saw a simulacrum of myself, once so totally denuded of that most atomic comfort, touch. Like the monkeys with poor substitutes, I turned so enthusiastically to hugs and next-best-thing comfort. I did it especially with the men in my life who loved me and showed affection. These men were my cloth-covered stand-ins for the father that didn't, or couldn't, love me.

The way the monkeys threw open their arms on approach to their own fake mothers was so reminiscent of the way my own limbs broke land-speed records to find the security of touch.

God, I know it sounds silly to say but I truly felt a probing sorrow for the little things when I watched those videos. True, it was a sorrow that extended to myself, also. How to put into words the magnitude of the thing we have lost that makes us grab so instinctively for a thing that will never, can never, replace what we had?

Those outstretched arms hold whole universes of hurt. It was true for the monkeys and it was true for me, too.

Curiously, in Harlow's study, there were key differences between the babies who were removed from their mothers at one week and those who were taken away after a month. The findings helped inform the Harvard study in Bucharest, and Nelson noted the implications early in the work's summary. Monkeys who had been separated from their mothers at one week showed 'profound disinterest in and concern for other monkeys' and preferred to be alone.

The monkeys who had been taken away at one month had an 'intense need to be with other monkeys and displayed heightened anxiety, clinging indiscriminately to whichever other monkey was available'.

In the simple mathematics of this equation, I was a one-month monkey.

Writing of his findings in the journal *American Psychologist* in 1958, Harlow touched on a kind of poetry I did not expect from the man who had so dispassionately designed these experiments.

He said he and his fellow researchers were surprised by the disparity between the young monkeys' desire for 'comfort contact' over nursing. It led them to consider that the 'primary function of nursing … is that of insuring frequent and intimate body contact of the infant with the mother. Certainly, man cannot live by milk alone. Love is an emotion that does not need to be bottle- or spoon-fed, and we may be sure that there is nothing to be gained by giving lip service to love.'

Neuroscientist David Linden gave a lecture in 2016 that I like because it helps remedy a nagging question: why do I care *so* much about this now distant injury?

His thesis is simple: people born blind or deaf at birth can and do adapt. They forge great minds and bodies; live wonderful lives.

'But if you are born with the biological components for a sense of touch,' Linden says, 'but you do not receive touch during your infancy and when you are a toddler, then a disaster unfolds.'

We know this, he continues, because of those Romanian orphanages. The orphans had no one to hold them. They rocked themselves back and forth compulsively as a way of soothing that hurt and then, as years dragged by, suffered cognitive delays and attachment disorders.

Damage was evident well beyond disorders of the brain and mind.

'Their growth was stunted and they had problems with the development of their gastrointestinal … and immune systems,' Linden says.

The Bucharest initiative brought in teams of people, including social workers and foster families – almost unheard of at the time in Romania – to begin giving the children what they needed most: touch.

'On the whole it was just breathtakingly awful,' Nelson reflected to the *Harvard Gazette* in 2010, a decade after the study launched. 'One of the eeriest things about these institutions is how quiet they are. Nobody's crying.'

The study found that for children aged over two it was very difficult, and sometimes impossible, to reverse the damage that had been done to them. But even half an hour a day of genuine, caring touch from volunteers – some hugs, some 'limb manipulation' and so on – before the age of two was enough to ameliorate some of the worst aspects of their institution-imposed disabilities. Timing was everything.

When placed afterwards in quality foster care, children regained the lost physical growth that had happened despite having been fed a nutritionally balanced diet in the orphanages. In other words, it wasn't the food that was affecting their physical form. It was the complete lack of love.

Their IQ scores leaped ten points on average, taking them from the border of intellectual impairment to a score that allowed them to function better at school and, later, in society.

The *Gazette* also noted: 'During one test, in which a stranger comes to the door and unexpectedly asks the child to come with him, 55 per cent of institutionalised children went with the stranger, while 25 per cent of foster children did. Just one of the community control children did.'

I have been that child at the door, sensing danger but choosing it anyway because the alternative is so numbing.

No other study has been so comprehensive over such a long period of time to even rival the findings of the Bucharest project. More work should always be done in any scientific endeavour, of course, but its findings are so horrifying and so solid that they have given scholars and policy experts the world over the sharpest insight we are likely to see for half a century into touch deprivation among children.

Our evidence comes from Romania, but at the turn of the millennium there were some eight million children in orphanages around the world. In exceptional cases in Australia, where foster care is not available or suitable, people under the age of eighteen with nowhere else to go are placed in residential care.

Then, as if turning eighteen is some magic biological marker of adulthood, these same kids are released from care the way other children are taken to the pub to celebrate a milestone of age, though not of maturity.

In an age of increasing, and justified, awareness of child sexual abuse there are formal and informal rules in place that govern how Australian children in care – both foster and residential – are looked after and nurtured, and whether it is ever advisable for carers to hug them or soothe them the way a parent would.

In 2019, I was giving a workshop on trauma. One of the women who attended was a foster carer. What she told me during that session haunts me.

'We are told not to touch the children, everyone is worried about how that can be construed,' she said. 'But I see the kids and I just want to hug them and love them like my own. You can see it, they want to be hugged.'

There must be a word for the ache those children feel, the one that signals such an animalistic desire to be held but for which we might not even have language. For years and years I ached to be held but I didn't know enough to articulate it, nor even to identify the source of that dull internal throb.

The poet Franz Wright captured this belated sense of revelation at the beauty we have denied ourselves, knowingly or otherwise, when he wrote: 'How is it that I didn't spend my whole life being happy, loving other human beings' faces?'

I want to take this further and ask: How is it that I didn't spend my whole life being happy at the touch of another human being? How could I have gone so long without being given over to that basic ecstasy of life?

What a squandered opportunity.

We must give ourselves permission to make mistakes out of ignorance, however. To have learned it is a gift in itself. The thing about trauma, though, is its ability to perpetually undermine high reason. In this sense, the progress I have managed to make thus far must be jealously guarded.

Jasmina was going to form part of that enduring work. I had hoped she might teach me to imagine an expanded world of comfort outside my dependencies.

It was not to be. Circumstance has a funny way of engineering our precise miseries.

It began with Séamus in 2014 and returned with him in 2020 when he moved into my apartment in Sydney's southwest, serendipitously timed ahead of the global lockdown that prevented us leaving our own homes and seeing other people.

Our narrowed existence was complicated by the fact that Séamus is an intensive care nurse who was, at the time, directly caring for patients with Covid-19.

The initial ritual we had developed in the apartment, a kiss and a hug in the morning and before we went to bed at night, was abandoned after his first potential exposure at work. Of course I knew the logic of this and I was consciously fully on board with the new directive: we could not hug or kiss after that first exposure.

It made sense. For a day.

I noticed the hunger crawl back into my skin almost immediately. It hurt, not in the upper floor of my mind where I make logical decisions with rational assumptions, but downstairs in the basement where the oldest part of my brain holds debilitating memories in its cells.

It was a starvation of such proportions that this ancient part of my mind began to radiate pain again. It remembered, even though I longed to forget.

How quickly I drifted back to the state of those anxious monkeys, antagonised by a penetrating nothingness. It was the worst kind of fear, in my experience, the one that attaches to nothing in particular. The kind of fear that hovers above you without rhyme or purpose, like an unmoored hot air balloon filled with lawyers.

Just days into the self-imposed dance of avoidance, I broke – not in any extreme way, but with the most gentle of signals. I reverted back to those old days and threw open my arms towards Séamus before bed one night.

'I need a hug,' I told him through one of those faces distinguished by the act of trying not to cry.

Séamus paused, uncertain of whether he should, having just completed another twelve-hour shift. Eventually he leaned in and took me into his embrace.

'I'm just trying to protect you, buddy,' he said as we held each other on the couch. Later he would tell me that it had been killing him, too, this lack of physical affection.

But right then, all I could do was whisper into his ear, 'I'd rather die from Covid-19 then go another day without a hug.'

It sounded melodramatic but I truly meant it.

I had been here before, many years prior, and I knew this one thing to be the case. To go without touch is a kind of death, a deletion of the soul, and I decided I wanted to live.

The Self

'Just try to keep your eyeballs nice and still,' the therapist says politely.

I cannot see her because my eyelids are closed. Her voice is soft and I try not to imagine her judging me from across the room. *Look at this idiot, can't even keep his eyeballs still.*

I am wearing a tight blue cap on my head with more than a dozen electrodes pressing into my skull. A series of wires, in the colours of the rainbow and running side by side in a flat cord, extend from the base of the cap to a strange box before being sent to a computer – her computer.

'Try and keep your eyeballs nice and still,' she coos again. I don't say anything out loud to her because I am trying to be a model participant, but I do think: *how the fuck am I meant to keep my eyes from moving?* They're closed. I think I'm staring straight ahead but, really, I'm not sure. When she reminds me,

I get nervous again and my eyes start darting all over the place behind my lids, like they would during vivid dreams.

Also, I wish she'd stop calling them eyeballs. It gives me the shivers.

She can probably see my unease because, at this precise moment, my brain waves are being sent raw to her display and she is, quite literally, getting a glimpse of my machinery. Mentally, I am undressed. Is this how motorbikes feel when you strip them for parts?

It's not good news that I cannot control my eyes, partly because I like passing tests, but mostly because of the reason we are here at all.

We are going to try to fix my brain. Keep eyes still, fail, move on to overhauling the entire architecture of the mind. Good luck!

For most of my life, my brain has been a distressing combination of desperately misguided optimism and highly specialised deficit-discovery machine. Balancing these two opposing programs meant a continuing invitation to confusion and despair.

The thing that still causes me friction is that I had been *writing* about trauma and its effects through the generations since 2017 without ever really considering that I might be a sufferer of trauma myself. I didn't want to be a candidate, but I did need to know what was causing my earth-splitting nervous breakdowns. Was this just garden variety anxiety and depression?

I have a friend who, with his flair for the dramatic, once told me that he kept going to the doctor thinking he had cancer, and each time he was told nothing was wrong he felt like he'd failed an audition on the *X Factor*.

'And the doctor was like, "Sorry it's not cancer this time; better luck next year,"' he said with mock resignation.

We laughed darkly when he told me this as a joke, but deep down I felt the same ripple of disappointment with each new psychologist and each new GP. Not a single one ever suggested something more powerful was at play. Their answers to my problems seemed so skinny and insubstantial.

After my first book, *One Hundred Years of Dirt*, was published I joined the writers' festival circuit which, as I understood it at the time, was a lot like the V8 supercars championship but with more syllables.

That is how I described it to my family who, though they loved me very much, thought it absurd that anybody would pay to listen to me talk about anything. They weren't wrong, either. But some good did come from the experience.

At the Newcastle Writers' Festival I was a panelist in a discussion about trauma. We were in the Playhouse Theatre and I was off in my head, scanning the steep-tiered seating for faces in the crowd. Any faces, really. I like to remind myself that this is a real thing with real people in the audience and, for reasons entirely inscrutable, they have chosen to come and hear us speak.

I was sitting beside writer and poet Dr Meera Atkinson, who began reading from her book *Traumata*.

'My body is at the ready for flight. I can't switch my nervous system off. It scans and calculates tirelessly, antennae out for threats,' Atkinson read aloud. 'The body remembers.'

She then described the results of a report titled 'The Neuroscience of Traumatic Memory' in which the authors Bessel van der Kolk and Ruth Buczynski studied the brains of traumatised people. They found that the thalamus malfunctions, resulting in people remembering sensations and images of the original traumatic event but not in context. 'Apparently, the brain forms maps of territories marked dangerous and safe. The brain of an abused child can become wired to believe, "I'm a person to whom terrible things happen, and I'd better be on the alert for who's going to hurt me now."'

I was still making a catalogue of the people in the room while Dr Atkinson read her passage. It was fun to imagine at least one member of the audience had stumbled into the wrong theatre and I was trying to guess which one. Usually the crowd has a certain look: like they want something profound and brilliant and will eat you if you fail to provide it. There are always some who make notes throughout the session, like all my psychologists did. *Ah yes,* they seemed to write, *this one is a difficult case.*

Atkinson continued reading.

> This [alarm] can't be fixed by talking about the event in the past, which is not in the past at all, but in the present, in the very sensations of the now.

In much the same way, I can still remember the shape of the sensation I felt right then on that stage when that line was breathed into the theatre. There was clarity in the air, an electric yearning for calm finally earned.

Trauma. It was trauma. I didn't just have anxiety and depression, though I did indeed have these things. Nor was my memory as exceptional as I believed it to be. The reason I had great recall, at least some of the time, was not because I was gifted. It was because I had been hurt. My body and mind needed these reminders to 'protect' me.

I was not just a boy with painful memories, I was an abused boy with a post-traumatic response that followed me like an unmuzzled dog into adulthood, growling at my heels when the imagery and provocations of those doom-filled childhood moments were triggered again.

Atkinson's simple explanation of trauma as something that lives – it is not merely remembered, it is reanimated – described what had been happening to me for years now. Those flashbacks of my dad kissing the nineteen-year-old governess, the white-hot fear in my chest on the 1000-square-kilometre cattle station when that seven-year-old boy felt so alone. A world of bones can live in that sense of isolation, can make themselves at home in your desolation. And they rattle and rattle for the rest of your days. Sometimes they clatter so hard they knock you right out of yourself. Dissociation, doctors call it. A phrase I had not yet come across and yet had lived.

'It's no accident. Evolution doesn't allow accidents,' Dr Roger Gurr tells me later from his office in western Sydney. Gurr is the clinical director of the Youth Early Psychosis program for the Australian government headspace centres. He's also a trauma specialist who has directed mental health services for a region of Sydney with 1.8 million people.

I'm cheating, somewhat, because Gurr is not my therapist. Our interview is for a piece I am writing about mental health reform in Australia. My interest is deeply personal and I steer the conversation to the things about which I was learning.

He explains that dissociation is when the brain literally re-wires itself to help a person, typically a child at onset, avoid the worst of the physical, sexual or emotional threats while they are experiencing them. This then becomes a permanent part of the mind's hardware as paths between different parts of the brain become fat with habit.

Trauma is the thing that happens to us. Sometimes just once, as in a major accident, or repeatedly as is often the case with complex PTSD. The response we form to this moment or moments, however, is ongoing. The body becomes thick with the weeds of it.

'Because a lot of the [onset of] trauma happens by three, a person cannot give you a language story about what happened to them,' Gurr says. 'The evidence is that your brain just moves all your resources to recognising the threat, running away, fighting or, worst case, playing dead and disassociating. You don't need language for any of that, so people don't lay down any language memory.'

No language, no story that makes sense.

It helps now to know what happened back then, right in the fleshy middle of my head. It started with the amygdala, a nub of the brain about the size of a walnut. (I didn't know how big a walnut was when I first read about this but struggled to find other foodstuffs of equivalent size. The amygdala is bigger than a grape, for instance, but smaller than a peach. Perhaps a touch smaller than a golf ball. Honestly, you'll probably have to look it up.)

Amygdalae are so old, evolutionarily speaking, that almost every animal that has lived on this earth has one. Given this, it won't be a surprise to learn this little structure in the brain is our most primitive. It's not here to help us read Proust, in other words.

'The amygdala controls the different parts of the cortex that need to be involved in fight or flight,' Gurr says. 'And so people with trauma have superhighways between the amygdala and those bits of the brain. So if the amygdala decides you are going to have to freeze and play dead, it switches to stimulating the parts of the cortex that deal with anaesthesia for pain and other things to help you survive that situation.'

When you begin to understand the processes that happen in the background, the illusion of control fades away. The point is not that we are incapable of being aware of these system mechanics, but that *we almost never are aware*, even when we think we are paying attention.

I find, even as I sit at my laptop in my apartment in Sydney, that the words I am writing seem to come from somewhere in my mind, though it is never a place I truly have access to. Sure, it's a useful illusion to *think* that I can pause and conjure the right phrases, but if I really interrogate that thought, they too seem to spring from some place totally ineffable. There is always a layer beyond which I cannot penetrate.

Try it with your own thoughts, right now. Can you pin them down?

It's not magic; it's just the circuitry in the brain doing what it has evolved to do. And so it was with the responses to my trauma. I never decided what to do in that moment I watched my family slip away from me, but my brain did. It kept the worst moments as warning signs for later – the amygdala determines which memories are 'emotionally significant', which allows them to become particularly stable and vivid – and deleted the rest. These memories are like high-resolution photos of some distant galaxy, all shiny detail in a vast field of black. To endure the rest of those weeks, the end-to-end pain of it all, my mind shut down. I left myself so often throughout the ordeal that, in sum, the events feel like they happened to somebody else.

That's the trauma survival plan.

And it worked that first day, so the brain tried it again. And again and again.

By the time a traumatised child reaches adolescence, these responses are well-worn pathways, like the smooth grooves in the concrete steps of ancient cathedrals.

And then the brain has a resources meeting with itself.

Here's the kicker: despite youthful protestations, we are not born knowing everything. We are born with a series of baseline equations in our heads. If X, then Y. If hot, hands burn. If aggressive, probably dangerous. If cute, needs protection. As children grow, information based on their experience is plugged into these equations so that they can populate a map of how the world works *for them*. Everyone is different, to a really fantastical degree, which is why we are born with the directions and not the destination.

The problem is, early on, our brains don't exactly know what information will be useful and what information is misleading or redundant.

When we mutate into teenagers, our brains stop growing indiscriminately and begin a process of culling. Your 1.3-kilogram skull-bound nerve centre was Marie Kondo-ing itself before Netflix ever commissioned the special, and this is significant for the traumatised mind and its coping mechanisms.

'The problem comes because the child's brain gets changed to help it in the toxic environment until puberty and then actually the brain changes, because it is programmed to change,' Gurr says. 'Now the brain is going to stop growing and it is going to be pruned for efficiency … and that can actually exacerbate the problems.'

In short, the brain ignores the neural connections that are of least use and preserves those that have been of great service so that they can be enlisted for the grand expanse of the rest of our lives. Playing dead, disassociation, the surging adrenaline and panic that once accompanied those terrifying childhood experiences come with us into adulthood, even if those toxic environments are left behind.

Remember those memories stored as warning signs we discussed earlier? This is where they come back into play. When a person later encounters particular triggers for their trauma the body's emergency system is activated. For some people, it might be a smell or sound – the cologne and voice of an attacker – or something visual, like the stylings of a living room. In my case it was a set of circumstances; men I love platonically shifting their affections.

When we talk about not having a language for our trauma, this is what we mean. The cues are subtle and they are picked up in the subconscious. It's not like a person smells a specific perfume and thinks to themselves: *That's right, this is the precise smell of the man who attacked me and even though I have no reason to believe the person wearing this cologne that I am smelling right now will harm me, I had better launch into an uncontrollable panic.*

Your brain thinks it is doing you a favour.

This was what I had come to unlearn, at the ripe age of thirty-two, at the hospital-white clinic in Sydney's eastern suburbs. This neurofeedback clinic was more calming than the first one I'd tried just a few weeks earlier, which did not look at all like the brain-science future I had imagined.

That one was in a low-rise brick house in Sydney's west, filled with dark-panelled secondhand furniture; the therapist sat behind a large desk next to some cabinets. There was also an occasional chair to the side of the desk, upholstered in mustard-brown-yellow fabric that was the colour despair would be if the person viewing it had synaesthesia.

I did not like that clinic, not because it wasn't any good but because I desperately needed to believe this process would work, and part of that charade, if that's what it all was, clung quite heavily to the decor. I wanted it to be more … space-like. Some things just need to be a certain way, psychologically.

For example, I want my aircraft pilots to have important sounding names, like Chesley Sullenberger III, who landed that Airbus A320 on a river and kept all 155 people alive. Once you know his name, you realise there was no other way that incident could have unfolded.

Now imagine the pilot's name was Darren.

I don't *want* the world to be this way, it just is – for me, at least. This is one of a suite of shortcuts my brain uses to tell itself – and me – that things will be OK without expending too much energy, without really knowing if things *are* going to be alright.

Like when your parents tell you there is nothing to be afraid of in the dark when, statistically speaking, the same frightening world you experienced during the day still exists at night, except this time the lights are out.

Still, give me the soothing platitudes, please. That desire is insulation against the world.

Usually when I walk into a therapist's office it is in a moment of deep personal crisis, an episode of trauma that has fired buckshot into every important element of my life so that I am not simply nervous but scarcely able to speak. This time I was visiting a neurofeedback clinic, though, so it was more exciting than anxiety-inducing. I am fascinated by the human brain, which, as far as we know, is the most complicated thing to ever exist in the universe. It has been noted that the brain is the universe's way of trying to understand itself. In my case, I was hoping it could help me by sorting itself out, with a little nudge here and there.

Broadly speaking, there are four types of waves – Delta, Theta, Alpha and Beta – produced by the electric hum of our brains. In a perfect world, these are in balance and help us perform at our peak. Delta waves, for example, are common in the final stages of sleep and almost exclusively present in the brain during the so-called 'deep sleep' stage. Too much Delta while awake, however, can overload the mind, making it difficult to concentrate or perform daily activities consciously. It's a similar story for Theta waves, a feature of daydreaming. Alpha frequencies characterise the resting state of the brain and, finally, Beta is a 'fast-wave' produced during consciousness or when our attention is focused on a task.

These waves are just building blocks, of course, and the combination of patterns in different regions, too much or too little, can create all manner of internal noise. There is no one perfect set-up, but it is usually obvious if parts of the brain or its output are dysregulated. It is these out-of-whack murmurs that are picked up by the electrical sensors during neurofeedback.

In many trauma brains, for example, the feedback through the sensors is chaotic and severely out of balance, as various portions of the hardware work overtime to surveil the environment for threats.

Our work, then, is to find the frequencies that are out of order, wherever in the brain they may be, and teach the brain to push them back within a normal range.

There is no quick zap. Ideally, I will have forty sessions over the course of a year as the therapist prods and nudges the electrical signals in my head. All I have to do is turn up, very much a bit-player in this exercise.

The endpoint of neurofeedback, we hope, is that the therapist will have to manipulate the brainwaves less and less and guide the behaviour of the 'bad' ones less often, until eventually the brain just accepts this new way of doing business and carries on without any external help.

One of the games I'll play, the therapist tells me, is Pac-Man. 'Play' seems a generous assessment. I'm about to be attached to her computer via the electrodes on my skull. There is no other game controller. Nothing for my hands to do. In fact, I try to keep them still like my eyeballs in case the movement ruins my chance of victory.

All I have to do is watch.

'It'll take a bit of getting used to because he'll only move when the brain is doing what we want it to,' she says. 'You'll think that you can make Pac-Man move yourself, but you can't. It's something your brain has to figure out. It'll start to realise what makes the Pac-Man go and then do more of that, because you both want to see the Pac-Man go.'

Both. Both of *us*. Me and my brain.

How easily the therapist and I slipped into the language of the two selves: the part of me that believes itself to be in control versus the operations-centre in my head that actually is.

The therapist dabs little dollops of ten20 conductive cream onto both my earlobes and a little patch of my scalp, right by the double crown in my hairline that makes a cyclone of my follicles. The cream is cold and contains within it the frisson of new adventure. What might the scan uncover, I wonder. Long forgotten ATM PINs? The vestigial background hum of the *Neighbours* opening credits? The precise frequency of my own happiness?

The little electrodes are attached, and we begin.

There are less frustrating ways to spend fifteen minutes. You could untangle tinsel for the Christmas tree, for example. Or attempt to teach a bunch of third-graders how to do quadratic equations. In each case, you would have more *agency* in the exercise.

With Pac-Man, I had none.

We started out fine, I guess, but very quickly the scenario devolved into one where the off-brand yellow dude froze repeatedly and turned black. The therapist was right, there was *nothing* I could do about it. I tried different tactics, like focusing my attention as specifically as I could on the little yellow monster.

Didn't work.

So then I tried *not* paying attention to him at all, as if I were hoping to catch the reflection of a shy ghost in a mirror. This seemed to work very briefly before Pac-Man entered his longest, most sustained freeze yet.

I tried looking at him but not thinking about him, and vice versa. Blinking really fast did nothing to change the score, nor sneezing (accidental), nor the repeated internal monologue barking at Pac-Man to 'move, goddamn it, you yellow fucking fuck' (deliberate).

During one session I experienced an unbidden erection, which I felt for sure would have derailed any progress made by the munching yellow circle, but this, instead, coincided with the most prolonged stretch of unobstructed movement.

Every time Pac-Man ate one of the little pills, the computer beeped loudly, an auditory cue that quickly became a symbol of success. Both my brain and I wanted to hear the beeps. We wanted to hear Britney Spears's hit single 'Toxic' and we wanted to hear our fathers say they loved us and, above all in these sessions, we wanted to hear the beeps.

But again, and I cannot stress this enough, I was just a spectator in this mission.

For the first time in my existence the usual order of things was exposed totally for me to see. I was conscious that my consciousness was not enough to fix the machinery of my brain, which was calling the shots and, frankly, being a bit of a dick about it.

Sit with that understanding for just a minute, please.

We spend our waking hours operating under the very convincing assumption that we are the masters of our own domain. We are not. You may think you have palmed off the boring, repetitive work of existence (like breathing or operating your arms) to the brain so that you can focus on more important things (like asking someone out or doing your job), but in reality it is the other way around.

Your brain has given you a modicum of control, much of it illusory anyhow, to keep you from messing things up. Most of the time, you are neither needed nor wanted.

Neurofeedback, then, is a way of turning up to a debate against yourself and making sure you lose.

This is what the father of modern philosophy, René Descartes, did, after a fashion. Over a period of nine years, the French thinker engaged in a program of 'systematic doubt', which involved 'uprooting from my mind any errors which might previously have slipped into it'. It was his own dreams that led him to the conclusion that even the existence of the world itself can be called into question. It makes sense when you really stop and consider the limited physical range of the brain. Unless you've had cranial surgery, that lump of grey flesh has never – not for a single moment in your entire *life* – seen the outside world. And yet, from that realm of total darkness behind your face, it has told you what the universe looks, feels, tastes, sounds and smells like.

If you suspect your brain has been lying to you, as Descartes did, good luck proving it wrong.

Descartes's process of conjured doubt did, however, lead the seventeenth century philosopher to his most famous deduction: *cogito ergo sum*. I think, therefore I am. After excluding everything else that could be a lie, he – whatever *he* was – was the only thing left that must be real, Descartes reasoned. He expanded on this later by imagining some 'malicious demon' with infinite power that had corrupted everything about the world. This demon could trick Descartes by turning every last road and shop, every other human and even his own hands and feet into an illusion. The mountains could be faked, the rivers too. And so might the sky and the earth beneath those sham feet, the sound of music (both the film and the sensation, I suppose) and the touch of one on another. It might all be the demon's trickery. All of it, except us.

Put it this way: if you can be aware that the demon has deceived you, then you are real. I am thinking, therefore I exist. Crucially, Descartes didn't see any need for the body in this equation. It could be illusory, too. He was only certain of his thoughts; that it felt *like* something to be him, the little driver behind his eyes.

We are all instinctive dualists – the Cartesian model proposed by our man Descartes – and remain so because we cannot today explain where our consciousness comes from.

During the worst of my successive mental breakdowns, beginning in 2014, I would catch myself in the mirror and not recognise the man staring back at me. Sure, he had my body, but if Descartes taught me anything, this was of little comfort. I moved and studied the way the reflection moved with me – of me but not quite me. Who indeed was running the show?

It wasn't until my life became disjointed by the whiplash of coming in and out of nervous breakdowns that I began to catch the details usually hidden from us by our own minds; not everything you think you saw, not everything you think you felt or heard or witnessed ever happened.

Months of being fed objectively unbelievable lies by my brain, which were so powerfully spun that I believed them anyway (such is the root of mental illness), were followed by patches of stunning clarity. The latter forced me to confront the mastery of the mind when it comes to deception. My brain – and yours – has everything it needs to completely upend our realities.

There are some who interpret Descartes's nine-year doubt spiral as a prolonged episode of mental illness, while others, quite generously, call it a sort of philosophical awakening. To butcher that old idiom, you don't have to be mad to start questioning the nature of your own reality, but it certainly helps.

Whatever it is we imagine *we* are – our mind or thoughts or spirit – we do tend to agree that this intangible entity sits just behind our face; like a little tractor driver in his climate-controlled cabin. When we imagine ourselves steering the good ship *Me* or *You*, it is never from behind the knee, for example. Nor do we picture our spirit hovering behind our groins, although I confess to believing this to be partly true during high school.

This is instinct.

Evidence of rudimentary 'surgeries' that tapped into the human skull can be found as far back as 7000 BC – thousands of craniums punctured with clean holes, some of which showed signs of healing. It's called 'trepanning' which, I'll admit, makes the procedure sound more fun than it is. Trepanation, in this manner, seems to have been conducted to treat head wounds or signs of neurological trauma, and the holes have been discovered in various locations around the skull, supporting this theory.

The plot thickened after researchers discovered a total of twelve skulls from a handful of different sites all within a fifty-kilometre radius of each other in the Rostov-on-Don region in southern Russia. These skulls were extremely rare because they all contained trepanation holes high and at the back of the cranium (at the obelion, keen students), which is a point of extremely high blood flow.

Boring a hole in that location is, in other words, considerably dangerous. It would have led to almost certain death. These specimens showed no signs of brain injury or disease – though such conditions do not always leave traces on the skull – so it raises the question: what, precisely, were our ancestors looking for in those holes?

It's possible, researchers say, they were looking for our selves. Or themselves.

Ritualistic trepanation may have been a way to release the bad 'energy' of mental illness, a term that would not be invented for another few thousand years. They drilled holes in the head because the basic intuition of our forebears was that we could be found in there, for better or worse.

Trepanation is our ancestors' attempt at neurofeedback. Our understanding has not come a long way since.

While in many ways I am writing this book from the comfort of having at least figured out the basic outline of what is happening in the gears of my mind, I still haven't 'fixed' the underlying issues.

True, I am at a point of stability I haven't felt in over a decade; but part of that, I know, is that I am in between trigger points. The sense of abandonment that sinks into me like sharp stones when I form close attachments to male figures in my life – friends, mostly – comes and goes depending on the imprecise alchemy of how I form those attachments. Currently, I have no such relationships that are so overpowering that the feared retreat of a man I have come to love would bring me undone. But I have had five or six of them over the past years and I've no idea if there will be more, or when. Worse, I've no idea whether my handling of that trauma response – which flicks on inside myself like a doomsday switch – has improved.

I want to improve it.

The very idea that consciousness – and with it, notions of free will – is so nebulous and vanishingly weak in comparison to the more assertive unconscious operation of our brains has run up against my studied instincts of optimism.

But does any of this self-aware searching actually matter? Does it re-code an ounce of my brain or overthrow the dictator in my own skull? So far I have not been able to regain control. My awareness, like the area covered by a sweeping searchlight, has extended only so far as to reveal the approximate volume of the stuff about which I am conscious but not actually in control of. I am aware of the extent of the operation of myself that runs far beneath the surface of my understanding but it is not mine to command.

One of the most common types of dream is the one where you know you need to run to escape some fast approaching danger but your legs won't move. You sense the total urgency of the moment, you beg your legs to work but you remain stuck. Or, somehow worse, you may manage a single, painstakingly slow step before having to focus all your might and attention on the next leg. All the while the thing that threatens you bears down.

We hate this dream because it severs our minds from our bodies. Yet, in our waking state, few of us comprehend just how detached our minds are from our brains.

This mental blockage was on – or in, I suppose – my own mind when I flew to New York in March 2020 to have what turned out to be a brain-bending chat with the philosopher David Chalmers in his office at New York University.

Chalmers has been described as a 'rock star' of the field, and his appearance, when he arrives at his office on a rainy Tuesday in early March, does nothing to dissuade me of this. His once long, flowing grey hair has been restrained somewhat to a shaggy crop of silver that stops before his neck. He's dressed almost entirely in black and grey and he has an easy smile.

If a wizard from some magical realm who speaks only in riddles was transported to modern New York and had to try and blend in, he would look and act a lot like David Chalmers.

The riddles are not deliberate, it's just that he specialises in what has become known as the 'hard problem' – a term he coined in 1995 – of consciousness. Which is: where the fuck does consciousness come from? The easy problem, by inference, is not really easy as much as it is knowable. *How* the brain processes data (like visual inputs and sound) and which areas approximately run which parts of the body or thought, are things we have figured out and are still working on.

But answering any of those 'easy' bits will still tell us nothing about why it feels like something to *be* us.

'The point of this book,' I explained to Chalmers, 'is, I guess, I'm trying to take control of some of this stuff now and yet I wonder how useful that might actually be. Because I feel like life got better once I became more aware of what was going on. And I think that helps, but I'm not sure whether that in itself is a solution.'

Chalmers was curious.

'You acquired a theory of yourself,' he said. 'That's quite interesting. A lot of people think that the only way we really access our minds is by theories and models of ourselves. The same way we model other people.'

There is a school of thought – illusionism – that maintains consciousness itself will never be explained because it is not real. It's just a story our brains spin to cover the biomechanical systems that underpin everything we do. Chalmers is not totally convinced of this, but conceded it is something that should be taken 'seriously, philosophically'.

'People have done various things to soften us up about the idea that introspection is not that reliable in many ways,' Chalmers said. 'We've been wrong about our consciousness. Typically, we might think we have a fully detailed visual field experience of the world, like a picture, but vision scientists themselves have told us that is not so. We only really get details of what we're attending to. Everything else is just big blobs. But somehow introspection makes us think that we're conscious of more than we are.'

In the now classic split-brain experiments conducted by Roger Sperry and Michael Gazzaniga in the late 1950s and early 1960s, people whose corpus callosum had already been severed to treat otherwise incurable epilepsy were drafted to study what happens when the left and right hemispheres of a brain can no longer talk to each other. The corpus callosum is a bundle of nerve fibres that acts as an enormous information interchange between the two halves that typically process different kinds of information, like visual cues and language.

In some versions of the experiments, patients were shown mood-altering commands such as 'smile' and 'laugh' written on cards that could only be seen through the left eye. Such visual cues like these, viewed from the left, are processed in the right hemisphere of the brain. This is a crucial point to understand because the right hemisphere has some basic language abilities – it appears to do OK at recognising the names of things, like 'pencil', but falls apart when the words are verbs, commands or contain more complicated grammar – but not quite enough to fill in the gaps, at least in the first year or so after a person's brain is cut in two.

When subjects were shown the words 'smile' and 'laugh' through their left eyes, they did in fact smile and laugh. But here's the mind-boggling fact: they could not explain why they did. As far as their right brain, which processed the signal, was concerned, it followed the command. But the complex language centre in the left brain was completely in the dark.

When asked why they just smiled or laughed immediately after being shown the written commands in their left eye, the subjects concocted a story that bore no resemblance to reality. It was a case of the left brain improvising on the fly to find a coherent narrative in the absence of all the information.

In another experimental set-up, a seated person was shown a written command through only their left eye to stand up. Researchers wanted to see whether the command registered at all and, if it did, whether the person could tell them about it. Remember, the signal would be processed in the right brain where language skills are inferior to the left hemisphere. Would the right side follow the command and leave the left hemisphere to concoct a story?

So it was.

The person in the experiment stood up. The instruction registered *somewhere* in their brain even though they had no conscious awareness of that happening. And they *followed the instruction.*

The person had no idea why they did this. When asked to give a possible explanation, their brain improvised a narrative that simply wasn't true.

'I needed to stretch,' the subject said.

Chalmers knows this experiment, of course.

'You know, the brain is very good at fooling itself,' he offered when I mentioned it.

Given all of this – the subject stands without knowing they have been told to, the Pac-Man moves without my direct input, we have braked in the traffic jam before we knew we needed to – what is the point of being conscious at all?

'Well, it's one of the big questions,' Chalmers said. 'What role does it actually play? No one has really found an essential role for anything you might want consciousness to do. It's very unclear why you need it.'

This isn't just some theoretical fox-hunt. These are very real questions with very real implications. Chalmers himself is a mathematician by training and neuroscientists have spent the last few decades trying in earnest to answer this same question.

And then there is me, this kid who grew up with a brain that has both rescued and tortured him. I long to know what might have been different; how things might still be different if the knot between brain and mind can be untangled just a little.

I mentioned some of this to an acquaintance when they asked what I was working on and they chirped in response: 'Oh, so you're writing a self-help book?'

After extinguishing my cigarette in the ashtray at the bar, I gathered myself in response. '*Look* at me!' I cast my arms across my body, like a used car salesman revealing a 1995 panel van for sale. 'I am not a self-help kind of guy.'

Yes, sure, I was trying to help myself, but I don't really have any answers. Have you ever paid $400 to go to a seminar with a positive life coach only for them to yell at the crowd: 'I've no idea what I am doing!'

Of course not.

(I've seen those self-help gurus and personal advertisements for the power of light-filled thinking or mindfulness. Smiling like their teeth are on fire, their lips having fled in opposite directions to freedom. I'd have to lose at least twenty kilograms just to be even faintly believable in the role and, besides, I never quite believed that *they* believed it. The stereotypical self-help success story strikes me as someone who is barely outpacing their own troubles, having decided they cannot be brought down if they just keep smiling and running and hula-hooping or whatever it is that they do now.)

My next session of neurofeedback is a wellspring of positivity. I'm shown a series of pictures on screen that reveal themselves square by square with a satisfying beep as each image begins to take shape. My brain wants the whole image. It is a greedy hedonist for the cute animal photos and landscapes.

There is a cheetah mum with five cubs lined up in a neat row behind her, their lithe frames stood atop the gentle rising curve of a tree on an open savannah. There is a photograph of three labradors – a chocolate, a yellow and a black one – side by side, grinning stupidly as if they were waiting for the encore at a community theatre production of *Cats*. There are photographs of regal elephants, tiny kittens, flamingoes, a grizzly bear on the top of a grassy knoll. There are snow-covered chalets and vistas of open fields, prairies and meadows, ravines and rainforests. It is as if all the motivational posters from the internet decided to hold a convention, at which I was the sole guest in attendance. They were beautiful and funny and I watched them slowly appear over half an hour, while the sensors on my earlobes and scalp sent signals back to the therapist's computer.

Novelist Vladimir Nabokov was in awe at the 'marvel of consciousness'; when asked in an interview for *Saturday Review* in 1976 what surprised him most in life, that's what he gave as his answer. He called it 'that sudden window swinging open on a sunlit landscape amidst the night of non-being'. Part of me expected to see such a vista in the neurofeedback program, a clue that something deeper was at work.

Sorting illusion from genuine advancements of the self prove difficult.

A week before I flew to New York to meet David Chalmers, a group of scientists published a stunning paper in the scientific journal *Neuron* in which they reported reanimating anaesthetised macaques near *instantly* with a tiny jolt of electricity deep inside their brains.

The monkeys went from being deeply, wholly sedated to waking up, looking around the room and reaching out within seconds of having their central lateral thalamus and the buried layers of their cerebral cortex stimulated. As the electrical stimulus stopped, the monkeys fell back into that total state of anaesthesia.

I was thinking about this exact study later in the year when I underwent surgery, the first time I had experienced general anaesthetic as an adult. Apart from my horror at the process of going under itself, one of the last things I remember thinking is how mad I'd be if anyone dared stimulate my central lateral thalamus.

The *Neuron* study is a mind-blowing development, though it is difficult to know what it means. The paper's co-author Michelle Redinbaugh from the University of Wisconsin told the website Inverse that the networking between these parts of the brain may indeed operate as the 'engine of consciousness'.

When I discussed it with Chalmers, he said he felt the discovery might be scientifically incremental.

'Who's to say about these creatures that wake up. Is it also possible that it's a wakeful state, not a conscious state?' he asked.

Chalmers said we can be conscious during sleep – while we dream, for example.

This raises another possibility for the evolution of consciousness: that we needed it for language, to tell ourselves and other people stories about how we are feeling, doing and creating.

The writer Cormac McCarthy, who has taken a special interest in such matters, wrote in *Nautilus* magazine that language is almost like a virus and infiltrated our species with a ruthless efficiency that natural selection couldn't hope to achieve. It simply arrived and commandeered the parts of the human brain that were the least busy.

His thesis, backed by scientific minds like those of evolutionary biologist David Krakauer, is that our unconscious was perfectly happy running the show for two million odd years before language showed up. That would explain why it still talks to us today in pictures and broad concepts – not words – and why we often have no idea what the hell is going on back there.

The subconscious is like an artist's inspiration, which might encourage the painting of a particular scene without any specific directive. Of course, like the subjects in the split-brain experiments, we can come up with a story later but it is just that, a story.

Language arrived well after our brains were built. We were not prepared for it and, in many ways, the subconscious has refused to adapt. 'The picture-story mode of presentation favored by the unconscious has the appeal of its simple utility. A picture can be recalled in its entirety whereas an essay cannot,' McCarthy says.

Take the condition known as trypophobia. While technically not a phobia, it is real – I have it – and it is born of a fear or disgust of closely packed holes. I can't tell you why these images make me recoil in horror, though researchers believe it is because of our ancient past. In the animal and plant kingdom, species with actual holes like this in their foliage or patterned on to their skin could be fatally poisonous. Before words could name the things, our unconscious mind had to find a way to keep us safe.

It did so using patterns.

McCarthy goes on to say that the facts of the world come to us as just that, facts, and that it is we who have to put them into narrative form. 'The simple understanding that one thing can be another thing is at the root of all things of our doing.'

Language, he means to say, is the engine that propels abstract thinking, which in turn is the driver of human ingenuity. Were it not for language, our internal world would have remained a very small and unimaginative thing.

In addition to unlocking creativity, the simple existence of language – spoken or otherwise – gave humanity a way to carry success, and memories of failure, through the generations. Language is the ability to 'save' your progress while playing a video game, rather than starting at the very beginning after each death.

I think this was patently a brilliant move for our collective success at civilisation – we established crops and then cities, harnessed forces to achieve heavier-than-air flight, put a man on the moon (but not a woman) and cured entire diseases – but it left something of a disjoint within ourselves.

The philosopher Daniel Dennett, something of an ideological nemesis to Chalmers, agrees with Cormac McCarthy's theory of the language super boost. He concurs that language hit us in the blink of an eye, too fast for Darwinian evolution to have orchestrated the change, and our brains have been trying to catch up ever since.

But it is this language that has played the role of out-of-body DNA, something that can be mutated and adapted at will to fit the world around us as it changes by our own hand. A useful discovery, certainly, but I wonder what happens when this precise grammatical and syntactical scaffold meets the amorphous nature of our subterranean mind.

It strikes me that this cognitive two-step was at least partly to blame for the apparent success, and then the stunting of, my therapeutic pursuit to get better. Putting what happened to me into a clear narrative provided an awareness not previously available to me about what had gone wrong. I used the front part of my brain for that, where higher order thinking is established. But after a certain point all my talk, that constant push for meaning from language, runs up against the ancient mode of the unconscious that has been using its preferred method of insight since well before the existence of words.

Just think about it.

The mere fact that I am here now, writing these words, is the result of some ancestor tens of thousands of years ago finding a way to express in more detail beyond rudimentary grunts how he or she was feeling and then *passing on the discovery.* That allowed people to communicate and collaborate with one another in a manner so intricate and finely tuned that our species broke the bumbling and painfully slow cycle of Darwinian evolution. It was a jailbreak that secured not just our survival, but our emergence as the dominant species.

Lot of pressure not to fuck it up, if you ask me.

It's a simple and well-established point. We tell stories of ourselves and about others and we do it because by now it has become a cultural imperative, the sinew that keeps our social species together, even if we no longer think of it that way. Our survival against the elements and the other animals depended on teamwork, and our teamwork became blazingly sharp when we learned to speak.

Language is the crack of light that fell across the darkness of our minds.

It did not, however, fall evenly.

There is a stream of trauma treatment called narrative exposure therapy where we coax people by themselves or in groups to give voice to one or more moments in their lives where they suffered greatly. The narrative slowly builds to include other events, even positive ones, so the person can establish their hurt as a single point on a very large canvas. Maybe it's many points, though the effect is the same.

In their book *Narrative Exposure Therapy*, authors Maggie Schauer, Frank Neuner and Thomas Elbert write:

> Trauma destroys the human kernel that resides in moments or acts that occur in a social context: communication, speech, autobiographical remembrance, dignity, peace and freedom.
>
> Trauma isolates the survivor, alienates life, and indeed freezes the flow of one's personal biography.

I like this theoretical approach and I think it has a lot of value, though I do not believe it alone is the answer.

Take my own story, for example.

It helped, oh how it helped, to assemble the fragments of my life into a thing with explanatory power. I spent the better part of a decade doing this, picking through the membrane that held my life together and identifying the way events and moments were connected. Most of it was like hacking through weeds, if I'm honest, but if you've been slack on the upkeep you have to move through the weeds to find the path.

And then the progress stopped. It wasn't for lack of trying; it's just an intractable reality when you come up against the two parts of ourselves. Introspection can lead us to the wall, and we may perhaps imagine what lies beyond it, but we do not easily control the unconscious, if at all.

How damaging to be the creature that invented language, lost to the fear network.

Consciousness is the slow drip of a leak from a dam wall, hoarding the total reservoir of our brain's processes behind it in a lake. We cannot see the lake, though we know it exists and every drop of awareness that has ever been visited upon us has sprung from that vast body of water.

Around the year 627, the Venerable Bede wrote *The Ecclesiastical History of the English People*, an account of Northumbria's King Edwin seeking advice from his counsellors on conversion to Christianity. One of his men compares the life of a single human being to a sparrow that has flown in one window of the king's banquet hall and out another:

> While [the sparrow] is inside, he is safe from the winter storms; but after a few moments of comfort, he vanishes from sight into the wintry world from which he came. Even so, man appears on earth for a little while; but of what went before this life or of what follows, we know nothing.

Consciousness, I think, is the span of flight that sparrow enjoys in that warm banquet hall. What happens beyond either window is a mystery immune to our best guesses.

Our observable universe is the same. It has a diameter of almost 100 billion light years, though we do not believe it simply stops at some distant border. We cannot see beyond this range (46.5 billion light years in any direction) because the universe is not old enough for that distant light to have had the time to travel to our eyes.

There is more out there: beyond the banquet hall, in the lake, in the universe, in our minds.

That is what makes the neurofeedback program so counterintuitive and so necessary. It takes me where talk and narrative therapy never could because it bypasses the reasoning brain and goes straight for the subconscious wiring. As Dr Gurr says, if you don't lay down a language memory of a traumatic event, the help must come from elsewhere.

Philosopher Daniel Dennett is among the most influential proponents who wonder whether our conscious mind is just another form of a 'user illusion' – like a desktop screen on your computer. Take the icons on your computer screen. They are each governed by lines of code and complex systems that form a set of instructions. The graphical user interface, created by Apple, was a breakthrough because it meant ordinary users didn't need to know the code to make the computer work, as long as these intricate functions could be represented by simple graphics, or icons. That's the illusion.

In much the same way, Dennett proposes, our conscious mind is a simplified projection of the brain that gives us the suggestion of control. In reality, he says, we know nothing of, nor do we need to know, how the code works.

Subconsciousness is subterranean, like one of those naked mole rats. If you want to bring that stuff to the surface you're going to need to put a nice coat on it so it doesn't scare the kids.

When I graduate from the Pac-Man game in my neurofeedback sessions I am allowed to watch a movie. The premise is similar. If my brain behaves itself, the movie plays as it should. If my brain waves enter territory classified as out of bounds, the screen becomes gradually shaded with an opaque filter, like somebody has rubbed toothpaste on it.

I can choose my movies from a cupboard, which doesn't look like it has been updated since video stores went broke. This isn't a bad thing. Life was a lot simpler when we had to go to a shopfront to get a movie. In the local video store in my home town of Boonah, sometimes all the copies of the one film I wanted had already been booked out on a Friday night, but this competitive spirit made me feel alive, animated with thoughts of delayed gratification and revenge.

I'm not saying this is a good thing, but where has that energy been redirected now, I wonder.

Without giving it much thought, I choose *The Matrix: Reloaded* from the sad cupboard because I wanted to feel like I was sixteen again, in the van with my friend's dad and my mates on the way to a midnight screening in the nearest town with a big cinema. What a funny thread that has connected my life in that moment to the one I am living now, trying to take the themes of the film seriously instead of just turning up for the fighting bits.

There's something eerie about the experience of being hooked up to electrodes on my scalp and ears as the Oracle tells Neo he 'didn't come here to make the choice'.

'You've already made it. You're here to try to understand *why* you made it,' she says.

Well, damn. Isn't that the very definition of the work we do on ourselves? We are trying to understand how the swallow came to be in that banquet hall and where it might have gone.

Leo Tolstoy's diary entry for 25 January 1851 is remarkably short and glorious:

> I've fallen in love or imagine I have; went to a party and lost my head. Bought a horse which I don't need at all.

We should very much like to know why it is we bought the horse.

This kind of thinking accords with the deterministic view of the universe, which sees our minds as just one more element in a physical system governed by the absolute laws of physics.

Our brains, though living tissue, are ultimately only collections of atomic particles. The same particles make the sun, the other stars, planets and gases. That is all there is, a constituency of bric-a-brac.

If we had the God-like power to know absolutely everything about absolutely every particle in the universe, none of what happens at any given moment would be a surprise because *there could only be one way for each interaction to unfold.* And those interactions would be specifically limited by the collision of particles that came before it, and the collision that came before that and so on, stretching right back to the time of the Big Bang.

In a game of pool, the billiard balls follow these laws of physics. Even with our inferior knowledge of the practical forces and velocity and angles involved, we have a fairly good idea of where certain shots can take us. With even more intel (and, let's face it, coordination) it would cease to be a game at all.

Most everything would be predetermined.

Our brains are pool tables, after a fashion, and the connections and synaptic responses are ultimately carried out by electrons and cells made of other particles. My decision right now to drink from the water bottle on my desk was made possible by an earlier decision to fill it up from the jug in the fridge but it was also set up by my decision to move back to Sydney late in 2019. These two apparent decisions could only have followed the countless tiny moments that came before them. And that medley of little decisions traces back even further, to my childhood and into my parents' lives and back through human history, the birth of the solar system and eventually to the Big Bang itself.

It's all just particles smashing into other particles and following the rules.

That's determinism, a concept that raises legitimat
about free will, the notion that we 'could have done

at any given juncture. I know this stuff sounds like the pointless distraction of sophomoric personalities, but most scientists agree we are just bags of cells buffeted by the forces of the world around us.

In my weaker moments, I wonder whether my search for a better brain even stands a chance. I mean, it's a strange place to begin with.

Just moments ago I awoke from a mid-afternoon nap and a single urge ascended into me. I say ascended because it really did feel like it had wafted up on a gentle breeze from somewhere deep in my subconscious.

That urge was this: play Delta Goodrem's 2003 hit 'Innocent Eyes'.

Now, I'm no Delta super fan and, if I had to guess, the last time I heard that song was five years ago. Before I had my nap I had not been speaking about her or anything connected with her and yet, when I awoke, there it was.

This thought, totally unbidden, had arrived and I was powerless against it. Try as I might to examine how it came to be, I am left with zero clues. Somewhere, in the latticework of my brain, a memory of this song broke free and drifted to the surface like a bubble of air in an aquarium.

And there it was.

So I'm writing this now, having just listened to 'Innocent Eyes', and I'm further plagued by the sense that each sentence here has itself come unbidden into my mind. There has been no instruction, for example, where I choose each specific word in the precise order I intend to write it. They just come and I, the stenographer, write them into the hansard of this book.

Becoming disillusioned with the idea that I might change my circumstances through sheer will is not a useful state of being, however. That's one reason why scientists and philosophers alike don't hammer us over the head with such observations. Sure, this thing may be true but knowing so does not help us in any practical way.

It is enough, I think, to know that we are not the sole authors of our lives.

This was Baruch Spinoza's revolutionary insight in the seventeenth century.

'Men are mistaken in thinking themselves free; and this opinion depends on this alone, that they are conscious of their actions and ignorant of the causes by which they are determined,' he wrote in *Ethics*, published the year he died.

> This, therefore, is their idea of liberty, that they should know no causes of their actions. For when they say that human actions depend on the will, these are words of which they have no idea.
>
> For none of them know what is will and how it moves the body; those who boast otherwise and feign dwellings and habitations of the soul, provoke either laughter or disgust.

Ouch.

It all sounds so defeatist, though I promise it is not.

Spinoza, a lens grinder who was excommunicated for his bold ideas, had a certain genius that turned the bald facts of life into something more profound. It is important to grasp what he has to say.

The philosophical solution to the riddle of whether we have free will begins with the notion of *conatus,* a sort of existential endeavour by which certain things 'persist in their own being'. This most obviously applies to all living organisms which have, to varying degrees, the desire to continue existing. Such things, unlike a grain of sand or a rock, have a strong urge to avoid danger and heal themselves when injured.

So far, so not rocket science.

In Spinoza's view, such things can possess more and more *conatus* until they become God-like, though never reaching or surpassing this 'God' in its endeavours. The key to reaching the higher chambers of *conatus* is the quest to understand and take as much charge as physical laws will allow over the condition in which we find ourselves.

Truth, therefore, is an act of personal enrichment. If we travel through the valley of disenchantment and remove the helpful illusions of our own existence (like free will), we can emerge on the other side to see the world as God would, enlivened by the complexity of its moving pieces.

It is not so odd that Spinoza, a man who sought to prove the existence of God, was branded a heretic, though I find no less solace in the idea that this God is not one of a religious bent. Perhaps this God is simply an essence of an already very strange universe, a cosmic emergence similar to consciousness that arrives from its constituent parts. Maybe God is just beauty, as we find it.

However we might understand it, Spinoza charts a course to freedom.

'If the way I have shown to lead to these things now seems very hard, still it can be found,' he wrote. 'And of course, what is found so rarely must be hard. For if salvation were at hand, and could be found without great effort, how could nearly everyone neglect it? But all things excellent are as difficult as they are rare.'

This is the kind of salvation with which I can get on board. Long before I read Spinoza, my guiding personal philosophy was one of curiosity. Ignorance should not, in itself, be punished. We are born ignorant and we grow according to our different capacities and access to resources. Being curious, however, is truly valuable. That it is ever invoked, to explain the world or ourselves, is the engine room of awe. And, as per Spinoza, it is the only way to truly be free.

I reminded myself of this during what unexpectedly became my final neurofeedback session, rudely interrupted as my appointments were by the worst pandemic since the Spanish Flu in 1918.

Was I getting anywhere with this therapy? Something was beginning to happen, though I'm not sure what.

Early on in my sessions, the therapist told me I would need to have about fourteen visits before I noticed any change at all and forty for the progress to be coded more permanently into my brain. We only got to six.

In the second last session before it was decided that rubbing a conductive gel on my ears and scalp constituted a public health risk, I left the centre feeling a little woozy. By the time I returned home I was beyond exhausted. Moving from the front door to the lounge felt like an uncommon effort. To an outsider, it might have looked as if I was a rhinoceros that had been tranquillised from a low-flying helicopter as part of a park relocation project. My movements were slow and awkward and when I finally hit the couch I didn't move again for three hours.

The sleep came heavy and total, as it did for those anaesthetised macaques I'd read about in *Neuron*. What whisker-thin marionette strings had been pulled in my mind, I wondered.

Perhaps it is too easy to say, as I want to, that it seemed fitting my quest for understanding my own mind had ground to a halt. Perhaps it is too easy to suggest that this was some kind of polite reminder that I was not going to be the one to crack the enigma code within us all. How presumptuous, even, to try.

I do know this, however.

My consciousness harbours an echo of some audible horror that happened a long time ago. Eventually, if we are lucky, the sound and fury fade away. Oh, I work at it. The *work* is sometimes all there is.

It does not elude me that my existence is in many respects an act of diminishment. Quiet the echo, quiet the source; quiet as salvation.

Per Spinoza, though, I need not write QED at the bottom of the equation. Asking is enough.

And it is true to say that I understand volumes more about my selves than I ever thought possible. I know that there are moments when my brain tells my body and me that we are under attack and I know those moments look a lot like abandonment. I know why I simultaneously crave and then burn acceptance. I know that sabotage is sometimes a revolutionary act but that, equally, it can hold a system in place against the imperative of change.

And then there is this.

When you try to catch a glimpse of yourself in a mirror – to see yourself spontaneously as others might – you always fail. It is impossible to capture that living frame as God or others might see it. There is only the blur of motion and light and a face looking back at you that knows the trick you tried to play.

Even on camera there is nothing that can show a person what it is to view themselves from the outside.

Our cognitive machinery is like this, too. We snatch curtains and covers in vain attempts to draw the outline of the self, the *real* self, and we see only the edge of shadows as the covers shift back into place. We interrogate ourselves and find only echoes.

In the end, these games we play in the mirror or in our minds reveal themselves for what they are. There is only you, looking back at yourself and asking for forgiveness.

Forgiveness

In late 2012, I was partying with friends at the Imperial in the Sydney suburb of Erskineville. The pub-turned-club was an icon of the city's drag scene and served as the opening venue for *Priscilla: Queen of the Desert*, a film that I loved but which was nonetheless my only natural enemy as a teenager in country Queensland.

There was nothing special happening that night but it was a Saturday and two friends and I were looking to get smashed and dance. No use pretending to a higher cause.

I was drinking rum and coke like it was water and, back then at least, could stay out all night without the need for performance-enhancing drugs. The caffeine alone could have restarted a dead buffalo. Eventually, the other two grew tired and asked if I wanted to leave. I didn't but it was also unusual for me to stay out anywhere on my own.

The idea of being the sad bloke in his mid-twenties drunk and dancing at a club was repulsive to me, but the little widget that regulates such disgust in the human body, the anterior insula, was at that point swimming in two litres of cola and spirits. So I stayed.

There was one man I'd had my eye on. He was slightly older than me, handsome and appeared to be with a friend. I couldn't have done anything about it, though. This was during a stage of my extremely delayed development. My making any kind of move at all would have been as graceful as a cruise liner doing a three-point turn on a motorway, so I did nothing.

This might explain my stunning pliability when the man came over to me and started chatting. The rest of the evening at the Imperial is a fractured mess of memory. I remember snatches, but nothing that could constitute a reliable narrative. I do remember being propositioned to leave, though, and getting into a car with the man, his friend and another ring-in: a lad from the country who had fallen in with this small group of strangers. I recall being surprised that the cute guy was able to drive and gave the situation a cursory thought – *hope they don't crash* – but said nothing.

In fact, *nothing* was a feature of my response that night. I fell into the slipstream of other people and let my self end up where it may. The guy from the country was in a state when we arrived at the nondescript apartment block. He was solidly built and reminded me of people from my past who chewed grass, checked rain gauges with silent concern and kept themselves emotionally hidden in order to survive.

'I don't wanna be gay,' he kept yelling in a mournful, drawn-out howl. We were in a lift heading up to the apartment of the two strangers and I was haunted then, as I am now, by this bloke's distress.

When we got inside, the other two men quickly disappeared and I sat with the country fella on a bed in another room and, through increasingly slurred speech, attempted to give him some gay wisdom.

I had not much to give. I had come out three years earlier and had only kissed a single person in that time. I knew what he was feeling because I still felt it, only he was clearly in his thirties and time had eaten away at him more than it had me. The grief I felt for him in that moment was also my own.

We tried kissing, though it was difficult for both of us. My body became increasingly paralysed and floppy and eventually I lay back on the bed wondering what it was I was even doing there.

That is when the two other men came into the room. What happened next was fast and purposeful and my response was only the faintest of recognition. Within seconds one of the men, the cute one I first spied in the club, had removed my pants and the other one was standing over my head. He shoved his dick in my mouth while the other one began raping me.

Here's what I need you to know about that moment. Right then, I felt mild surprise and nothing more. The next morning I told a friend I'd 'lost my virginity in a foursome' and made mirth of it. There was no sign of anyone when I woke up that morning. The sun was high in the sky already and the apartment silent. I gathered my things in a stupor and called a cab after looking for the address on Google Maps. I still can't remember the suburb.

I have no memory, either, of telling my friend that the men had given me ketamine, the horse tranquilliser party drug famous for the near-paralysis 'ket-hole' it can induce. There is not even a whisper of recall in my mind, certainly not of actually taking it.

And that is how I thought that story would end, as a self-deprecating humorous anecdote about this awkward sexless young adult who somehow stumbled into an orgy the first time he ever 'had sex'.

Somewhere below the choppy waters of my conscious mind I knew this wasn't true. Spinning it as a voluntary, enjoyable encounter had resulted in an obstruction of my being. I came to understand it was doing me harm. It was barely a register, at first. I was still telling new friends in 2017 the story as an in-joke, laughing with them until they asked for details on how it happened.

I watched their faces grow unsure with each new reveal until eventually I stopped, not wanting to unsettle anyone else at the table. Maybe I didn't want to unsettle myself, either, though the truth of it is that I didn't care.

One of the defining characteristics of the person who has survived some form of developmental trauma is that it usually takes a lot of convincing for them to know – really know – they are loved or even worthy of its graces.

The thing that should have shaken me on that night I instead understood as the normal consequence of life for someone like me: that bad things would happen to me and they would be right to happen because that had been the enduring lesson of my years to that point.

I joked about being raped, and struggled, when I was alone, to even see it for what it was, because the evidence of my worth had been arranged in such a way for so long that other conclusions were unavailable.

When I was trying to find the right words to articulate this sensation, I came across an interview the actor Thandie Newton did with *Vulture* about the pernicious effect the entertainment industry's racism had on her own sense of value.

'It just made me super-vulnerable to predators,' she told the publication. 'That's the truth. Because there's so much about not having a sense of my value. I suffered quite badly for a couple of years from anorexia, and it all feeds into this. Just wanting to disappear. What happened for me was I had a very complicated relationship with … I never chose. I let other people do the choosing for me. That saddens me.'

That last line about outsourcing the very act of choosing sent a bolt of recognition through me. I was like, *hey, who took this photograph of me?*

When abuse takes place within a family, researchers have found that the trauma is made all the worse by a betrayal of trust. The same goes for other places where children are supposed to trust adults: schools, religious institutions, sporting clubs.

Researchers Wei-May Su and Louise Stone write in the July 2020 issue of the *Australian Journal of General Practice:*

> In betrayal trauma, symptoms are more likely to be severe, and survivors often lose their capacity to detect unsafe behaviours into adulthood. For this reason, they are more likely to stay in unsafe relationships.

On that night back in 2012, even while pickled in Bundy and coke, there were so many red flags. The 'cute' guy I kept looking at was sketchy as hell, he drove wasted, the vibe was totally off.

There is a tendency to think the abused child in adulthood has a sense of innocence – why else would they go with a suspicious stranger into the night and take on such a risk? This misses the point, though. In most cases, myself included, it's not that we are naive. Truly, we've seen more than we should ever have. Instead, our behaviour flows from a violation of trust that infects everything else. We seek to reinforce a view of our worth that has already been so degraded.

And there is the shame.

'If a child is abused at a young age, they tend to believe they deserve it,' Su and Stone write in their journal paper. 'This pervasive sense of shame can be difficult to shift.'

Outward appearances mean nothing here, as Su and Stone say. The survivor of such a fundamental betrayal can be highly regarded, loved and otherwise doing well in life and still their minds and bodies succumb to shame.

These all exist on a spectrum. I did not languish in a Romanian orphanage, for example, but I have been betrayed at a crucial moment of my development in a way that made temples of hurt in later life. Part of the reason the rape was so confusing for me is that it did not feel how I expected it would, psychologically. It bubbled away in memory and attached itself to feelings of disgust and shame but, ultimately, could never rival in intensity the prototypical hurt of my childhood.

They call these risky behaviours maladaptive. It is an unwieldy word that essentially means *not helping*.

I am writing this now to regain some of that agency.

It is not as simple as changing your thinking. Anyone who tells you that, especially if you suffer the physiological consequences of cumulative emotional battles, is a bit of a fuck. And I say that with empathy, for haven't we all been that person?

I'm detailing this story now because it is important to correct my own thinking. Of course, it's private and in some ways embarrassing. The ordinary day-to-day fear response in my brain that is meant to protect me from getting mugged or raped is curiously atrophied, yet on the other hand this has allowed me a strange bravado in writing about such things, too. At a certain point, you realise no one else can ever make you feel worse about yourself than you do, which is a kind of win.

I'm not doing this for the fun of it, though. I had to tell this story so that what follows has any meaning at all.

I forgive my rapists.

It has been eight years since I was on that bed, drugged and largely non-responsive. I'm not even sure if these men used a condom, which was the most unsettling part of the experience. It was my first time. There wouldn't be another for six years. They stole something from me that night that will never be replaced.

Yet I forgive them.

If this could have been done any earlier I'd have been glad for it, though that isn't how any of this works. Forgiveness is not itself a resource that can be marshalled; it is an emergent phenomenon that springs from its parts. Empathy, kindness and understanding all play their role here, but they do it in concert with due scepticism and restraint.

Put it this way: just saying 'I forgive you' is not going to cut it. Sure, for the recipient of that phrase it might be enough to send them on their merry way. But for the wronged, offering forgiveness is not simply a phrase.

Forgiveness is a garden in bloom. You are never guaranteed the beauty of those flowers, though your best chance is and has always been to tend to them nonetheless. We practise true absolution when we have tended to the parts of the whole.

I don't know the men who assaulted me. It will never be clear to me whether they simply wanted something they saw no need to ask for or whether their intent was more predatory even than that. There is no map of their histories; who they are when they are not in that room of my mind – nor in that room itself with me – remains a mystery.

The room on the night is like a theatre stage in my head. Its walls were white and featureless. The apartment was modern but in the way cheap new developments often are.

Across the floorboards of this proscenium stage trod the three men and myself, playing our roles in the production of my abuse. This is dissociation in action. I am watching the four players as if from the stalls, a theatre critic alone in the dark trying to parse the drama for meaning.

In truth, I didn't say no that night because I didn't love myself enough to think it an option. The responsibility for abuse lies with the abuser, always, though I can't escape the idea that being able to forgive them came only after I was able to forgive myself.

I have known mercy.

It can fall on a person the way a single drop of rain overwhelms a beetle on the concourse of the earth; suddenly, like a flood. It can leave you gasping for air.

There is love in that ministry of forgiveness, though it does not travel the way we think. When we love ourselves first, we can then forgive others. There is a recognition that to do otherwise would be to stoke the coals of hate, which is itself an abuse against existing hurt. Hate is oxygen to the fires of pain. It is both source and sustenance.

To understand the physics of forgiveness, we must start with the wound itself.

The wound is real. Whether it is physical, emotional or psychic: the wound is real and so is the hurt. Accept this.

It has happened. The thing cannot be undone, in the same way an egg cannot be unscrambled, nor the bread unbaked. The thing cannot be reversed.

But as the writer and poet David Whyte writes in his book *Consolations*, forgiveness can change our relationship to it.

> Forgiveness is a heartache and difficult to achieve because, strangely, it not only refuses to eliminate the original wound, but actually draws us closer to its source.
>
> To approach forgiveness is to close in on the nature of the hurt itself, the only remedy being, as we approach its raw center, to reimagine our relation to it.

Many are the times I have needed forgiveness but greater are the times I have needed to forgive.

In the 1930s, Swiss psychologist and child development researcher Jean Piaget attempted to build a scaffold for forgiveness as a moral good. He noted that children, before they became teenagers, rejected the idea of an 'eye for eye'. In one example, when Piaget asked a ten-year-old boy why he did not strike back another child who had just hit him, the boy replied: 'Because there is no end to revenge.'

It is easy to impart a sense of wisdom on to children, though of course they are all different. Still, left to their own devices and without the interference of our own learned inadequacies, I have found them wiser than adults in the realm of intuition.

Antoine de Saint-Exupéry, author of the children's classic *The Little Prince*, asks any child 'who may read this book to forgive me for dedicating it to a grown-up'. He says, 'All grown-ups started off as children (though few remember).'

What did that ten-year-old boy understand at a deeper level about his reflex against revenge? That it has such potential to extinguish the person who has wronged – an appealing notion if they are particularly odious or cruel – but that the flames of vengeance are not so easily contained to one person.

They burn more widely.

In the late 1980s, psychologist Robert Enright developed a model of forgiveness – and how to measure it – which broke the concept into six stages, five of them containing conditions that are imposed on the person who is being forgiven. Only the last stage promotes a 'true sense of love'.

'Because I must truly care for each person, a hurtful act on his or her part does not alter that sense of love,' Enright says. 'This kind of relationship keeps open the possibility of reconciliation and closes the door on revenge. Forgiveness is no longer dependent on a social context. The forgiver does not control the other by forgiving, but releases him or her.'

I don't want anything from my abusers and I have not forgiven them because, for instance, a religious code demands it; one of the conditions in Enright's hierarchy. There has been no social pressure brought to bear on my thinking, so the forgiveness I offer is not in deference to society at large.

It is an unconditional gift, an act of love.

'Forgiveness as an expression of abstract identity welcomes offenders into the human community, perhaps like no other moral concept,' Enright says in a 1994 paper in the journal *Human Development*. 'It fosters the belief that offenders are of considerable worth, a part of our human community.'

I think there is considerable value in forgiveness if you can realise it at a personal level, though the literature on its value for people who have suffered significant trauma is mixed. There should be no forced expectation of it and, where there is, people who have said the words but only out of a sense of duty can be hurt even more by the giving of it.

And what of mass atrocities?

In 1998, after South Africa established the Truth and Reconciliation Commission (TRC) following decades of violent apartheid, the commission's chair Anglican Archbishop Desmond Tutu said this:

> Forgiveness is an absolute necessity for continued human existence.

The reality of those hearings – which required confession, forgiveness in the form of legal amnesty decided by a committee, and restitution – is far more complex of course.

Cape Town's Institute for Justice and Reconciliation executive director Stan Henkeman has said the TRC did a 'sterling job', but conceded it could never have been a silver bullet. Any move towards peace must start with acknowledgement but, more than two decades after the commission began, many have become stuck in a new cycle of despair. The process has been criticised for making the guilty parties feel better about their crimes while requiring little in the way of enduring behavioural change. This isn't a violation of the stages of forgiveness because in these cases the abuse is still going.

'If we look at the young people today, especially black, young people who are still experiencing the struggles of poverty, unemployment, and exclusion that their parents went through, they are extremely critical of the TRC,' Henkeman told Public Radio International's *The World* in June 2020. 'In fact, they call the TRC a whitewash of white atrocities.'

McMaster University Professor of History and Global Human Rights Bonny Ibhawoh noted in *The Conversation* that, since the 1980s, truth and reconciliation structures have been used in countries like Chile, Sierra Leone, Rwanda, the Philippines and South Korea. Despite the limitations of the model, South Africa's is considered the gold standard.

In his article in *The Conversation*, Ibhawoh quoted from Dag Hammarskjöld, who had been the secretary general of the United Nations in the 1950s. Criticised over the limitations of the UN, Hammarskjöld had once said the UN was 'not created to take mankind to heaven, but to save humanity from hell'.

Ibhawoh likened South Africa's Truth and Reconciliation Commission to the UN, arguing its purpose was not to turn South Africa into an 'idyllic utopia', as that would have been unrealistic following 'a century of colonialism and apartheid'. Its purpose, he said, was 'to save South Africa, then a nuclear power, from an implosion – one that many feared would trigger a wider international war'. He determined: 'To the extent that the commission saved South Africa from hell, I think it was successful. Is it a low benchmark? Perhaps, but it did its work.'

I like this concept of forgiveness as a detour around personal hell. The truth-telling part, if we are to move on from anything, is ground zero.

We've had no such acknowledgement in Australia and, really, no attempt at it from those in power. And it's not for lack of effort by First Peoples, either.

Indigenous people in Australia have had such truth-telling customs in their culture long before overseas governments first tried them in the 1980s. Like, tens of thousands of years before. I know, right?

In Yolngu-Matha language the process of healing that begins with truth-telling is called Makarrata and it has been proposed as a reconciliation policy solution in Australia since the late 1970s. In 2017, the bid for constitutional recognition of First Nations people through the Uluru Statement of the Heart process coincided with growing calls for the establishment of a Makarrata Commission.

The omission in our own history is just as harmful as the alternative, sanitised stories we have told in its place.

I didn't learn much about the intricacies of Aboriginal and Torres Strait Islander culture in school. Oh, there was much about the First Fleet and the penal colony and occasional spotlights on figures like Neville Bonner and Truganini (though I knew nothing of the horrors she endured until I went looking for penguins on Bruny Island with my mum and came across a lonely sign in her honour).

But there was nothing substantial in that education that alluded to *what non-Indigenous Australians did.* In high-school

English we watched the film *Rabbit-Proof Fence*, and discussions ranged into the fertile territory of dispossession and attempted genocide. (I would learn nothing of the Frontier Wars until my mid-twenties.)

Institutionally at least, there was always the sense that Indigenous people were standing in the way of an overwhelmingly white narrative of progress and conquest.

I had more reason than most to know at least a little bit about what came before white settlement: my father and his ancestors had grown up side by side with Aboriginal people on the edge of the Simpson Desert. Though these relationships were always by their very nature unequal, the two groups adopted much from the other.

I could not distinguish between the peculiar accent of my dad and the Indigenous people in that corner of far-west Queensland that runs into the emptiness of South Australia; they were one and the same.

These were superficial observations, however, and I would go through life painfully unaware of anything more than that.

In early 2020 an internet acquaintance of mine – it's a big world out there – messaged me on social media with a screenshot from a new book about the Coniston massacre by Michael Bradley. The passage contained a single reference to a 'Nugget' Morton. My friend asked: 'Any relation?'

I had never heard the name before, though my general rule of thumb in life was to assume that any Morton west of Dalby in Queensland and into South Australia and the Northern Territory must have been a relation.

My father's family had settled on the Birdsville Track by the turn of the twentieth century and then ruled it with malice and blunt cunning for a century. Everyone knew that name and everyone knew the violent echoes of their bloodline.

I was immediately intrigued and began weeks of searching through ancestry records and old newspaper clippings on Trove, that gem of a platform hosted by the National Library of Australia.

In 1984, the year my brother, Toby, was born, the *Canberra Times* ran the second in its series of excerpts from the book *The Killing Times* by John Cribbin, a fictionalised account of the massacre of the Warlpiri people. Thanks to Trove, I was able to read the extracts and, as I moved my eyes through the archived newsprint, a feeling of dreadful recognition coursed through my body.

Nugget Morton was a 'frontiersman' who had moved into the harsh landscape of central Australia 'prepared to shape it to his purpose'. As Cribbin tells it, Morton was in his mid-forties at the time. Although a cattleman for most his life, his venture to establish a holding along the Lander River with a mob of cattle driven south across the desert was a bold one. There were no fences, nor any buildings. In fact there was nothing there at all to announce to the world proper that Nugget Morton had claimed this land as Broadmeadows Station.

'It was a raw tract of open bush where the stock were allowed to forage free,' Cribbin writes. 'Broadmeadow offered the most primitive subsistence to those who settled it but, in a sense, this suited Morton for beneath the exterior of this 20th century white [fella] was a most primitive man.'

Sure, he was a man of immense proportions; nearly as wide as he was tall. His arms looked like other man's legs, as if they didn't belong on his enormous shoulders. 'But the primitive man showed most clearly in his face,' Cribbin writes, 'broad fat features, the nose hammered across it, the skin made leathery by the sun, and small primeval eyes which held the world under incessant, angry surveillance.'

Cribbins's account was a creative retelling of the events, though it matches historical records, including firsthand interviews with and diaries of both Warlpiri people from the time as well as Nugget and his contemporaries.

Nugget's appraisal here was also an eerily precise description of almost every man in the Morton family going back as far as I knew, with only the rare one or two – my father and great-grandfather – turning into drought foals, lean and undersized. In my first book I called my forebears 'barrels with legs' and have, to a smaller degree, inherited some of their flat-footed gracelessness.

Now, of course, I had to know if this man was a distant relative. The similarities were uncanny, both physically and in his character.

Bryan Bowman, who later became the owner of the titular Coniston Station, called Nugget the 'cruellest' human being he had ever known. He said Nugget rode about the land with a gun always within reach and trailed by two particularly savage dogs, Nero and Tiger, who did his bidding.

If terror could manifest as physical forms, it might look much like Nugget stalking across his leaseholding.

Although the key events of this tale took place in 1928, an 'uncommon insight' into the man can be found via the personal diaries of T.G.H. Strehlow, an Aboriginal affairs patrol officer in the then Commonwealth-controlled territory, who had been sent in 1937 to investigate Morton's suspected breaches of the Aboriginal protectionist legislation. Strehlow wrote:

> Nugget Morton was keeping a Western Australian lubra [woman] there for his stockwork: she had tried to run away – as well as some of the girl victims mentioned below – but Morton had got her back (and the other two) each time and inflicted a severe hiding as a deterrent against further attempts to run away.

> Nugget was since employing as 'stockmen' (he has no male abos. working for him) one or two other little native girls, 9 or 10 years of age, whom he had raped. Another little girl he had given to his nephew 'Shrimp', who was about 17 years of age.
>
> Ben Nicker, who was working for Nugget, was similarly using a little girl, and both Ben and the girl were suffering from gonorrhoea.

The entries are considerably detailed, furnished with derogatory terms common for the time, and somewhat matter-of-fact. That the depravity of these acts should still leap off the page is testament to the horrors inflicted on Indigenous people, horrors that would march on through time and become harder to hide.

I've written elsewhere about the amorphous secret involving my grandfather George Morton's abuse of an Aboriginal woman. Whether it was above-average violence or sexual assault or rape is unclear, but the extended family do know my grandmother provided a false alibi as leverage to secure an education for her seven children. Until that moment, these Aboriginal women and girls had been kept as quasi-prisoners for free labour on the 6600-square-kilometre Pandie Pandie cattle station south of Birdsville.

On my father's side of the family, they were not just witnesses to colonial violence. They embodied it.

It was Nugget's use of 'lubras' – Aboriginal women stolen from their people by white men, for domestic work and rape – that was contributing to rising tensions in the Coniston area in the late 1920s. He also treated the local Warlpiri and any visitors with total contempt. He beat them savagely, often breaking their bones for being 'cheeky' and flailing them with a whip.

'Nugget was an immensely powerful man. He showed his disdain for Aborigines by always sitting with his back to them in any camp,' historian Dick Kimber writes in his twelve-part re-creation of the events surrounding the Coniston massacre.

One of those Aboriginal men so disdained by Nugget was Alex Wilson, who worked for the old man when he first arrived in the Centre. Wilson had his wife, an Indigenous woman from Halls Creek, summarily taken from him by Nugget and was flogged mercilessly with the cattleman's stock whip when he protested. The whipping left open wounds from shoulder to waist.

Kimber writes:

> Fifty years later Alex … lifted his shirt to show me the huge scar. Alex had no reason ever to respect Nugget, but every reason to fear him – as did most of the local Warlpiri people.

Around the same time, the region had been hit by the worst drought in three decades. Cattle brought into the interior by pastoralists were drinking waterholes dry and competing with native animals for food.

'The old ni—ers reckoned we were sitting down in *their* country,' Nugget Morton told Strehlow during an interview in 1932, 'and they started frightening our stock boys by telling them that they'd start shoving spears into them if they didn't go back to their own country and take their cattle too. They reckoned that there wasn't enough grass or water in the country for our cattle and their damn kangaroos.'

It is unclear if any specific thing triggered the attack on Nugget's neighbour Fred Brooks, but certainly it was born in this environment of fear and torment. Brooks was set upon and killed by a group of Warlpiri men and women in the first week of August 1928. His body was stuffed in a rabbit hole, with one leg sticking out into the open air. Weeks later, on 28 August, it was

Nugget's turn to face the consequences of his brutal reign.

Nugget was camping out on the Lander River. Accounts of what happened next agree to a startling extent. The oral history of the Warlpiri people accords almost entirely with the version of events given by Nugget who escaped – just – with his life.

The group of fifteen men that had ringed Nugget's camp at dawn sent in three of their quickest, and youngest, to lead the attack under the cover of asking the whitefella for food. Nugget was unusual among white settlers in the area in that he knew a number of Indigenous languages well enough for basic conversation. The best account of the ensuing fracas comes from Nugget himself as he gave it to authorities at the time. It is corroborated by Indigenous oral history from the time.

> After sunrise the next morning [28 August] I was having breakfast when three natives walked to my fire. I knew them, some by name. I told them to go back and sit down.
>
> Immediately one blackfellow walked to my fire again and said he was hungry and wanted beef. He spoke in his own lingo which I can speak and understand. Without looking up I handed him a piece of beef from the dish. He immediately seized my wrist my right wrist, swung behind me and caught the other arm behind me. The other two were on me in an instant. While endeavouring to throw them off I saw a mob of blacks rush out of the titree in front of me.
>
> The only thing I could do was make for the revolver that was in my swag. The three who were holding me hit me with their closed fists, anywhere they could get a hit on me. On gaining my revolver I was belted over the head with a nulla nulla.
>
> I don't remember how many hits I got, but I got more than one. The hits on the head put me in a very dazed

> condition. One big Aboriginal was standing over me with a nulla nulla going to bash me over the head. I was then standing up wrestling with the other fellow who had hold of me. I shot the Aboriginal who was standing over me, in the head. The others were still belting me.

Nugget was belted with a nulla nulla, or hunting stick, on the chin, face and head and had his thumb broken clean as he reached for the revolver.

> I held my left arm up to save my head and was just about all in when they left. After I tied up the cuts on my head from which I was losing a lot of blood and suffering great pain I got my horses and made my way back to my main camp which I reached in a very weak state from bruises and loss of blood.

I hesitated to include these details here because, to a certain eye, they make Nugget look heroic. But the fact is, he was a violent man whose history caught up with him. And he would descend into weak rage alongside the mounted policeman William George Murray, long considered the leader of the Coniston massacre.

Between 14 August and 18 October 1928, at least thirty-one members of the Warlpiri, Anmatyerre and Kaytetye people were killed in a series of ranging executions led first by Murray and subsequently by Nugget. The real death toll may never be known but it is likely to be as high as two hundred.

The agreed version of events between Murray and Nugget, told at the official inquiry in January 1929, is suspicious on more than a number of fronts. Still, Murray and Nugget admitted to killing fourteen people between them at Tomahawk Waterhole, the nearby Circle Well and on the Hanson River, which runs alongside the Lander. Nugget claimed he recognised the 'blacks' who set upon him at each attack.

Kimber makes an interesting point here about the Tomahawk killings. By this point in Murray's telling of the events he had dismounted his horse and been attacked on 'probably' ten different occasions. As with previous attacks on whitefellas, had these things happened as Murray claimed, he would certainly have been struck with waddies, boomerangs and yam-sticks. He might also have been knifed, speared or tomahawked dozens of times over.

'And yet there is no evidence that he needed the slightest bit of medical attention or bandaging. This is truly remarkable. His luck held in the next attack too,' Kimber says.

Remarkable, too, that another police patrol happening at the same time as this one managed to *arrest* twenty men, not kill them.

Film-maker Bob Plasto, who directed the documentary *A Shifting Dreaming* and the dramatised film *The Killing Times*, once interviewed a very old Alex Wilson, the young Indigenous man who had escaped Nugget Morton's violent rule only to find himself stuck in the murder party.

Bob asked him: 'Did they shoot in self-defence?'

Wilson was adamant in his reply. 'No! They shot 'em like a dog.'

Wilson told a friend of Dick Kimber long after the events of 1928: 'They never got off their horses. They shot them down in cold blood.'

Wilson was not asked to give his account at the offical inquiry by virtue of being 'half-caste' and illiterate, two facts which somehow rendered his testimony unreliable.

What are we to do with such a painful truth?

Bear in mind, this massacre happened almost a decade after Australian soldiers, including Indigenous men, finished fighting in World War One. Many went and some returned, having now established what millions still today consider the values of a fledgling nation. For most of the country and its people, this was no longer some lawless colonial experiment. It was a functioning democracy with a constitution and a criminal code; it had citizens who thought themselves proper and law-abiding. To the extent that these manners and customs were assumed by most of the white population, even in the interior of the continent, they never quite applied to First Peoples. In many ways, despite the modern appearance of legal oversight and appeals to justice, these rights afforded the non-Indigenous were still mere suggestions for those whose ancestors date back 70,000 years on this land.

We don't need a Nugget Morton in the family tree to find the current state of affairs abhorrent, though I find the idea that I might be related to him particularly troubling. Confusion creeps in because it's understood that this particular Morton had moved from Anningie station to Amaroo by the early 1930s.

Nugget and his wife were still on Amaroo (apparently it is spelled interchangeably with one 'm' or two, depending on the source) by 1949, but within four years it would be owned by C.C. Morton and Sons. Celcus Charles Morton is my great-grandfather.

I can find only one glancing reference to the change of ownership buried in the records, which says the surnames are entirely coincidental. The 14 April 1950 edition of the *Northern Standard* notes in a section called 'Around the Territory':

> Mr. and Mrs. W. 'Nugget' Morton and Terry seen in AS [Alice Springs]. They spent a busy time bidding their many friends farewell. They plan to live in Victoria. Strange coincidence that the new owners of Ammaroo Station should also possess the name of Morton.

Nugget had made his way to the interior from Melbourne decades before my extended family moved to the Birdsville Track in the late 1800s. Nugget Morton is not related, per this single newspaper clipping, to my great-grandfather.

The Morton name is everywhere in the region, spanning many decades. There are stories about Banjo Morton and Milly Kemarre Morton; Nigel Morton is the chair of a Northern Territory health service. But these are Aboriginal people and my family is not. For years and years, I assumed there had been marriages (I was naive, and possibly still am) or close connections. My great-grandmother's closest friend was an Indigenous woman called Ethel, I am told.

But their surname, Morton, did not come from my line.

In my frenzied searching to find out whether I was related to Nugget, I came across the website of the Short St. Gallery, which represents an accomplished artist by the name of Milly Kemarre Morton. She is an Alyawarre woman and her bio on the website was illuminating.

> Milly grew up on her mother's Country, Aherrenge. She was born in the bush, with no walls around her and has very strong ties to country and is amongst the best hunters in the community. Milly's father worked fencing the boundaries of Amaroo station, this is where the family was led and as was common they took the surname Morton, being the station owner.

They took their name from a murderer: Nugget Morton. There was no choice in it. Choice, for most people who weren't white landholders, was a degraded and famished thing.

It is not my place to make a case for forgiveness on such a broad acreage of violence and genocide. This hurt is not mine.

The concept of Makarrata gives non-Indigenous Australians like myself a place to start. Merrikiyawuy Ganambarr-Stubbs is a Gumatj woman and principal of Arnhem Land's Yirrkala School. In 2017 she told the ABC the word is a layered thing which literally means a spear penetrating a person, usually the thigh, as a form of justice 'to calm them down'.

'It can be a negotiation of peace, or a negotiation and an agreement where both parties agree to one thing so that there is no dispute or no other bad feeling,' she said.

We cannot agree that which we do not admit.

Scrolling through Twitter, where I unfortunately spend most of my life, I came across a surprisingly civil argument about how to deal with racists. The discussion was between two people who would have experienced racism, though one was proposing cutting racists more slack and bringing them into the fold. The other, lawyer Nyadol Nyuon, who was born in an Ethiopian refugee camp after her family fled the second Sudanese civil war, was unconvinced.

'This is a deeply personal choice,' she said. 'It shouldn't be an expectation or a demand. If I can't give my forgiveness willingly, if there is a pressure to seem reasonable, to forgive, to be the better man, then that is also not improvement in "race relations".'

Nyuon's considered analysis, something I particularly love about her presence in the Australian media scene, gets to the heart of the matter. Forgiveness cannot be forced; it is more like an essence that flows when the necessary work has been done, either on yourself or when it has been offered by the other party.

Personally, I did my time carrying hate around with me. It was a closed fist inside my chest. There was so much of it that it poured out through my fingertips during the nascent years of blogging. It filled my pockets, and my boots. I hated religion, my father, not having enough money to live, everyone else who had enough money to live. I loathed people who were well dressed (because I wanted to be) and I scorned those who seemed to be able to have fun – real, joyous fun – without drinking a bottle of rum first. There was vitriol reserved for people whose parents sent them money or chipped in for home loans, and resentment not for my mum but the social and economics forces that meant I had to do those things for her. It broke her spirit and mine. Oh, it was a time totally soaked with animus. I kept my distance from other gay and lesbian people because I did not want to be 'associated' with them. I didn't want to be like them. I *was* like them, but that was kind of the point.

I had many good friends but I also made friends with people who did not treat me well, and whose own poisoned outlook on things came to infect mine even more. I was the Cheryl Sandberg of hating things – I leaned into it because, well, what else was there to do?

Above all, I hated myself. I was not loved because I was gay. This kernel of truth, as I saw it, became the source of every other wild fantasy of anger. The boy who felt these things was so wounded and so fragile that the force of rage sent outward was the only thing holding his constituent pieces together.

Look, I know I'm not the first person to have a moody teenager phase, even if mine didn't arrive until my early twenties and then outstayed its welcome. It didn't stem from some overarching philosophy of nihilism or performative disdain.

I was hurt, and hurting. There was not enough life in me then to know all that hating was making me sick. If someone had told me in those years that forgiveness was an option I might ider, I would have scorched the earth with my fury. I would mething like, *If you think that is a possibility then you suffered enough to know otherwise.*

Let me say this now, as someone who has largely shed this self-inflicted violence: it was cell-bustingly exhausting. Around the same time, my friend Bridie used to quote something to me, a line taken from some place I've long since forgotten.

'I hate so many things I have to get up four hours early just to fit them all in,' she would say, and I would laugh.

But here's the thing. It was fucking *true*.

You won't find me sidling up to some tortured soul like a door-to-door tout and asking them if they've tried forgiveness. That's just not how any of this works. But I think even the smallest part of me then needed desperately to know that, when the work was done, it might be possible to feel kindness and mercy for those around me. More important still, I needed to at least believe some version of myself in the future could step into the weightlessness of that same grace.

As far as clear thinking goes, I've had more relapses than the Betty Ford Center has had patients. I will fail or forget my own advice. So don't think of this as some gospel I found at the top of a mountain. Think of this more as a messy, living document. A thing that does not presage perfection so much as encourage progress.

In May 2020, during yet another of my sinking attacks of past trauma, I was sitting in my therapist's office in suburban Sydney. He had a large canvas picture leaning against a wall that said:

> Mistakes are proof that you are trying.

I wanted to push that poster out into a lake on a little boat made of wood and then set fire to it. Motivational posters have never done it for me, but on that day, I found that one particularly offensive. Platitudes always miss the person, I thought.

During our usual back-and-forth, the psychologist said something to me that I had not heard from any of his predecessors. (Psychologists in my life are like characters on *The Bold and the Beautiful* or *Neighbours* – they disappear from the show for months or years at a time and then come back when the scriptwriters need them.)

'You are not that seven-year-old boy anymore,' he said to me in his pleasant, anodyne room. 'You have to let him go.'

I wasn't prepared for those words spoken in that order, and nor was I in the kind of mood where I thought tears were on the cards.

And then the sobbing started. It was one of those ugly cries, where you look like the victim of a workplace accident at the Clag Glue factory. Bubbling snot, eyelashes matted together, that sort of thing.

In time, there may be better ways to describe what that felt like. But for now it seems appropriate to say it struck me as absolution.

It's not that the adult me hated the child who had to endure what he did, though there was a significant stretch of blame that spanned the time and space between age seven and age thirty-three. That child did the best he knew how with the frankly embarrassing amount of resources available to him at the time.

I pardoned that little boy then, in that moment. And I hope he knows that I love him and that, perhaps, I always did.

Animals

A few years ago, without warning, Mum decided that she no longer felt comfortable killing mice in her own home. Part of this resolve may well have been to do with my then young sister, Lauryn, who begged for a halt in the systematic destruction of mice-kind. A mouse still twitching in the spring-loaded bar trap only served to strengthen Lauryn's intervention.

Never has an American invention so commended itself to the Australian people. As a child, I knew people who had calluses on their fingers that could be directly linked to the bar of one of those devices. With faux seriousness, my father said other people, who actually were missing fingers, had lost them on account of run-ins with the traps during the setting of the springs.

I couldn't have known it then, but some of the traps on the market have a force of almost ten newtons, which is almost precisely the same as the pull of gravity on a one kilogram object – enough to drag it to the earth at a rate of 9.8 metres per second squared.

This isn't quite enough to sever a human finger, but what do young boys know of classical physics?

It remains unknown whether time itself mellowed my mother, or a more nuanced revolution regarding animal care took root in her mind. Simply, one day I noticed that the old traps had been thrown out and new ones had arrived. These ones were little cages that trapped the mice alive. I liked the idea of less suffering in the home, but the logistics had me stumped.

'I like them, Mum, but they don't exactly solve the problem,' I told her one morning in the kitchen. 'What do you do with the caught mice?'

I have developed a keen sense for when Deb Morton is scheming. There is a faint smile that is crowded out by the shining eyes of a fanatic; the kind of eyes that belong to someone who knows they are right even if they may not be.

'When I release them, I point them in the direction of the neighbour's yard,' she told me, shimmering with pride.

This was a perfect solution, if mice weren't engineered through millions of years of evolution to simply turn around on a whim. As I understand it, the ability to turn left or right or even 180 degrees forms a major plank of their survival strategy.

'Mum, they're just going to come straight back,' I told her.

Throughout my teenage years, the period of time in which my eyes deteriorated and I was fitted with optical glasses, Mum handled a losing argument with me with a single riposte: 'Oh whatever, four eyes.'

On this occasion, however, she didn't admit defeat. She admitted something else instead.

'They don't come back,' she said.

She made it sound sinister, like an old Soviet space director talking about the passenger manifest on the first orbital craft. Indeed, it was uttered as a *direction*.

'You couldn't possibly know,' I replied, 'if the mice you catch again are new ones or the same ones!'

Even as I was saying it, I saw her spirit rise and I knew, somehow, that I was wrong.

And so, having beckoned me to follow her, Mum led me down the creaking steps at the back of the house. She was wearing a mismatched ensemble of dressing gown and slippers, each in a state of disrepair such that they gave her the air of somebody who had founded a doomsday prepper cult and then couldn't make the payments on the bunker.

'Come here. Look at this,' she directed when we reached the gate that opened to a path leading underneath the house. The old Queenslander home is raised a level by stumps, but we never had the means to do anything fancy with the concrete expanse below. It became a warehouse for scrap metal, old appliances and spare parts; the sort of place that could give a home stylist an aneurism.

At first, I couldn't see what Mum was trying to show me. It was just like the rest of the downstairs industrial-asylum aesthetic: empty paint tins, bottles of WD-40 and at least three-quarters of the parts necessary to build a combine harvester.

My eyes had to adjust to the light, certainly, but my brain couldn't have known what puzzle it was trying to solve. Then Mum pointed specifically at the tiny little paint brushes, all dabbed with colour.

'Mum,' I said. 'No …'

She grinned, nodding her head vigorously. 'I've been painting their tails. That way I know if we get any re-runs.'

The scene presented itself in the manner of a mystery-thriller flashback, where the hero has figured it all out and the clues from earlier in the investigation pop into their head like signposts.

And here's the thing: Mum was right.

We never did get a recurrence of the same mice turning up in the traps with paint-covered tails, rodents with highlights. Unless, of course, they discovered a vat of turpentine and launched an elaborate rebirthing operation the way criminal enterprises launder stolen cars.

I wondered, then, what had happened to them. If we weren't getting the mice back, were they perhaps turning up in other traps and giving residents across my home town the chance for that sensational jolt of wonder, the kind that only comes when reality departs so severely from expectation.

This is simply a curious tale of rodent painting, in isolation. I learned much later, however, that it was something more akin to a habit.

In his late twenties, my brother, Toby, purchased a domesticated rat that he named Bam Bam. He lived with it in a room at the back of Mum's house. Nobody else went into the room, but occasionally the rat was brought out for a run in the rest of the house. Mum never warmed to Bam Bam, shuddering at his presence.

And then, as if fate were obsessed with mockery, my brother was sent to jail. His rodent friend was temporarily orphaned and it fell to Mum to care for it. In the fever dream of a mother's anguish, Deb hit upon the idea of writing a letter to Toby in prison and decorating it with the painted footprints of Bam Bam.

Thus ensued a tiny struggle as Bam Bam was marched through a tray of paint and coaxed to run across the piece of paper on which the family letter to our incarcerated boy had been written. Mum screamed, my sister laughed, the rat developed a deep and enduring faith in reincarnation; the better to believe its next life would be more dignified.

As much as Lauryn and I teased Mum about these vignettes, the truth of it is that I have always admired her sensibility when it comes to animals. Through her, we were taught that animals could love us just as fiercely – and often more consistently – than other human beings could.

Serious people would counsel not to anthropomorphise an animal. Our minds are not their minds. To intuit the emotions of another non-human life was, to these serious people, a folly of cognitive biases.

Still, it never stopped Mum, Lauryn or myself from turning our animals into vehicles for elaborate radio plays, each with their own idiosyncratic style of speaking. Rosie, our miniature fox terrier, had – for reasons that are unclear to me – a speech impediment, while the chickens emerged from our own minds as elderly women in a nursing home. Jack, the blue heeler, was pensive and erudite.

Sparky, our beloved cat, was just a cunt.

When she died, Sparky was eventually replaced with Charlie, the most strikingly beautiful cat I have ever laid eyes on, who became Mum's favourite immediately. To my sister and me, denied the opportunity to truly bond with him because of his attachment to Mum, he was a male model; a magazine cover star who had made the turn to starring in bad arthouse movies.

While writing this book, it occurred to me that so many of the best elements of my own life were mediated through animals. I wanted to interrogate what it was our pets had done for us as a family but, more broadly, how all animals have enriched us as a species.

I begin by asking Mum about our habit of projecting ourselves on to the animals and, without skipping a beat, and with total earnestness, she asked: 'Did we give them our personalities or did they already have their own?'

This farce brought us closer to what we imagined were the interior lives of our pets, but it also rendered the entire animal world alive with the possibility of feeling.

In his now famous 1974 paper in *The Philosophical Review*, Thomas Nagel asked readers to imagine what it is like to *be* a bat, part of a larger thought experiment to pick apart the intractable problem of consciousness that he called 'hopeless'.

Bats make for an 'exceptionally vivid' problem in this regard because although these mammals are somewhat similar to human beings they nonetheless possess sensory and activity systems – like echolocation – so undeniably strange that it becomes harder to imagine what it might be like to be one.

Even without the guiding light of philosophy, Nagel concedes anyone who has ever been trapped in an 'enclosed' space with a hyperactive bat 'knows what it is to encounter a fundamentally alien form of life'.

His assertion, with which I happen to agree, is that the bat – or an alien life form humanity may meet in the future – is so fundamentally different to us that we can never hope to *really* know what it feels like to have the subjective experience of being a bat.

Blind people who manage to develop an imitation of sonar by clicking their tongues to identify objects in their way will come closer to the experience than the rest of us. But neither the blind nor anyone else will get it completely right.

That, however, is no reason, Nagel says, to deny that a bat or alien life form has experience. Similarly, they may not ever be able to get inside our heads either, but we would be offended at the suggestion we have no inner life.

'To deny the reality or logical significance of what we can never describe or understand is the crudest form of cognitive dissonance,' Nagel says.

The philosopher was accelerating to a bigger point about consciousness and human experience, but I like to let the fixation on the bat sit with me because it speaks to a core human desire, I think, to wonder what it is we left behind.

If you go back far enough, all animals share a common ancestor, a single-celled organism which, for ease of reading, we will call Barbara. At one point, these lineages branched out this way and that, like spiderweb cracks in a sweeping pane of glass. Not every animal is our direct ancestor, but each one of them was once on the same trunk as us.

Granted, you have to go back a very, very long time to meet Barbara or the other common forebears who existed before yet another split in the family tree. You have to go back, past the moon landing and the Industrial Revolution, the Bronze Age, zip past the Agrarian Revolution (while yelling *wrong way, go back*) and through the ice ages and beyond the dinosaurs.

The other forms of life and us – intimately connected eons ago but now so isolated – are like former lovers who spent so long together they can never forget what it was like to hold the shape of the other's body, yet now view the other's inner life as unfamiliar.

Why were we together in the first place, we can feel ourselves ask. We bask in this strangeness.

After my parents' divorce, in the late 1990s, my brother, Toby, and I were visiting our father on the sheep station Comarto, slightly more than fifty kilometres west of Wilcannia in the deep reaches of New South Wales.

Here the land is perpetually thirsty, rain so rare it was the perfect climate zone for the movie director George Miller to film the original dystopian *Mad Max* films in nearby Silverton. When the wet finally came that summer it hit so heavily we ended up having to stay for an extra two weeks.

Something that appeared to my young self to be magic happened in that soaking rain.

The pools of muddy water that sat in the clay pan earth across the station exploded with life forms unlike any I had seen. They were shield shrimp, a desert crustacean that looks like an oblong frisbee with a mesh-like tail that ends in two thin strips that jut out in a V-shape.

I was transfixed.

It would be another twenty-five years before I found out, while researching this book, what they were, so rare are their appearances. The eggs of these creatures can lay dormant in the normally arid soil for up to seven years before bursting to life with the rain that propels them into a hyper-speed life cycle again.

Toby and I studied the hard-headed little things in their ponds. To me they looked just like the extinct trilobites I had read about in the course of my youthful obsession with dinosaurs. In fact, I convinced myself that we had found an ancient form of life long thought to have been lost to human knowledge.

For all the cattle station's later troubles, and the marker of cataclysm it would become in my own life, my siblings and I were lucky to have our childhood in outback Australia and we were doubly blessed that our mum, Deb, was there to imbue it with a love for the natural way of things that might otherwise have passed us by.

While Toby satisfied himself with the life he could see, I was obsessed with the old and the new. In particular, a few years before my discovery of the shield shrimp, I had been on a serious mission to find a dinosaur. Preferably alive, though I knew to focus my efforts on unearthing a skeleton.

A very big sauropod – a long-necked thumper, if you will – was found on a cattle station called Durham Downs north of Roma in western Queensland in the 1930s. This was a sign that dinosaur hunting was in my blood because it was on this station that my mother met my father, albeit quite a bit later.

This twelve-metre-long beast was given the unfortunate scientific name of *Rhoetosaurus brownei* and probably died from embarrassment sometime before the onset of the Cretaceous.

I wanted to find my own.

My quest was complicated by a preponderance of bones belonging to the cattle on the station we called home. Further frustrating my efforts was the not insignificant fact that my enthusiasm for discovery outshone any capacity for skeletal identification.

It was in such a state of general ignorance that I would occasionally bring home the femur of a dead cow and present it to Mum with totally unwarranted optimism.

'Is this a dinosaur bone?' I would ask her.

'No, darling, that is the thigh bone of a steer,' she would respond.

She always encouraged me in the pursuit of the natural sciences, no matter how wrong my avenues of inquiry. I collected bones like an unprepared anatomy professor on his first day of class. If my selection was indiscriminate, it was only because my hopes were sweeping.

What about this? And this? Or that? Mum, could the dinosaur have died so recently that bits of its flesh were still being picked from the bone by meat ants? Why not?

I never did find a dinosaur but, rudely, our next-door neighbour did.

In 2004 the fourteen-year-old son of graziers near Eromanga (which contained our nearest pub and is the farthest town from the sea in Australia) found what he thought to be an interesting-looking rock while mustering cattle. His name was Sandy Mackenzie and the station was Plevna Downs. His family had helped my parents in those horrifying hours in 1994 after my brother was burned on Mount Howitt station but before doctors could arrive. We knew them well. They were good people.

I only learned of Sandy's discovery when reading the newspaper sometime around 2009.

He'd discovered Cooper, the largest prehistoric giant to ever have risen from the earth in Australia, and several other entirely new species of dinosaur.

Mum could not contain herself.

'After all those cow bones! Oh, Rick! After all those cow bones!'

But the cruel hits would keep coming. Years later, when I was thirty, I was wandering around a sheep station outside of Barcaldine on assignment with the newspaper I was working for and I noticed the owner had a perfectly preserved jaw bone from an extinct giant kangaroo on a shelf.

I told him the story of my long-ago abandoned attempts at discovery and, thinking he was helping, he barked at his young son.

'Tom! Go find Rick a fossil,' he said.

And here's the thing. *Tom did.* They had so many sitting in situ on the drought-cracked land that his primary school–aged son could go out blindfolded and pluck one from the dirt.

I was grateful but also on the verge of lodging a police complaint over the unfairness of it all. I thought I was owed a part of this past on account of my interest in it.

The frustration I had was a tiny slice of something more pernicious, a skeletal symptom of our species' lust for control and ownership over the animal kingdom.

Animals have long captured our imagination. They have comforted us, terrified us, eaten us, performed our work, fed us, infected us, provoked our amusement, carried us and been subjected to our experiments and tests.

As a species, human beings are the confident spruikers in the office project management team who have taken credit for the work of their colleagues at bonus time. To concede late in evolution that we are this far advanced largely on account of the animal kingdom is, for some of us, embarrassing. I'm interested in this idea because I've seen firsthand on the cattle station how it feeds a specific, unearned, idea of strength.

Animals lived in our service. The cattle fed and, once sold, clothed us. Working dogs were not to be spoiled. Horses existed to be ridden for mustering or sport. If anyone else, including Mum or myself, dared articulate a view that perhaps we had much to gain from animals beyond mastery, it was dismissed as weakness.

There was – for my father, the jackaroos on the station and also many women who had bent to the harshness of the environment – a refusal to engage on this matter because it required an admission of vulnerability.

Here, strength was defined only through the language of violence, dominion and control. To be vulnerable was the cause of great distress. The closest my father ever came to loving another animal was his working dog Mother, a mean old thing who had a habit of killing her own litter of puppies. He respected her because she was a great working dog. Those that failed to measure up, like my blue heeler Tyson, were shot.

Let's consider dogs.

Every dog alive today, and modern grey wolves, are descended from an extinct common wolf species that lived around 15,000 to 40,000 years ago. Scientists cannot agree on precisely when we tamed some of these wolves and began the lineage of the modern dog, though estimates from various DNA sequencing studies range from close to that 40,000-year mark to between 14,000 and 6400 years ago.

Anthropologist Brian Hare told the *Smithsonian Magazine* in 2018: 'The domestication of dogs was one of the most extraordinary events in human history.'

And how did we repay these dogs?

To redesign them for our aesthetic pleasure by artificially breeding them. We obstructed their airways by flattening their faces, shortened their legs and generally moulded their bodies into shapes uniquely unsuited to the ordinary requirements of being a dog.

Before we managed to go absolutely hog-wild on this type of extreme genetic selection, our ancestors were doing it already, without thinking, and presumably with one of those extinct wolves that was somehow open to being befriended by humans.

Maybe it was injured and needed food and they provided it; maybe it was just an unusually amiable specimen. We do know it happened.

And in that gentle bringing together of two species, once competitors in the same wilderness, a striking change took place. It has become the hallmark of tamed species, first identified though not totally explained by Charles Darwin.

The wolves' snouts shortened, their ears became floppy and brains shrank an average of 20 per cent. The concentration of certain types of neurotransmitters in dog brains also changed dramatically.

We have been able to watch this in real time with the remarkable study of silver foxes in Russia, which began in 1959 at the Institute of Cytology and Genetics in Novosibirsk in Siberia.

Researchers led by Dmitri Belyaev and later Lyudmila Trut (who remains in charge today, six decades hence) selected a group of wild silver foxes that seemed, in relation to their peers, to be calm and accepting of human beings. With each new generation of foxes, the researchers chose the top 10 per cent of animals that seemed most tame and bred them, and so on and so on.

As evolutionary biologist Lee Alan Dugatkin noted in the 2018 *Evolution: Education and Outreach* journal, the effects were almost immediate. Beginning with a population of essentially wild foxes and breeding them for tameness – and only tameness – produced within six generations:

> … a subset of foxes that licked the hand of experimenters, could be picked up and petted, whined when humans departed, and wagged their tails when humans approached. An astonishingly fast transformation.

The changes kept rolling in. After less than a decade, the newly domesticated foxes developed floppy ears and curly tails. By generation fifteen, stress hormone levels (glucocorticoid) had halved. The adrenal gland, which produces this hormone, had become smaller and smaller. Serotonin levels rose, creating 'happier' animals. Over the life of the experiment, the tamed foxes had also developed mottled 'mutt-like' fur patterns and 'they had more juvenilised facial features (shorter, rounder, more dog-like snouts) and body shapes (chunkier, rather than gracile limbs)'.

In short, the animals became *cuddlier.*

It's not that we made them cute and baby-like because of our efforts, but rather this was a long-established fact of nature, and humans are instinctively wired to pick up on it. Animals that *look* fierce, historically speaking, usually *are* fierce and ought to be avoided. Exaggeratedly round, adorable animals that look stuck in a juvenile phase? Harmless. We are drawn to them as if to light.

There is something about the healing power of connection with species other than our own, even those we imagined.

I know, in some small but tangible way, the chickens Mum bred in our backyard helped her through those first years after our family was split with violent precision. At first there was Hector the rooster and Hessie and Ida and later Sammie and Billy and a cast of others – and a pause after they each passed away.

Deb's recent decision to raise a new flock of hens immediately struck a hurdle when two of them turned out to be roosters.

'I have a dilemma,' Mum texted our family group chat. 'Gladdie and Dixie might be Glennie and Dickie.'

Mum returned them to the woman who gave them to her and instead inherited a hodgepodge of already fertilised eggs for her only hen, a scrappy little game bird called Pearl who was fiercely on the cluck.

'At least Pearl likes me,' Mum lamented during the crisis.

Pearl was still laying her regular eggs when we attempted the switch; she had found a favoured spot under the old Queenslander home. It was an old tub filled halfway with teaspoons that Mum used to collect. Pearl's nest became one big egg-and-spoon race as Mum fretted about building a new chicken coup for mother and babies when they finally hatched.

For this, she enlisted the help of my brother, Toby, who had, once again, moved back into her house without any discussion. I won't say he had gone back to his old self because it felt impossible at that stage, but he had stopped using ice in the year or so before and much of his good-natured humour and amiability had returned. Still, he had no job, no house, very few prospects and a mountain of debt.

He had lost none of his skills from his former work as a trained carpenter, however, and was happy to help Mum build the new home for Pearl and her chicks.

Unlike Mum, Toby lacked the natural intuition for a chicken's needs. When Mum tottered off to work one day, having left him in charge of building a ladder to get hen and brood to the roost, she had more faith in its faultless delivery than was warranted.

What Toby built was indeed a ladder, and a mighty fine one. If you had a leg span of thirty centimetres or more.

'They're chicks, Rick!' Mum said to me down the phone after seeing the ladder. 'How the hell are they supposed to get up there? They don't have wings!'

My brother took a while to process the physics of a newly hatched chicken before conceding he might have made the ladder in such a way that a baby bird would simply fall through it.

No one in my family had ever watched *Arrested Development* but that didn't stop me from remarking for a week with a borderline psychotic glee: 'Has anyone in this family ever even seen a chicken?'

It was nice.

Pearl remains unaware of her status as a family mediator but this project, this collective desire to build a home for new life, was such a gentle moment of mother and son bonding. There were no seismic shifts undoing the damage of the past. Just two good people taking steps so small in their capacity to bridge hurt and fear that they might have fallen through that ladder, too. It was enough and it made me glad.

The chicken coup itself is more like a mansion. It may well have been the most significant construction project in Boonah since the global financial crisis, I told Mum, though she demurred.

Chickens are a known quantity. Cattle, for the most part, I can deal with. Dogs have been a feature of my life since the day I was born. Birds are a delight, cats a mysterious binary of pure love and ruthless derision, horses grace.

While childhood gave me a privileged access to the world of animals, it would be some years before I discovered the mind of the cephalopod.

This class of squishy sea creatures – octopuses, squid, cuttlefish and the nautilus, to be precise – are some of the most startling animals ever to have arisen on the planet. Appraising them even momentarily, one is convinced that the cephalopod is an article of tomfoolery. The cephalopod is what happens when evolution develops a gambling addiction, pawns its belongings to make rent and then has to buy back an eclectic mix of odds and ends just to survive.

With the exception of the nautilus, the molluscs all lost their external shell about half a billion years ago, either getting rid of it entirely or internalising it, as in the brittle central bone of the cuttlefish.

They have beaks. And up to eight arms in which, in some species, more than half of all their neural cells are located. In other words, most of their brain can be found in their appendages, which is a state of affairs well known to some human men.

The eye of the cephalopod is very similar to ours, in that it works just like a camera, though these creatures do not have a visual blindspot as humans do. In cuttlefish, the iris is shaped like a W or an old-timey moustache on a cartoon villain. They can tell the difference between an actual object and a photograph of that object, and use the difference in left and right eye visual fields to calculate depth with astonishing accuracy.

Octopuses are such skilled hunters that, as Aristotle observed in the fourth century BC, their very presence in fishing nets could literally scare a crawfish to death.

'Thus, this animal is so overmastered and cowed by the octopus that it dies of terror if it becomes aware of an octopus in the same net with itself,' Aristotle wrote in *Historia Animalium*.

In the 1910 translation of Aristotle's work, it was noted that Jean 'Georges' Cuvier, a renowned French naturalist at the turn of the nineteenth century, said that 'the octopus is detested by

Mediterranean fishermen because of the havoc it works upon the choicest lobsters and crabs'.

In the third century AD, Roman rhetorician Claudius Aelianus wrote in *On the Nature of Animals*:

> If a field, or if trees with fruit upon them are close by the sea, farmers often find that in summer octopuses … have emerged from the waves, have crept up the trunks, have enveloped the branches, and are plucking the fruit.

His descriptions fill me with a particular joy.

> The octopus feeds first on one thing and then on another, for it is terribly greedy and for ever plotting some evil, the reason being that it is the most omnivorous of all sea-animals.
>
> The proof of this is that, should it fail to catch anything, it eats its own tentacles, and by filling its stomach so, finds a remedy for the lack of prey. Later it renews its missing limb, Nature seeming to provide this as a ready meal in times of famine.
>
> Mischief and craft are plainly seen to be characteristics of this creature.

Imagine the raw cunning of the octopus that men should write about it so.

Little has changed in the hundreds of years since. In December 2020, researchers from Portugal and Germany released a scientific paper in which they observed octopuses punching fish during cooperative hunting in the Red Sea. Usually this was directly linked to the molluscs trying to keep the fish in line – either to remove them from the hunt or make sure they were doing the work needed to catch prey – but on at least two occasions, the study team watched an octopus raise an arm and strike a fish for *no apparent reason.*

It was this that gave rise to a medley of wonderful headlines such as: 'Octopuses observed punching fish, perhaps out of spite, scientists say.'

Aristotle might have been kinder if he had known the octopuses were stalking the seafloor and coward-punching unsuspecting fish. The philosopher called them 'stupid creatures' because, for the most part, they don't live much longer than a year and are properly ancient if they make it to two.

One stunning exception is the deep-sea octopus. A single female from the deep-ocean-dwelling *Graneledone boreopacifica* species was observed from 2007 guarding a clutch of her eggs on an underwater rockface. She stayed in that precise position for *four and a half* years. No other animal on the planet has brooded on its eggs for longer. It is also not clear that she ate during that time, as she was seen to brush crabs and other potential food sources away when they came too close to her eggs.

When her young hatched, the octopus died.

All this is to say: as a species, human beings should be thankful cephalopods live fast and die young because they are preternaturally intelligent and we are only just beginning to understand how.

Take the blanket octopus. This species appears to be immune to the powerful toxins of the jellyfish-like Portuguese man-o-war, or bluebottle, and has been spotted by researchers tearing the barbs from the floating fortresses and wielding them as spears for defence. Another much rarer species of octopus was caught on camera dragging the entire corpse of an egg-yolk jellyfish around, trailing the stinging tentacles behind it like a deadly cape.

This behaviour is intriguing because it fits with observations cited in a 2019 paper written by Piero Amodio and others from the University of Cambridge, published in the journal *Trends in Ecology and Evolution*.

The researchers noted the cartoonish habit of veined octopuses, which collect pairs of coconut shells as a sort of mobile fortress, carrying them around for use in the future, and referred to footage from David Attenborough's *Blue Planet II* (2017) that showed a common octopus ambushed by a pyjama shark.

At first, the octopus jams its tentacles into the shark's gills to stop it breathing, forcing it to let the octopus go, and then something remarkable happens. The cephalopod makes a dash for some rocks on the ocean floor and attaches them one by one to its sucker pads on its arms, then curls into a ball, arraying the stones on the outside as both a disguise and a suit of armour, like a crafty armadillo. The shark is totally outwitted.

Amodio and his colleagues suggest these behaviours are 'candidates for complex cognition' because they involve making tools.

'This rare example of composite tool use in invertebrates might be evidence of complex intelligence for two reasons,' their journal paper says. First, it might be an example of a behavioural innovation that provides security to the octopuses in environments where rocky shelters are hard to come by. 'Second, because coconut shells are transported to meet apparent future needs and through considerable costs (eg. conspicuous locomotion), this behaviour might rely on planning capabilities.'

Those words – 'future needs' and 'planning' – are key because they establish something that is thought to be vanishingly rare in the animal kingdom outside humans: a sense of time.

To imagine a future seems easy for us. We do it even when we don't wish to. My own anxiety has me in places I've never been at times I've not yet stepped into, playing out scenarios that might yet happen. I also project into the past, revisiting times I've long departed, imagining what might have been. It's exhausting.

But, to be fair, we wouldn't be here as a species without it.

Understanding time and that certain beneficial or ruinous things *might* happen to us at some point in the future has allowed us to break the shackles of evolution and wield tools to enhance our own chances of survival in the *right here and now* and our anticipated survival just beyond the horizon of our mind.

That cephalopods might join the great apes (not monkeys, though) and ravens on the spectrum of animals that can conceptualise a future moment is a spectacular notion, particularly given that they may well have arrived there independently and with a neural architecture that is at once familiar and altogether other-worldly.

Amodio and his team write in their journal paper that there ought to be a rigorous program of research to study the behavioural flexibility of cephalopods and their cognitive foundation. There may be much more going on here than even we suspect. Is it possible that these animals can attribute mental states to 'predators, mating rivals, or cooperative hunting fish'? That would be a truly astounding development.

If this turns out to be true – and it seems at least likely that evolution diverged long before the dinosaurs to give us both the cephalopod brain and the human brain – it means the intelligent mind was created independently *twice* on earth.

I want to spend some time on the cuttlefish, which, to me, is the most remarkable of all the cephalopods, as it illustrates an irresistible beauty and queerness in the animal kingdom.

Cuttlefish are the most skilled animals at camouflage on the planet. They can imitate not only the intricate webs of colour and shading found on the ocean floor, but also the three-dimensional *texture* of those environments. To do this, they have little muscles under the skin called papillae that can be raised and locked into position to form bumps and spines or that can move to mimic the rolling curves of a bank of seaweed or the pockmarked surface of a coral. They can do this in what seems like an instant, a matter of seconds.

Some species can display *two* completely different sets of camouflage on their bodies. None has employed this trick quite so deviously as the mourning cuttlefish, named for the tear-like blue tinge at the edge of its eye and common in the waters off Australia's east coast from Sydney to the northern tip of Queensland.

In 2012, researchers from Macquarie University caught one male specimen on camera in between a female and a rival male. To the female, the cuttlefish beamed a display of his manliness; but on his opposite side, where he might have provoked the competition of the rival, the cuttlefish changed his skin pattern and tone to mimic that of a female. It was *Rocky Horror Picture Show* meets *Finding Nemo*, or the Kinks' song *Lola* if the titular character was a titillating cuttlefish.

In other words, he had his fake and could eat it, too.

The curious life and minds of cephalopods have been studied well in experiments – they can open jars for food rewards, from the outside or inside, they can complete simple mazes – but often the most telling revelations are those that happen when a cephalopod, especially an octopus, simply does not wish to take part.

'The most famous octopus tales involve escape and thievery, in which roving aquarium octopuses raid neighboring tanks at night for food,' Peter Godfrey-Smith writes in his book *Other Minds: The Octopus, the Sea and the Deep Origins of Consciousness.* 'But here is a behavior I find more intriguing: in at least two aquariums, octopuses have learned to turn off the lights by squirting jets of water at the bulbs and short-circuiting the power supply. At the University of Otago in New Zealand, this game became so expensive that the octopus had to be released back to the wild.'

There are countless other stories like this. Specifically, there are countless stories of octopuses shooting their jets of water at researchers they have taken a dislike to, new people in the labs they don't yet trust or those in specialised experiments whose job was to scratch the octopuses with a bristly broom while others in identical uniforms gave them food rewards.

You can guess which ones the octopuses singled out for their water torture. Every single time. They can tell the difference between individual humans, a fact made all the more astonishing by the nature of their solitary lives in the ocean: cephalopods are almost uniquely anti-social creatures. They live alone, die alone and, even when mating, risk being eaten alive. Their mind is not like ours, in the sense that it didn't evolve to deal with complicated social cues and the life-or-death need to belong in a group.

And yet, still, here they are, figuring us out. A totally different species in some form of communion with us.

In her book *The Soul of an Octopus*, Sy Montgomery recounts how she befriended an octopus called Octavia and marvels at the seeming electricity of the bond between them:

> Being friends with an octopus – whatever that friendship meant to her – has shown me that our world, and the worlds around and within it, is aflame with shades of brilliance we cannot fathom – and is far more vibrant, far more holy, than we could ever imagine.

Our reverence for other creatures need not be confined to an appreciation of their intelligence. There are some noteworthy beings out there that have developed ways of living and, indeed, thriving that deserve contemplation and admiration. The ones that exist when the odds are truly stacked against them are particularly cause for wonder.

Consider the ocean sunfish, for example. An animal with precious little to live for, this giant frisbee of a thing mocks the very idea of evolution. To consider the sunfish is to ponder deep within one's own mind the necessary conditions for total failure in the animal kingdom.

This animal, the largest boned fish in the world, has no swim bladder and barely formed fins. Its mouth, a sort of beak with fused teeth, is permanently open so that the animal looks very much like it has been told it has only months to live, which it probably does.

Sea lions appear to take delight in playing a sort of underwater football with the ocean sunfish, tearing its fins from its body and biting chunks from the animal before leaving it to either die or eventually recover and look like a cartoon biscuit for the rest of its life.

Just when you think Nature has created a bit of a dud, consider this. We laud the existence of the sunfish today almost entirely because it lays more eggs than any vertebrate on the planet – some 300 million at a time. It is therefore proof that your worst efforts can achieve positive results if only there are a lot of them.

Beautiful, isn't it?

Of course, there are other stunning creatures. Quite literally, the pistol shrimp which I have come to consider the cowboy of the ocean. There are actually hundreds of such species but them are capable of firing underwater 'bullets' by coc comically oversized claw and snapping it shut so of water is forced out of a pincer, creating a bubble of air that is crushed within milliseconds by the surrounding wall of ocean water. This process creates a sonic shockwave that the shrimp use to stun or even kill prey within range. And get this. The sound is louder than an actual gunshot and the collapse of the bubble briefly creates a heat flash that burns very close to the surface temperature of the sun.

The US navy used these distinctive ambient sounds quite deliberately to conceal its submarines during World War Two. They parked their crafts near pistol shrimp colonies to mask the submarines' noise, making this perhaps the only time in US history one of its forces was happy for a weaker minority population to be armed.

There are horrifying animals out there, too. I'm thinking of all those parasites that take over their hosts' minds or, in the case of that river fish in the Amazon, its host's tongue.

The jewel wasp, by way of nightmare introductions, drugs cockroaches and turns them into puppets of the damned. It first stings the roach in its body to temporarily paralyse its legs – but this is only a set-up for the clincher. The second sting has to be breathtakingly exact – right into a specific section of the roach's brain – which then disables the victim's survival instinct to get the fuck out of there (a technical term, as I understand it).

Thus zombified, the wasp then chews off a section of each of the roach's antennae and effectively uses these as a leash, taking the insect back to its little burrow, as though it were a cavoodle in a gentrified suburb. The wasp then lays its eggs inside the cockroach (which, I must stress, is still very much alive), where the resulting larvae chew their way out within days.

Sleep well, everyone.

When I was a kid I used to love reading about stuff like this, totally enthralled by the brutal, often clinical, efficiency of the natural world. We witnessed much of this on the cattle station and I learned more when my maternal grandmother gave me her collection of 1960s *Encyclopaedia Britanica*, horribly out of date by the time I got them in the mid-1990s. Entire species of animals had gone extinct during that thirty-year period. I couldn't have known it, though, turning the pages as a primary schooler a full decade before reliable internet arrived in my area.

I cared deeply about individual animals, as did Mum, but this connection to them never really extended to an overarching understanding of what we do to them so that we might live. While it was considered weak or silly to assume that they ought, at the very least, to be considered sentient, it was a greater mistake to even consider dulling the impact of our own progress so that we might tread less heavily on the earth. This is a phenomenon that extended beyond my own family. Regional Queenslanders in particular, or at least the ones in my general experience, especially loathe environmental protesters. Didn't they understand we need this dam?

During a brief stint at a pop-culture website in early 2012, I flew to Los Angeles and interviewed the Muppets, Kermit and Miss Piggy, ahead of their latest film release. Entertainment was not my natural set of interests, however, and I spent a great deal of my fifteen-minute one-on-one with Kermit telling him about an Australian species of frog, the wallum sedge frog, which has, at various times in its career as an infrastructure-busting amphibian, been implicated in holding up the completion of the Tugun Bypass, a minor Gold Coast airport landing systems upgrade and a construction project near the Bruce Highway north of Brisbane.

'Wow,' Kermit said. 'That's an expensive turn of events. Maybe I could stop some bridge-building?'

I went on to quiz him about his sex life with Miss Piggy but am, unfortunately, contractually obliged not to discuss the details.

I'm not sure why I used my brief chat window with a Muppet to grill him about southeast Queensland infrastructure projects but I suspect it has something to do with my training as a news reporter.

We were always taught to frame stories as conflict. This is largely true in other forms of narrative work, but the imperative is many orders of magnitude more compressed and less nuanced in news reporting. Everything must be a battle between two opposing sides.

Could a frog stop a bridge? It could! And that meant the bridge, a thing that was probably useful but certainly not alive, became the automatic underdog, especially in the parochial tabloids of my youth.

It would take the better part of a decade before these deficient paradigms would shift in my own head. It wasn't malice that kept my thinking in place, just a sort of bumbling intellectual lethargy that I was still trying to shake off in my twenties.

The connection between all that I loved about animals and their place in the world that so controlled, maimed or killed them was a jagged line that made several detours through inscrutability.

Strange, I know, especially when we consider that one of my strongest early memories is being reduced to a sense of doom while watching the 1983 sequel to *Dot and the Kangaroo.*

The original book that spawned the films carried a dedication in 1899 from its author Ethel Pedley:

> To the children of Australia, in the hope of enlisting their sympathies for the many beautiful, amiable and frolicsome creatures of their land; whose extinction, through ruthless destruction, is being surely accomplished.

The films never shy away from this message and in the sequel, in which Dot finds Funny Bunny pretending to be a kangaroo joey lost by the mother kangaroo in the first film, the characters end up on Battle Beach – a stretch of sand filled with corroded US army trucks and the detritus of war. It is a wasteland.

'They were fighting here, all around here,' Dot tells Funny Bunny when he asks what it was all for.

'Why?' the little bunny asks.

'I don't know,' replies Dot. 'My father told me but I didn't understand. I don't think he did either.'

And then, as Funny Bunny asks what they do in war, the film cuts to real-life footage of atom bomb tests at Bikini Atoll, conducted between 1946 and 1958; the bright flashes are sliced with footage of wildlife and a baby bird left defenceless in a nest.

'They have guns and bombs,' Dot says, 'and they fight each other and they hurt and lots of them are killed. Sometimes women are killed, too. The mothers. And there's children left behind with no mothers and no fathers, and no one to look after them.'

Funny Bunny begins to sob.

I can't tell you exactly what four-year-old me was thinking when he saw these images. Certainly I didn't know much about nuclear fission or its world-ending promise. I can say with some assurance that it hounded the ease from me, the way a bomb's shockwave strips the ground of anything that dares grow out of it.

There is a lot to be said for children's films that impart challenging, important lessons. Perhaps we can agree on this: children should be taught about death. One of my favourite poets, Wislawa Szymborska, had this wry observation about death's far from total dominion:

> Many are the caterpillars that have outcrawled it.

I love that line but ultimately, as we know, all that lives must die.

This necessary education does not require children to join a hunt. At least, not anymore. Nor do we need to take our young aside, one by one, and explain to them in explicit detail that their parents will die, and maybe even soon because the universe is capricious like that.

Look, all I'm saying is I was not ready for talks on bilateral denuclearisation from Dot at age four. I was not ready, even, by the time I left high school, because my brain was still largely a mess of poorly arranged wires, like at a construction site that is close to lock-up but where the electrician has suddenly died.

The movie was not so much formative, as it was spiritually ruinous.

I don't mean to focus just on the nuclear issue, except that it's one symptom of humankind's broader instinct to act now and think later, a habit that has been tremendously unkind to the rest of life on earth.

Just a few days before my birthday in 2011, I was at my friend Candice's house in St Peters, Sydney, when a magnitude-9 earthquake struck off the northeastern coast of Japan's main island, Honshu. The quake was the largest since Japanese records began in the 1800s and the fourth most powerful ever recorded on earth. It permanently jolted Honshu island 2.4 metres to the east and shifted the planet on its axis anywhere between twenty-five and one hundred centimetres.

Bad news, in other words.

It was early evening in Sydney by the time I arrived at Candice's house and, rather than indulging in the planned drinking, I watched tsunami waves roll over the Japanese coastline, beamed live around the world by a Japanese news crew in a helicopter. I was transfixed.

Estimates varied, but the wave height was conservatively at least twenty metres in some parts of the country. It crested over the tops of pine trees in fields, surging inland for miles.

Almost 16,000 people died. The damage wrought came in at more than A$300 billion. A nuclear power plant went into meltdown in three of its reactors. A decade later, they are still removing radioactive soil from the region. In stages, the Japanese government has been allowing some 160,000 evacuees to return to areas within an original twenty-kilometre 'no-go' zone. Progress is slow.

The nuclear disaster was declared the same day as the earthquake struck, but authorities first revised the evacuation zone from two kilometres to three kilometres. The day after the quake, officials twice shifted the exclusion area – to ten kilometres and then to twenty kilometres within a matter of hours.

In early 2020, as I was preparing my research trip to Japan, a friend told me a tour company was offering semi-sanctioned visits to the radioactive Fukushima zone. When I arrived in late January, the Japanese government was preparing to reopen the rail line from Namie station to Tomioka in the Fukushima prefecture. It had been severed for almost ten years.

I signed up for a tour of the reopened areas – and a very fast drive-by within one kilometre of the crippled power plant itself – which was largely allowed on account of government messaging designed to prove that everything was absolutely fine.

That did not appear to be the case, however.

As my tour bus approached Namie, the local roads became clogged with convoy after convoy of trucks with green or black tarps covering loads of radioactive soil. Indeed, the trucks *were* the traffic. These streams of vehicles were conveyor belts, which have been operating for more than nine years, removing about 14 million cubic tonnes of contaminated soil and locking them in black plastic wrappers that resembled oversized body bags. This particular clean-up operation, involving 70,000 workers and 355,000 trucks so far, had been billed at almost A$40 billion.

Japan was nearing the end of winter when we were driven through the abandoned countryside, much of which had been turned into fields of these toxic bags piled so high they resembled Mayan temples. These structures rising from their fields were a reminder of what was lost and what still cannot be contained. There was a deep chill in the air, the grass and trees still dry. They had taken on the colour of rust in the freezing temperatures. Together, the elements painted a picture that matched the dystopias in my head from a younger age. Without human intervention, one of the caesium isotopes released into the surrounding ecosystem will haunt the area for at least three centuries.

The Japanese government had yet to find a permanent home for this bagged soil and so, for the time being, it sat there in the open.

My fellow tourists and I were each given dosimeters on this trip – they were yellow and looked much like the Pikachu pet game I had as a kid, which also doubled as a pedometer and allowed me to gamble on virtual slot machines for prizes to feed my Pokemon – and they beeped with a static-like fuzz as they measured the surrounding radiation.

In Namie, where vines had eaten entire homes, the meter held steady at a low reading. Here, it was safe to leave the bus.

We walked through the town, past a school that had been abandoned the moment the evacuation was ordered. The school children had left quickly, wearing only their indoor shoes; their joggers were still waiting untouched in pigeonhole boxes at the main entrance. In a classroom where the kids had been learning English – the alphabet was plastered in big letters on the wall –

drawings they had made of themselves and their families were still hanging.

Glassware and crockery remained on tables in local restaurants. Unopened bottles of Asahi beer kept them company. Windows in almost every building in the town were shattered or cracked, and mostly boarded up. Paint had peeled from abandoned apartment complexes.

On our way to nearby Ukedo, on the edge of the Pacific Ocean, I was confused by what looked like a line of silver-white cloud very low to the horizon. It ran in a perfect line across the tops of the tall yellow grass. Everything else was barren. All around were scarred fields of open dirt, the only people the occasional construction crew.

It wasn't until we were almost at the coastline that I saw that the strange cloud had a recurring octagonal pattern stamped into it.

Then I realised what it was. Not a cloud at all, but a brand new concrete seawall, nine metres high, separating the edge of Japan from the churning ocean on the other side. This was one sparkling new stretch of a A$20-billion project to build 400 kilometres of seawalls following the 2011 tsunami. Despite recent experience, this concrete barricade was about six metres shorter than the wave that rolled through Ukedo and wiped the town there from the face of the earth.

One building survived: the local elementary school, a two-storey concrete fortress that was almost entirely submerged by the mass of water that swept from the coastline, just 200 metres away. A large, radio-controlled clock near the top of the main building froze at 3.38 pm, the moment the tsunami struck. All of the eighty students there that day survived.

Authorities erected giant white pens in the place where Ukedo used to be; inside each of these pens, as big as football fields, was yet more radioactive soil, piled high in black bags.

The closer we ventured to the Fukushima Daiichi (number one) nuclear reactor, the more difficult it became to process the scale of what had happened here. The countryside reeked of misery and death. It was stamped with the futility of human endeavour in the face of overwhelming natural and man-made odds. We passed within one kilometre of the power plant and could see its blown-out roof – a result of a hydrogen explosion – from our bus windows. We could not stop there because the radiation levels were too high and we had no protective clothing. Our dosimeters sparked furiously with high-pitched warning beeps as we drove past, leaping past a reading of 3.8 microsieverts per hour. People naturally take in about two to three *millisieverts* (2000 to 3000 microsieverts) each year, so it's not like we were in any danger (I took on more radiation flying to Japan in the first place), but it's not the kind of place you'd like to hang around.

On this stretch of road there were police patrols and guards vigorously motioning at our bus driver to keep going. A Sega Sonic game centre sat in ruins next to a chicken shop. None of the former residents would be moving back here anytime soon. The land had necessarily been relinquished to the centuries ahead.

I wasn't there to become a morbid spectator.

My curiosity was piqued when I first heard about a local cattle grazier, Masami Yoshizawa, who refused to leave his farm even as the power plant went into meltdown and orders to evacuate were given.

Yoshizawa, aged in his sixties, had 260 head of cattle on his property – fourteen kilometres away from the Fukushima Daiichi plant – when his world changed forever. As evacuation orders came in, some of his fleeing neighbours left behind their livestock.

Yoshizawa showed our tour pictures of animals that had been abandoned in feedlots, reduced to skeletons held together by decaying skin.

'Nobody took good care of them. No feed, no water, so they had to die like this,' he told us through a translator in early February 2020 when we visited him on his farm, now called Ranch of Hope.

In May 2011, two months after the tsunami and subsequent disaster, government orders were given to destroy all remaining livestock on landholdings within twenty kilometres of the plant. Yoshizawa initially fled the disaster but came back for his cattle. He would not be leaving them to die, one way or another.

'According to the government, you could save your pet such as dogs and cats, you could save that but not the livestock,' he told us. 'But I myself didn't obey the order of the government. I broke the barricade and I came to my house and saw that my cows had survived.

'I understood that when I came into the restricted zone I would also get radiation. But even though it is a danger to myself, I decided to keep my livestock. I thought about the meaning of taking care of the cows.'

I couldn't help thinking of Mum's Dulux mice when I visited the radioactive cattle and this man who, under extraordinary circumstances, had gone from selling them for slaughter to spending a fortune keeping them alive. Granted, Mum was under no such duress when she made the switch from killing mice to setting them free like a pack of writhing Crayolas. But it was a moral reckoning nonetheless.

Yoshizawa didn't speak much English, but he all but grabbed me as I was leaving and told me in English that he was 'a cow terrorist'. That made it sound as though he existed purely to torment his cows, but what he meant was that saving those animals had made him a thorn in the side of government and, more specifically, of those who would argue that nuclear power is safe if only we do it well enough.

For years, the Japanese thought they had. The water pumping stations that routinely kept the fuel load of Fukushima Daiichi's power plant cool were located four metres above sea level and the plant itself ten metres above the ocean. None of this was enough. The tsunami there reached fifteen metres high, submerging the turbine halls under five metres of seawater and disabling multiple supposed fail-safe back-ups, such as diesel generation and the residual heat-removal cooling systems. Even the 125-volt DC back-up batteries failed as a result of being flooded.

Hubris had damned the nation and it had doubly damned the animals who had no control over any of it before or since.

I do not come from animal rights activist stock. Indeed, half of my family have been involved in a cattle station empire that alone would have shipped more than a million beasts off to slaughter over the decades. I tried to imagine what my cattle grazier relations would have done in this position.

Sure, they cared for their animals within the prism of the livestock industry, but theirs was not a gentle love borne of true feeling. It was a requirement of the job: well-fed animals who are not stressed during their lives make better eating. Bad news for the cows, good news for me if anyone were to contemplate frying me on a hot plate – I've been very stressed for a long time.

Yoshizawa confronted this system of convenient care, at great risk not only to his livelihood but to his life. He went back for his animals and he stayed, on his own, with little understanding of what that venture might turn into.

I asked him if he was ever lonely.

'I feed these cows every day and I have a strong feeling they are my friends,' he said. 'So my two hundred and sixty cows, they live peacefully and they show what is real peace.'

Then he switched to English: 'I am cowboy. Resistance. Kamikaze. I am cow Godzilla.'

Godzilla, created in the angst of the threat of nuclear war, is not the villain I once thought he was in the ignorance of my youth. In Japan, he is the king of the monsters, a kind of tough love check against the worst of humanity's impulses.

In philosopher Ludwig Wittgenstein's elaborate reckoning with language, he famously remarked: 'If a lion could talk, we would not understand him.' It is a small amusement to me that we have spent the seventy years since that line was published wondering what the fuck it actually means.

We know the essential problem: the life of a lion – even if the lion had access to the English language and the ability to communicate with us – is so fundamentally different from that of our own species that its *experiences* would be incompatible with ours. Even if the lion possessed the right words, it would be next to useless thinking we could fathom from it what it is like to live, feel and *be* as that animal.

There is a whole school of language and philosophical scholarship that picks apart competing theories about whether Wittgenstein himself was arguing this or something altogether more nuanced. After all, in the paragraph immediately preceeding that famous line, Wittengstein wrote of the same dilemma when travelling to a foreign nation with completely different customs and ways of living. Even 'given mastery of the nation's language', Wittgenstein said, 'we do not understand the people. We cannot find our feet with them.'

I'm not here to interrogate Wittgenstein, though given half the chance I absolutely would interrogate the lion. And I think the endless theorising about whether we *could* make sense of the results misses the point.

We may never understand animals as they appear to us, but all this proves is that they have minds unknowable or ungraspable by our own. I might also never understand the meaning of my own life, but there is beauty in the effort.

Beauty

In 1929 Friedrich Georg Houtermans, a German physicist who was known as Fritz, went for a stroll one March evening in Berlin with a 'pretty girl' after completing one of the most important essays of his career.

'As soon as it grew dark the stars came out, one after another, in all their splendour,' Houtermans later wrote of that night. '"Don't they shine beautifully?" cried my companion. But I simply stuck out my chest and said proudly: "I've known since yesterday why it is that they shine."'

Houtermans had only just discovered the then revolutionary notion that stars use nuclear fusion to burn for seemingly an eternity. Right then, on that clear evening, he was one of only two people in all the world who knew the secret of that blazing dark.

I think about Fritz Houtermans a lot. The man was a gifted scientist, but he was also one of the funniest people I've had the pleasure of coming across in history.

His was a sense of humour forged in adversity.

Fritz left Germany as Hitler came to power, migrating to England, which he found intolerable. His friend Hendrik Casimir recalled in his own writing that Houtermans had a theory about the natural limits of the former Roman Empire and how any civilisation or group of people could be judged by the way it prepared potatoes.

'If they were just boiled with salt you were certainly beyond those [limits],' is how Casimir explained his friend's theory, as quoted in a 1992 article for *Physics Today*. England had been adjudged and found to be lacking.

Here was a man who blended skill, serious work and a wonderful commitment to good humour and silly pranks. He got fired from a job as a tour guide in Rome after telling one of his guests that the street they were on was called 'Via Latrina'. Houtermans made his own good fortune in other jobs but was perhaps singularly unlucky on the matter of living arrangements. He voluntarily left England for the Soviet Union, driven by his left-wing politics and idealism, but was eventually deported by Stalin's regime and sent right back into the mouth of Nazi Germany, where he was imprisoned by the Gestapo.

He was released by the Nazis in 1940 and got a job at *Forschungslaboratorium für Elektronenphysik*, a private laboratory in Lichterfelde, a suburb of Berlin. There were rumours the physicist had sold out on his values in order to save his own life from the Germans but that wasn't true, according to his colleagues left behind in Stalinist Russia, to whom he sent his meagre rations so that they might live.

And, still, he had some cheek about him.

Houtermans lost his job at Lichterfelde at the beginning of 1945 'under rather curious circumstances', Iosif Khriplovich writes in a 1992 article for *Physics Today*. An 'incorrigible' smoker at a time when German tobacco was in short supply, Houtermans was able to persuade 'Nazi big shot' Abraham Esau, the nuclear research supervisor, that 'one could extract heavy water from Macedonian tobacco'. The research was considered '*kriegswichtig* (important for the war effort)' and Houtermans was given a bag of tobacco for his troubles.

'When that had been smoked he managed to get one more,' writes Khriplovich. 'But that was too much. It attracted the attention of the Gestapo, and [Manfred] von Ardenne was ordered to fire him immediately.'

Here is a man, I think, who has come to understand that beauty can be extracted from the fuzziness of ordinary life; that it can be found in the right kind of laughter which runs perpendicular to stress.

And, sure, I have on occasion been jealous of his walk along the streets of Berlin in 1929 with his 'pretty girl' – Charlotte Riefenstahl, also a physicist, whom he would later marry – thick with the knowledge he had unveiled about the stars above. Imagine how it must feel to be able to look up and believe the universe has presented this information to you specifically and that, for this brief moment in time, the charm of this appreciation was yours alone.

It could be said that everyone who has ever encountered an irresistible scene in art or nature, or a story that has moved them so, is the first to it. They hold it as if it is theirs alone. And it is.

Whatever it is that we call beauty, no two people will ever leave its presence in quite the same way.

In 2015, on the phone to Mum, I was listening to her trying to tell me a story about someone we know who had been head-hunted for another job. I say 'we' but it's really only Mum who knows him; because we are from the same country town she assumes I know all the same people, which I don't and never her usual delightful fashion, Mum mangled the was trying to deploy, the linguistic equivalent boat in the water from a cliff top.

was head-honchered,' she said to me.

I suppressed one of my routine giggles. 'Do you mean head-hunted?' I asked her.

Deb turned the upset into a victory with stunning speed. 'I'm an explorer,' she told me, shimmering with a pride I could feel down the line. 'I discovered a word.'

And though I teased her mercilessly at the time, this sentiment captures the way each of us tangles with the sublime. The moment of electricity that sparks when you see a gorgeous painting or the terrifying expanse of Australia's interior, beautiful in its dimensions – that spark is yours and yours alone.

Every preposterously luminescent ray of light in the dark of winter and all the portraits of human dignity that fill the shelves of your mind are a single set of disappearing footprints, never to be travelled again.

What makes anything beautiful at all is that we possess its full grace for a breathtakingly small moment. And then we must give it back and that is OK, because we will find more when we leave open the possibility for discovery.

It is possible to find such things even in the hot breath of misery.

Viktor E. Frankl's account of finding an atom of hope in a Nazi concentration camp is perhaps the best known illustration of this notion, though it bears closer inspection.

I don't know if Frankl, who spent three years in Auschwitz and other death camps, ever met or knew Houtermans, but I imagine the two might have got along. In Frankl's *Man's Search for Meaning*, the psychiatric neurologist calls humour 'another one of the soul's weapons in the fight for self-preservation'.

I count the ability to divine absurdity in difficulty or despair as a kind of beauty – if it's good for the soul, it's beautiful. But Frankl presses even further into territory that is at first surprising.

> As the inner life of the prisoner tended to become more intense, he also experienced the beauty of art and nature as never before.
>
> Under their influence he sometimes even forgot his own frightful circumstances. If someone had seen our faces on the journey from Auschwitz to a Bavarian camp as we beheld the mountains of Salzburg with their summits glowing in the sunset, through the little barred windows of the prison carriage, he would never have believed that those were the faces of men who had given up all hope of life and liberty.
>
> Despite that factor – or maybe because of it – we were carried away by nature's beauty, which we had missed for so long.

There was other art in the camps, too. Violins were played, little theatre events took off and became so popular that already starving men would miss their daily soup to attend. We know that while food and water keep the machine of the body alive, such maintenance is worthless without the sustenance of art and the meaning we make of it.

Perhaps it is no coincidence then that the first piece of music I ever remember truly affecting me in a profound way was the theme from Steven Spielberg's *Schindler's List*, composed by John Williams and performed by violinist Itzhak Perlman and the Boston Symphony Orchestra.

My Year 11 English teacher, Roxane Scott, had designated analysis of the film as one of our key assignments for the

The principal task – and I stress this was for a group of almost entirely white teenagers in regional Queensland most of whom, certainly not me, had never met a Jewish person – was to choose a moment in the film and create a new scene or new ending for it, then produce the scene and act out the roles on camera.

I can't remember what some of the other students ended up producing, perhaps as a protective mental blackout, but I was responsible for editing my group's magnum opus.

I must have listened to the haunting violin of Williams's theme score dozens of times as I clicked the wheel of my editing mouse frame by frame in an attempt to align the soulful music with the bumbling boys shooting for depth on screen.

The violins in the piece were less a sound and more of a physicality, as if the instrument's bow was being played on my viscera. I did not listen to the piece so much as it played me, all of me, and my body moved with the ebb and flow of its parts.

The years before this moment had not been marked by a particular love or affinity for music. I liked the stuff that made me want to dance but the collection at home was slim. We had Billy Joel, Kenny Rogers, the Beach Boys and the *Lion King* soundtrack, but none of these featured what I would describe as especially awe-inducing lyrics.

Stephen Dunn, a poet, provides one explanation that I think is helpful here. Beauty is whatever leads us to desperation. This idea is twinned, I think, with the concept of meaninglessness,
…h titles one of his poems. You yearn for it, this moment of
…, and then it releases you.

…promise in the music we had at home; no threat
…was mostly syrup and I enjoyed it all very
…age of my simple existence had never
…the distinct sensation that what I was
…forever and that this was indeed a tragedy.

To be awakened in this way is the same as experiencing the faint stirring of first love; you may be ruined by the very idea it cannot last.

This is how we sieve the marble of beauty. This is how we make it mean something.

In Leslie Paul's *Annihilation of Man*, there is a darker interpretation but one that, I think, attaches evidence to my case.

> All life will die, all mind will cease, and it will all be as if it had never happened.
>
> That, to be honest, is the goal to which evolution is travelling, that is the benevolent end of the furious living and furious dying. All life is no more than a match struck in the dark and blown out again.
>
> The final result is to deprive it completely of meaning.

Light a cigarette, if you must. We should sit with it, if only to consider how this argues the opposite case.

Instead of depriving it of meaning, doesn't the understanding that life is inevitably finite mean it is weighed with the deepest of meaning? Isn't that very impermanence the birthplace of all majesty?

Anyway, this is a long way of saying I never asked these questions while listening to Billy Joel's 'We Didn't Start the Fire', even if learning the lyrics off by heart gave me something approaching the sublime during karaoke.

To love anything or anyone we should be able to inhabit the loss that comes with knowing anything to be temporary. To do otherwise would mark us for despair and I've spent enough time in that dark place trying to turn the electricity back on.

The devastation of living in despair, if we fail to move beyond it, will only poison us against the sequence of marvels that await.

..‥en composer John Williams first saw a rough cut of *Schindler's List* he baulked. 'I really think you need a better composer than I am for this film,' he said.

Spielberg took the bait. 'I know,' he said. 'But they're all dead!'

Frankl would have approved.

It turns out there is a specific reason why Williams's Academy Award–winning work is so affecting. In fact, it is used in most of the songs that make you want to rip your heart out and wear it as a jacket.

In composition it is called an *appoggiatura* and it functions like a little musical speed bump that ruptures the listener's expectations about what note should follow in the melody.

Williams, for example, uses the drop from a B-flat to an A in one measure and an even bigger drop – a full step – from the B-flat to a C during one of the most evocative passages in the theme track. It is the musical equivalent of coming home after a difficult day's work thinking there is nothing to eat and then remembering you had ice cream in the freezer; overwhelming.

In 1991, British psychologist John Sloboda tested how reliably such devices could make people cry. He asked eighty-three adults to nominate three pieces of music in which they had felt a range of 'thrills' – shivers, tingling, the pinprick of tears and so on – and then had them pinpoint as near as they could the moment of onset.

In eighteen out of twenty cases where the music produced tears, Sloboda's subjects identified the range of the piece that featured the *appoggiatura*.

'The physical responses described are part of the innate autonomic response system of all human beings. They do not have to be learned,' he says in the paper published in *Psychology of Music*. 'This approach links emotional response to various classes of creation and violation of expectancy or implication within musical structures. Most of the ten significant structural features are clearly linked to such violations.'

Now, I am to music what seagulls are to jet engines. We rarely have anything to do with each other but when we do, I can really ruin the pitch.

In primary school we were given the opportunity of joining a subsidised music program and, apparently because I didn't hate myself enough already, I chose to learn the clarinet.

Why the clarinet? Only the Lord knows. I wasn't very good at it. The clarinet is neither reliably cool, like a saxophone or drum kit, nor in the top tier of acceptable classical music instruments like the piano and violin. It ekes out an existence in the shadowland of odds and ends alongside the triangle and the recorder.

Although many have loved the clarinet, to me it was a lonely thing that plied its workaday trade in the third-rate offices of musical acceptability. But then, if you search clarinet masters, there is a man called Julian Bliss and I refuse to believe a person so-named could be wrong about any of their choices.

All this is to say: do not ever ask me for music advice.

I was curious, then, to see what the eighteen pieces of music with *appoggiaturas* in Sloboda's study would do to me, the boy who thought woodwind was a medical condition.

The prototypical tear-jerker, according to Sloboda, is the opening six bars of Rachmaninoff's Second Symphony. It doesn't disappoint.

I also try Beethoven's *Fidelio*. The tense musical feature appears in Act 1 No. 3 bars 14–22 and Act 2 Finale bars 173–7 and bars 192–7.

Look, it took me well over two hours to find and crosscheck whether I was at the right part, but the theory holds up. And then I was sad for a bit and went back to the *Schindler's List* music to really lean into the sensation.

Alarmingly, one of the physical responses marked by the participants in Sloboda's study was 'sexual arousal'. Almost 40 per cent of them said they had experienced musically linked horniness (not a technical term) in the last five years. And then the paper proceeds to make literally *no other mention of this*, which, funnily enough, has left me unsatisfied. (This isn't important to the larger discussion on beauty, of course. But you can't just dangle that information out there and expect me to go gliding over it in pursuit of literary fidelity.)

I wonder if Fritz Houtermans ever felt that the piercing insight he had into the fuel source of stars had robbed them of their beauty. I'm not sure he would have conceded it, because in my experience the knowing simply adds another layer of apparent magic on top of the experience.

We may now understand more about how certain songs can provoke physical emotional responses in listeners with the use of an *appoggiatura* – among other things – and we can even know something of the psychology behind this, that violent clash between expectation and reality.

But *why* should we be primed to react that way at all?

Because this is the scale of the natural world. We are born to it, in the beginning, and know that it could kill us at once. Our time on this earth was and is a period of grace given to us by the natural order. We are, as Leslie Paul says, that match struck in the dark. Beautiful. How could it be anything else?

The matter of how our brains interpret the mechanics of particular musical melodies and beats to wring pain or joy from [illegible] rs is quite another thing. I wonder now if there [illegible] n music never existed, when even animal songs fell [illegible] our ancestors with dull utility. As with language, [illegible] at the ability to intuit harmonies and patterns of sounds in ways other than as pure speech came only with the hijacking of underused parts of the brain?

Theories abound. We may never know the answer.

It is enough, or ought to be, that these arrangements can move us to deep sorrow, the thrill of excitement or, if things are a bit sparse elsewhere in life, even sexual arousal. I'm not here to judge. If Strauss or Puccini get your motor running, buckle up and enjoy the ride.

The puzzle of art lies in the waves of emotion it can engineer. I've had to reckon with this more than some, perhaps. Beauty I could find in the everyday quite easily – where else was there to look? – but I was not raised with any affinity for art, as I have now come to understand it.

There were no paintings at the cattle station and, when our family split in two, none in our new life either. Mum collected the occasional chicken print to hang in her kitchen (at one stage my sister Lauryn and I counted more than thirty different chook-themed statues, quilts, wall-hangers, ornaments and other decorative flourishes in the one room), but that was the extent of it. I'm not here to hang scorn on her pursuits. Deb's love for her chickens is absolute and piercing, and any art gallery would do well to earn the same devotion from its visitors to the work on display.

I had never been to an art exhibition at all until I was in my mid-twenties, and even then it was to attend some free networking drinks for journalists put on by a consulting firm at the Pop to Popism show at the Art Gallery of New South Wales. Apparently the more scrappy journos would attend these events, sink some nice wine and canapés, and then make a beeline for the exit. It was disappointing to discover the consultants had clued into this caper. They had mandated thirty minutes of 'mingling' time before anyone was allowed to check out the show (code for sneaking out), which might actually constitute entrapment.

Here's the thing about art made for high-end appraisal: it seems to require a specific stylistic or aesthetic education that, once possessed, grants greater access to hidden treasures of the heart.

If you come without it, like I did, things can get confusing.

As I stood in front of one enormous work – I couldn't tell you by who – I overheard two women discussing the piece.

'I love the way he has managed to bring out the mood with those brush strokes,' one of the women said to her friend.

Isn't that the point, I wondered to myself. He was hardly going to use scissors. Unless he was a scissor artist, in which case I would have expected the tool to be used in aid of such emotive output and not, say, a paint brush.

It's not that I didn't think these works were beautiful. Some of them had me in a meditative awe. But I didn't trust what seemed to be overly wrought explanations for why *other people* said they were beautiful.

One of the marquee exhibits was David Hockney's *Portrait of an Artist (Pool with Two Figures)* and it had me transfixed without a language for the feeling. In the painting, a youngish looking man in a pink jacket and white pants peers into a pool cut by sunlight into tessellated shapes. In the water, another figure in white underpants is submerged and swimming towards the end where the jacketed man is standing. The swimmer's body is distorted by the refracted light.

The pool itself forms the edge of the built environment. Beyond, the scene drops down into a valley of green forested mountains with just a hint of autumnal change rippling through the foliage.

I had never heard of David Hockney, nor seen this particular work even in passing. In that way, I came to it totally free. We met for the first time that day and the love was instant.

Imagine my surprise, then, when I read just a few years later that the work sold at auction for more than $90 million, making Hockney the most valuable living artist in the world.

Ninety. Million. Dollars.

The figure made me feel instantly violated, though not enough to sever the connection I had felt with the work. Given substantial resources, I wondered how much I would be willing to pay for the same piece and at what indistinct point the emotional value of the painting is swapped out for a financial one. Does it matter?

Shortly after I turned thirty-one I spent a strange, eighteen-month period living in Canberra where I worked as a journalist in the federal Parliament House press gallery. It felt the opposite of art, where politicians routinely said things like, 'Look, governing isn't always the most elegant of businesses.' It was an odd place, its inhabitants filled with clinical cunning and an almost pathological aversion to curiosity beyond the wielding of power.

As an antidote, I took myself off to see the Monet exhibition at the National Gallery of Australia, not entirely confident it would be something with which I could connect. It was a quiet Monday, but the crowd was still thrumming with keen observers and, presumably, a smattering of others like me who were trying very hard to look serious and engaged.

A delightful older couple sailed past me at one point and the woman said to her male companion: 'That's a Monet.'

'Yes, darling, I *know* it is,' he whispered harshly through his teeth.

To be fair to her, the exhibition also included a scene-setting display of artists such as Gustave Courbet, James McNeill Whistler and J.M.W. Turner.

It was at this exhibition that I learned the Impressionists were named derisively by the art critic Louis Leroy, who, on singling out Monet's *Impression, Sunrise*, condemned the whole lot of his peers for their sketchy, seemingly unfinished works.

Leroy said of Monet's submission that 'wallpaper in its embryonic state is more finished than that seascape'. The young artists, including Cézanne, Renoir and Pissarro, among others, were then dismissed as nothing more than a bunch of 'impressionists'.

Sick burn, Leroy.

The exhibition featured some of Monet's notable works, including the surprisingly small *Impression, Sunrise* that had so irked Leroy. The water lilies were gorgeous, but I was not particularly moved by them. *Haystacks, Midday* was bewildering to my untrained eye. I suppose Monet managed to get the shimmering heat haze right but the shadow on the largest haystack was off-putting. I mean, this clearly isn't a criticism of Monet. I literally could not draw the shape of a triangle until just before I started school. It was such a problem that each time I drew a square house and a rectangle roof my brother, Toby, would become frustrated and yell at me.

La Pont de l'Europe, Gare Saint-Lazare – a painting of a train station – was visually the most exciting piece, but maybe that just makes me a fan of trains. By the time I got to *The Japanese Bridge*, it felt like Monet wasn't even trying anymore. As far as impressions go, I had to be told it was a bridge.

Again, not a criticism of Monet. I'm mad at myself. And I'm mad that I'm mad at myself.

In our fairly grim childhood and adolescence, it seemed the height of privilege to even consider art at all, much less visit it and engage with it in person. On the edge of survival, what luxury! But that is unfair to people who have few resources and still maintain an interest in the arts. I think that is part of the problem with the industry, or society. Many assume opera is not for anyone on Centrelink. In this regard, I think the poverty that affected my family was as much cultural as it was financial. It isn't just that I started out my life living 1200 kilometres from the ocean, or that we moved from there to other regional areas. It is more to do with the realisation that it had not been taught to us, at least not in any systematic way.

Mum allowed herself to find wonder in her animals, for which I am forever grateful, and admired fine sunsets with the rest of us. This is all well and good, but often these encounters are a matter of merely waiting for the right moment. Beauty's task, I think, is to make us look for it.

Third-century philosopher Plotinus links beauty with its true form, love.

> This is the spirit that Beauty must ever induce: wonderment and a delicious trouble, longing and love and a trembling that is all delight.

I like this, though had never heard of the quote when I left high school. Still, I think this is what I unwittingly chased when I began to cultivate a nascent interest in photography as a young adult. It helped that I had bought a brand-new SLR camera on a credit card I could not afford to pay back – but if someone can fork out 90 mill for a Hockney, I'm allowed to make one dumb and life-altering decision in the pursuit of 'delicious trouble'.

Photography, I found out, was a way of seeing the world anew, even when you didn't have a camera with you. Before phone cameras evolved from potatoes, my newly acquired eye for detail in the environment often provoked a sense of loss, especially in the late afternoon 'golden hour' when the light came in low and near horizontal, washing the landscape with warmth and building shadows in the most unlikely of places. Fleeting moments, if not captured, felt wasted.

Over time, however, the photography itself wasn't even that important. Shooting became a means to an end, an excuse to be ever vigilant for a pleasing architectural line. In Hong Kong in 2019, for example, I came across two buildings. One featured a series of circles on its exterior – it looked like a silver game of Connect-Four – and the other, across the street, was a violent clash of lightly spaced vertical steel. From the right angle, you could eliminate the sky between the two towers. In the frame, they merged together as one jarring collision of shape and form.

I cannot explain why this sight pleased me so, but I do know that I would never have noticed it without more than a decade of curiosity through a lens. This wasn't something I could turn on or off anymore, it was a default mode of looking at the environment. Whether the photos that resulted were technically any good or not was beside the point; I remember my favourites with a sparkling clarity not afforded other moments in life.

That is another gift of beauty: attention.

Philosopher Alexander Nehamas, a professor at Princeton, says beauty is:

> … an emblem of what we lack, the mark of an art that speaks to our desire.
>
> Beautiful things don't stand aloof, but direct our attention and our desire to everything else we must learn or acquire in order to understand and possess, and they quicken the sense of life, giving it new shape and direction.

New shape and direction, certainly, though I find the moment of attention is a way to slow time. You will recall these temporally swollen pools, when the ache of universal splendour held fast your awareness. Each of these heart-stopping encounters can run for what seem an eternity, feeding on the re-routed circuitry of your own mind. Resources are marshalled and deployed to attend to this one unexpected, astonishing thing. The stopwatch in the brain is abandoned in favour of presence.

See how the light carves ribbons through the forest. How ants marching in formation resemble dark waterways across a savannah. Let time run like molasses by observing a vista so remarkable in its expanse that you feel crushed by it. We have *Die Hard* (yes, the movie) to thank for the butchered quotation of Alexander the Great who is said to have wept 'for there were no more worlds left to conquer'.

Except, that wasn't what he said at all. It seems likely the quote attributed to Alexander came via Valerius Maximus, a Latin rhetorician who wrote a book of collected 'anecdotes' about everyday life in ancient Rome. Here the phrase is translated by Henry J. Walker:

> Alexander's heart had an insatiable longing for glory. When his friend Anaxarchus told him, following the authority of his teacher Democritus, that there were innumerable worlds, Alexander said, 'Alas, poor me, because so far I have not even gained possession of one!'

The great conquerer shed tears because he had not even tamed a single world, let alone all of them. He wasn't at the end of glory, he was at its beginning and still felt devastated by his insignificance in its magnitude.

Ain't that grand, though? To be struck dumb by the powerfully extravagant and time-stoppingly sublime is to be administered life itself.

There is no telling how many of these moments we get between cradle and tomb, though one thing is clear. The precise quantity of fierce love, mediated through the beautiful, is entirely up for grabs.

When I was in my last year of high school, on a *Lord of the Rings*–themed trip with students and teachers to New Zealand's South Island, my friends and I became lost while attempting to walk down Queenstown's Ben Lomond mountain in heavy snowfall.

It was my idea. We had ridden to the peak on a gondola and the snow was falling in gentle flutters but, from the summit, there was a cold and brooding path visible. It was blanketed with snow and disappeared into the gloom created by the dense ceiling of Douglas fir trees. I had seen snow before but never like this; never as if it were presenting a profound mystery to the senses. And so, despite being short of time, I convinced my friends to walk down the mountain and we promptly became ensnared in the shiny, crisp-white prison of its features. The forest itself was still so wet and warm, and the snow so cold, that it created its own fog, which further obscured our progress. The only direction we knew was down, although at times my friends and I debated even that. I could hear their quickening breaths as we scuttled over exposed rocks and slid down embankments on our backsides.

All else was whisper quiet.

My friends wanted to make it back to the school group in time for the jet boat ride on the Kimiākau, though I had lost all sense of my place in the world I had left behind. It was as if the ordinary restraints of time and space had been replaced by a shimmering borderlessness. Moments of penetrating beauty had seized me before and many times since but this serves as the prototypical form in my mind. It was a perfect encounter.

I carried a secret knowledge as we made it to the base of the mountain and back into the dull ache of ordinary existence. Beauty's gift is that we may spend a lifetime within a single moment.

And so I have lived.

Masculinity

The men in my life, at least at the beginning of it, were not the kind who loved fiercely. Ferocity, at least as a form of passion, was a feature that never managed to attach itself to love.

Theirs was a version of masculinity that mapped to the landscape. It was barren, scalding to the touch and capable of instilling great fear. If water flowed on the surface, it was something of a miracle. We told stories about the times we had seen great emotional floods, though they were marginal events in the broad acreage of our existence.

What these moments – these crackles of static interrupting usual programming – showed us was a glimpse of a way to be a man that had not been modelled to us in any substantial way. They came, too, accompanied by shame or espionage humour to disguise the many secrets of feeling.

I remember visiting my father during school holidays when I was around the age of eight. He was then managing Tambo station, in central west Queensland, and had become concerned about my behaviour. I wasn't firelighting and getting into fights like Toby, my older brother, though Dad would have been happier were that the case.

Instead, I was what might best be described as *pre-gay*. Effete, a small child showing a distinct lack of interest in stereotypical boyhood. These were troublesome traits in the regions. Indeed, as I would come to discover, it was a problem all the way to the coast.

At some point during that school-holiday trip, Dad and I were sitting in the stark, hot living room of the homestead when he opened a box as high as my waist filled with softcore pornography magazines. It was tits for days.

'You like them?' he said to me, attempting to disguise what was an inquisition as a joke.

'What?' I said.

Look, I'm not an idiot. Even as an early-primary-school kid, I knew what he was getting at. I didn't know I was gay, but I was aware that I didn't quite fit in. In any case, I knew enough to make Dad articulate the precise point he was trying to make before admitting to anything.

'You like those boobs?'

There is a version of the Turing Test for young queer kids in which they play the role of the computer attempting to befuddle the user into believing they are speaking with a real human: they have to convince their parents that they're not destined to be gay.

I put another twist on it: to embarrass my father into submission.

'Yeah, why wouldn't I?' I said.

You just can't come back from this level of devastating riposte. It's not like he had any evidence with which to confront me: no browser history, string of ex-boyfriends or even declarations of love for boys in my journal (which of course I kept – and kept hidden).

He had nothing and, so defeated, the box was sealed up again.

Despite my success, the incident rattled me. It was the first real example in my life that the men around me were bent to shape, as hot metal in a forge. Departures from the approved form were not just frowned upon but, in cases where it might reflect on the observer, they were to be feared.

Why?

I was vexed by this question over the years and decades that would follow. Dad's intuition was right, as it happens, but it was not the question of whether he had a functional gaydar that kept me up at night.

This type of man, it now seems obvious, is terrified of those close to them being gay or *appearing* to be gay because it represents a crossing of boundaries. There is the old trope that a gay man must want to hit on the straight man, a situation which would render anew the usual interactions between men who hit on women. Suddenly, they might be dealing with *other* men who matched them in power and persistence.

No doubt this was part of the equation, but the bigger antagonist here is a built-in sexism that finds men who model female characteristics – no matter how subtle or even imagined – to be totally objectionable.

It is this hardwired notion of the primacy of the man above women, even the ones they profess to love, that drives disgust at homosexuality and femininity alike. They are, in the eyes of a particular fellow, one and the same.

Not everyone acts on or even feels these impulses, and you can find these men around the world living in the comfort of their own self. For those who feel it, unconsciously or not, the instinct is a prison that curtails much of who they could, or may want, to be.

Homophobia is just as damaging to straight men as it is to gay or queer kids.

Take a look at young boys playing with their male friends. Before society gets to them, they hug and kiss and cuddle. They hold hands, not because some interfering busybody has demanded it of them, but because they want to.

Even now, as I write this, I am at my friend's house with her two-and-a-half-year-old son Hamish and his 'mandatory best friend' Declan – mandatory because the parents of both boys are close friends. The boys are brash and bold and can whack one another with the best of them, but they are also delicate, gentle and generous with their affection.

They have been taught and encouraged to hug, and will continue to, but even so I know deep down that as they grow older there will be external pressures on them to be less effusive in their affection, even as we ourselves grow more wise about the manacles of such expectation.

Doesn't it make you mad?

In Christos Tsiolkas's 2019 novel *Damascus*, a sprawling imagining of the early days of Christianity, he writes of Saul:

> He had last known joy sitting in a circle of boys, listening to the recitations of their teacher. On becoming a man that had been stolen from him. He had to surrender to labour, and keep vigilant and futile watch over his disobedient body. Manhood had corrupted friendship and poisoned hope.

I underlined that passage as soon as I'd read it because it spoke of an irreducible truth about the lives of men. It told me something I had only discovered in my twenties: that we mistake unhappiness for duty.

That we are incarcerated by our disfigured understanding of masculinity is bad enough. To learn we also built the prison? Well, that just hurts.

And I don't mean you or me personally, but men, all of us, over thousands of years.

This should not be read as a defence of men and the systems we erected in our honour. But nor do I hate men. Some of my best friends are straight men! I'm gay (well spotted, Dad) which means I am also somewhat a fan when they get it right.

Further, I am a man.

Perhaps these are obvious points, but we must concede I have several horses in this race. Perversions of masculinity, though, are at the root of so many cultural ailments that have women as their principal targets. In the war on women and other minorities, men become our own collateral damage. What, you think upholding the abusive and controlling apparatus of The Bloke is entirely without cost?

Look at it this way. We bear the costs of an appalling lack of imagination in applying the rules of masculinity. We are overrepresented in drug overdoses, suicides, injuries, premature deaths, all forms of violence except as victims of intimate or family abuse. The list goes on. And that's *with* all of the structural advantages afforded to masculinity.

Pity is not needed here.

Surely, just maybe, reform of the worst aspects of *being a man* could do everyone a world of good. As Tsiolkas says of Saul, these butchered notions have stolen joy from us. And we have abused and killed or maimed, unleashed pain and trauma on ourselves and everyone else before allowing the repatriation of joy.

That's a problem. A solution would require a collective investment.

I asked some of my friends what masculinity means to them and their answers were, predictably, amusing.

Without skipping a beat, Tom replied: 'How many heavy things you can hold in your hands.'

Not to be outdone, Perry came through a few minutes later.

'Pretending to dummy pass an item when you're passing something to another man in the office,' he said.

Mick's was largely unprintable but started with a well-worn truism: 'Not asking too many questions about your mates' mental wellbeing.'

These were jokes but they are also instructive.

We don't need to look far to find these tragicomic representations of manhood reflected back at us as serious propositions. Kleenex has marketed 'man size' tissues; and in the United States the laundry brand Bounce developed fabric softener sheets 'for men and people who smell like them'; and, for a brief period, the yoghurt brand Powerful was labelled as 'brogurt' for its positioning as a protein-enhanced super treat for men.

In 2014, Unilever released a toothpaste for men, presumably because the science on whether women actually have teeth is still out. Colgate, recognising a new market segment among image-obsessed men who also still wanted to brush their teeth, did the same thing.

If a man wishes to bathe but not appear gay in doing so, he may wish to purchase a bath bomb shaped like a hand grenade and soak with a 'hero's explosive rush of black pepper and rosemary'. There are bronuts and bread for men, mancandles and cotton buds from Q-tips sold as 'men's ultimate multi-tool' so that cleaning one's ears cannot be mistaken for both having and enjoying penetrative sex with another man.

DudeWipes exist. Lint rollers for men have been developed.

Mancan developed a wine in a can under the pretense that 'we believe wine is for drinking, not pairing'.

'And our "notes" are more rock than classical,' the marketing copy reads. The tagline is a brusque, efficient: 'Shut up and drink.'

Remember, if you're a bloke and you talk, then you are probably a woman.

At the other end of the spectrum, but part of the same twisted universe of gender norms, objects considered to be 'manly' or simply utilitarian have been softened for the delicate sensibilities of women and girls. You can buy batteries in pink packaging, replete with unicorns, if your stored energy needs are more feminine. A tape dispenser 'just for girls' is also pink. Women who wish to write in ink have access to a 'pen for her', which appears to perform the same function as every other pen, though I confess to not having bought one on account of being a man.

Some of these products were too damn stupid to last very long, but the rest are still out there. They press on precisely because there is a market for them, of men and women so bound up in their own gender stereotypes that it would be unfathomable to use a soap product every day while having to yell 'Not a homo' at the shower head as it washes over you.

I'd like to say I was comfortable enough in my own skin back when I was at school and in my early twenties not to have gone along with any of this, but the truth is I was deeply afraid and ashamed of my own sexuality and what this meant in the eyes of everyone else, especially men.

Everyone and everything that was out of favour in high school was 'gay', with remarks ranging in severity from 'that's so gay' to 'you're a fucken gay cunt'. I was never the target of this stuff, but I didn't need to be to be affected by it. I knew what not to be – and that meant presenting as straight as possible. That meant being a *man* even when I scarcely knew what that was.

As I mentioned, though, this is not a problem peculiar to the gay kids in school. All the other boys were performing the same routine and some of them had come from broken homes, like me, or had fathers who hit them. Others had dads who never touched them, not even to hug them, and I wondered what that must do to a boy.

I remember one night in Year 8 when I stayed over at a boy's house. I'm going to call him Greg, but that's not his real name, for reasons that will become obvious.

On that Saturday, Greg's dad questioned him about not putting the bins out earlier in the week. When Greg attempted to explain himself, his dad punched him right in the head for talking back. I was just standing there, mouth agape. It wasn't a gentle tap in jest or mock anger; it was a bone-thudding whack.

Greg was straight. But I knew in that moment that even that wasn't going to be enough to protect him. He, too, would have to be a *man*. And what better place to learn masculinity than at the end of your father's fist?

So throughout high school all of us boys were acting out the roles as best we knew them, performing feats of manliness to establish our credentials as (a) not gay and (b) not a pussy. Pussies, in our understanding, were weak people, such as girls or boys who act like girls.

To the extent that the boys knew about lesbians, they were OK with them as long as they were classically hot and making out with each other for the benefit of other men. Otherwise, lesbians were an affront to men simply because these women excised men from their desires, pleasure or emotional attachment. The boys assumed all lesbians secretly wanted their dicks in the same way that all gay boys must have lusted after them, too. I guess you could be forgiven for thinking all roads lead to you when the roads were built to service you culturally, financially and personally. Still, get your hand off it.

In his debut novel, *On Earth We're Briefly Gorgeous*, the poet Ocean Vuong writes about the prickly passion between Vietnamese-American 'Little Dog' and a whitebread, all-American ball of anger and hurt called Trevor.

There is no finer book, and his assessment of the trap of masculinity was a punch in the gut for me.

> In his backyard, an empty dirt field beside a freeway overpass, I watched Trevor aim his .32 Winchester at a row of paint cans lined on an old park bench. I did not know then what I know now: to be an American boy, and then an American boy with a gun, is to move from one end of a cage to another.

Here's what I think Vuong means when he speaks of a cage. It is not one put there by women or people with different-coloured skin, nor those with a galaxy of sexualities. The cage belongs to all men, put there by all the men that came before us, and blaming others for its existence can never free us from it.

Men, we need to get our own house in order.

What we deny ourselves in this strange, sad affair is love. Not the emaciated, sclerotic substitute we've been taught to accept, but actual, real love. For many men, even love is a contest. Vuong goes on to write:

> To arrive at love, then, is to arrive through obliteration.
>
> Eviscerate me, we mean to say, and I'll tell you the truth … by then, violence was already mundane to me, was what I knew, ultimately, of love. Fuck. Me. Up.
>
> Sometimes being offered tenderness feels like the very proof that you've been ruined.

This was certainly how I came to collect the evidence of my own demise. When you see the real thing, tenderness, for the first time it is a cataclysm precisely because there is no escaping the horror that you have gone this far without it. Certainly, in my case, I was undone by that realisation.

I began to challenge my own aversion to vulnerability in my mid-twenties and it was almost impressive how much I was hewn by its absence. I almost had a panic attack about wearing a pink sweater to my eighteenth birthday drinks with my newsroom colleagues on the Gold Coast, for heaven's sake. I'd bought it from the now defunct Roger David chain store (a store on the edge of acceptability for *men* and then only if you were going out clubbing or had a court date). It was the first item of pink clothing I had ever owned and I loved it. But I wasn't out yet and I was steeped in the kind of bullshit culture that sells a pink Stanley knife to women so that others know they are neither men nor lesbians when they attempt middle- to industrial-strength craft or home improvement projects.

On closer reflection, I think the sweater was actually a sweater vest which meant I had bigger problems to worry about at the time, but I was consumed by the fear of being outed as gay. In this way, the clues my friends and I used to triangulate a person's sexuality were next to useless. We were modern versions of shit archaeologists who unearth an ancient burial ground containing feathered jewellery and a rudimentary windmill before concluding the now dead inhabitants must have been really into the Moulin Rouge.

I wore the sweater and exactly nothing happened. I fell off a bar stool while drunk and had a good time, but I can still recall so vividly the stress leading up to that night. And that's just one tiny example in a hall of fame chock-full of other accumulating stressors.

Like most of the other men in my life, I had shrunk myself to avoid social injury. We sharpened our edges to ward off approach, stooped low into ourselves and held this position with a laser-focus bordering on the deranged.

For me, this project was an overcorrection. It kept violence and embarrassment at the hands of other men to a minimum but it also made no room for love.

I was not loved and I did not love because that was not my experience of masculinity. The men around me were more or less on the same path, kissing and hugging their mates only on nights out when they were so 'fucked up' – remember, love is ruin – or after playing team sports and the notion of victory was so masculine in and of itself that it became OK to pat your friend on the bum or embrace them in ebullient relief at having won.

It's not like they didn't want these same things when they were sober. Rather, they were incapable of asking for them; they were so deeply afraid of being assumed gay or effeminate by reaching out in consolation or happiness that it was easier to stay rigid and strong.

We were all of us statues commemorating the wrong thing.

An analysis of two decades' worth of data by researchers from Duke University and the University of Arizona and published in the *American Sociological Review* in 2006 found that white, heterosexual men have the fewest friends of anyone in the United States.

Between 1985 and 2004, the 'discussion network' for most people shrank from almost three people to slightly more than two. Most of the time, however, these were a person's spouse or parents. This is particularly significant for men as they age.

You will have witnessed this in your own circles. The number of confidantes a married woman may have as she grows older will shrink, as it does for us all, but typically these will always include some other women or men outside of the marriage and her immediate family.

Straight married men, and I'm speaking broadly here, just do not know how to hold on to their mates. As the researchers note, they rely more and more on their wives for emotional support despite deriving less satisfaction from these relationships than they do from their friends.

A 2014 study released by Beyond Blue in Australia suggests one-quarter of all men in their middle age – that is aged thirty to sixty-five years old – 'have no-one outside their immediate family whom they can rely on'.

> This is an unspoken phenomenon: those experiencing it would rarely feel able to bring their 'neediness' up in conversations and it is rarely, if ever, a topic of public discourse.
>
> These men often lack the skills, the pathways and frequently the drive to remedy their lack of social connection and instead tend to bear the misery and shame of their situation with a stoic, masculine pride.

It might never be said in these terms, but many men know this one thing better than they know themselves: it is weak to ask for help. Even calling a friend and asking them to catch up is an act draped in the silent oppression of gender 'norms'.

Is it gay, and therefore 'woman-like', to ask a mate out for a drink? Is it gay to have good mental health?

For a particular subset of men, the corner pub or local and national sport are the only acceptable outlets for socialising, and even in those contexts it is generally forbidden to speak of personal troubles or loneliness. As one friend put it to me: 'You go there so you don't *have* to talk about it.'

You see this kind of thinking in pockets everywhere, but never so densely as among the working class and the working poor. These are the people I know best. Men who have shaped me, for better or worse, have typically come from these hard-knock backgrounds where their hands and backs were put to work and the work served a purpose and that purpose was unyielding in its purity – to have wife and child.

Whether it was a significant minority or even a majority of fathers over the last century, we'll never know, but I think it safe to say many of them never knew enough themselves to teach their own sons that the needs of a family may yet stretch beyond food and shelter.

Those things are important, absolutely, but it would have been just as helpful to advise all sons who wished to be fathers: if you're going to focus on, and even demand, the antiquated role of being the *provider*, than you'd best learn a thing or two about the provision of emotional and intellectual support, too.

In other words, you'd bloody well better learn how to love.

Times are changing. The arrow of time moves through its seasons. It just goes and goes and goes and throws upon its scrapheap the people locked so deep within themselves that they cannot be assured of progress. The recession in Australia that started in 2020 is unique in that it is the first in our history that has disproportionately affected the jobs of women. Manufacturing, for example, and its mostly male workforce has never accounted for such a low chunk of the economy. But in cafes and retail, the caring workforce of the aged and disability sectors, in offices, it is women who dominate. And more women are working than ever before in all types of jobs like accounting and law. This was their economy to lose; a unique state of affairs in the h
the country. It is fair to say, then, that the slow pivot a
manual labour in the West to a services and knowledge

has liberated real estate in the male brain that was typically on ice on account of the physical exhaustion of its owner.

Adjusting to this new state of affairs and away from a role in the family dynamic where you might have been both too necessary and too tired to let your mind wander is no small thing.

John Steinbeck captures this tired desperation in his masterwork, *The Grapes of Wrath*, when a poor man called Black Hat is fighting with the equally destitute Pa about undercutting his already woefully inadequate salary. They are both starving men with other mouths to feed and the tragedy of their circumstances has driven Black Hat to anger before. In resignation, he says:

> I dunno. I jes' dunno. It's bad enough to work twelve hours a day an' come out jes' a little bit hungry, but we got to figure all a time, too. My kid ain't gettin' enough to eat. I can't think all the time, goddamn it! It drives a man crazy.

In the context of a survival situation, this rings true. It's the constant *figuring* that grinds a person into the ground. But there are matters of mental bandwidth, too, for men who have come out of these roles without ever having been taught to sit with themselves and make friends with the person they discover there. We are not shown how to be vulnerable nor taught that the embrace of it is a kind of relief.

A while back I was having dinner with my mates, the aforementioned Tom, Mick and Perry, when we came to a discussion of therapy and its relative merits. We usually take it in turns to go through periods of distress and I can't remember who was having a go this time (it was probably me), so Mick asked the obvious question: 'But is it helpful?'

Perry, a boy from the Central Coast of New South Wales who still roasts a whole pig on a spit each year with lads from his high school, responded with a mixture of jest and deeply held belief. 'Look, people who do it swear by it,' he said. 'But, again, it's one of those things. I've never put Premium in my car either and it's fine.'

(Perhaps six months after this episode I was driving Perry back to Canberra from Sydney where he had left his car because it had just stopped working. I'm not saying this incident was definitely related to the petrol issue because I honestly have no idea how cars work, but not quite enough time had passed for me to forget his argument and the episode didn't reflect well on his credibility.)

The fact we were even talking about mental health, as three straight men and a gay guy, is something of a monument to the times, I suppose, even though we all dragged our own hang-ups to that dinner like four weary travellers with more baggage than places to put it.

Outside my friendship group there is a fragility among some men that I find truly confronting. An entry in this low-stakes hall of fame comes from a Snapchat user called Kevin who posted a picture of a deep pink sunset with the tagline: 'I'm straight but … that's incredible.'

I feel genuinely sorry for Kevin who, through his personal and broader social networks, has come to believe that finding beauty in the world is the sole preserve of women and gay men. As if only raw sexual energy can intuit the rolling charm of our reality. Of course, it is fun to imagine a world where that masculine fear is an actual physical law; where a straight guy cops one look at van Gogh's *The Starry Night* and ends up sucking an acre of dick behind the bike sheds at a local sports ground.

Don't come for their state-based beer, either.

As 2021 broke, I had finally made it home to Boonah in Queensland to see my mum. On a rare trip to the state capital, I was passing the XXXX brewery in Milton and decided it would be funny (jury's out) to post a photo of me giving the building the finger. I have no particular feelings about the brewery one way or the other but it has been a feature of my upbringing in the state and I am fond, certainly, of its place in local lore.

The reaction from men – it was only men – was swift.

A man called Archie, whose profile photo is a vintage car, replied: 'Keep going, show some respect.' Others like Shane told me to 'fuck off home then', presumably to New South Wales where I am now based. Another said I was 'quiet [sic] welcome to go back to plague city, champ.' Nothing stings as much as being champed by an older bloke. Matt took a different angle, at least, commenting only: 'That's a fat hand.'

A fat hand! I pictured him sitting at home, shaking with rage, plotting his defence of the brewery's honour.

It is strange the hills on which people will die, metaphorically and also literally. Just days after the beer skirmish, pro-Trump domestic terrorists staged an insurrection by storming the Capitol building in Washington DC on the day lawmakers were due to certify Joe Biden's historic victory over the one-term demagogue who had occupied the White House since 2016.

The fascist mob scaled the walls of the Capitol, smashed windows and used makeshift battering rams to infiltrate the seat of American Congress. Security forces, objectively more sympathetic to the rioters than they have been to Black Lives Matter protestors, were overwhelmed – in part because of those sympathies and otherwise because few among their leaders had ever taken the threat of right-wing violence seriously despite its meteoric rise as the primary domestic threat in the years prior. Vision from inside flooded social media, posted by news crews and the proud men and women who had seized the building for a man who could not care less about them. One police officer died after being hit in the head with a fire extinguisher. Video showed another being crushed in a sliding door, screaming for help as the mob bayed. One right-wing extremist, a woman, was shot and killed by the Capitol police.

This event was in part a disease of misogyny. That might seem an odd thing to say. There were women there! How could it be an example of misogyny?

Firstly, it is important to state upfront that much of this hysterical moment has its roots in a fundamental hatred of the *other.* Racism helped birth the conditions, most recently with the election of the first Black president in American history. That was perceived by racists as an injury for which the country needed radical surgery. As ever, though, there were other forces at play in the background.

The DNA of one of those constituent parts, Gamergate, turned up at the Capitol Hill riots. For those who live their lives blessedly offline, the 2014 Gamergate histrionics will mean nothing. But it is important to understand how a disgruntled posse of video game bros made life hell for women over the course of some months through a targeted online harassment campaign.

Gamergate started after Eron Gjoni, the ex-boyfriend of video game developer Zoe Quinn, wrote a blog post in which he falsely accused Quinn of an 'inappropriate' relationship with a gaming journalist. He was angry about their split and dishing the 'dirt' as payback. #GamerGate hashtag users picked up the baton, many hiding behind their gamer names but some in full view, and coordinated a harassment campaign.

However, to say Gamergate was solely about Quinn is a farce. Beneath the thin veneer of that excuse was a magma chamber of hatred directed at feminism, and progressivism more generally, and its influence on video game culture. These were bros who did not wish to account for their behaviour – or ever change it – threatening rape and death, revealing her phone number and residential address. They stole nude photos from Quinn in revenge porn quests as if it were one of the games they themselves played in a rich online fantasy world. But this was real life.

'My breakup required the intervention of the United Nations,' Quinn writes in *Crash Override: How Gamergate (nearly) destroyed my life, and how we can win the fight against online hate*, her memoir about the frenzy.

Others might draw a direct causal link between this episode of culture war violence and what happened on Capitol Hill, though it is no less powerful to look solely at the facts and understand how its core features bobbed around in the soup of shadowy online discourse before emerging more fully into the world with fanfare after the election of Donald Trump.

These were people who only ever wanted permission: to be their authentic grotesque selves without fear of consequence. Others helped pave the way before and after Trump's ascent to the White House. The once in-demand alt-right figure Milo Yiannopoulos – now banned from most social media platforms and broke as a consequence – sensed an opportunity in Gamergate.

In 2013, only a year before the controversy, Yiannopoulos called gamers 'saddos living in their parents' basements' in a column for the now defunct *The Kernel*, which he founded. He wrote: 'There's something a bit tragic, isn't there, about men in their thirties hunched over a controller whacking a helmeted extraterrestrial?'

What these new-age reactionary grifters lack in humanity they also lack in ethics. They are exceptionally good, however, at monetising opportunities of righteous indignation. Gamergate was one of them. Yiannopoulos hijacked the 'rebellion' against political correctness in its infancy and helped catalyse its natural mutation into full-blooded right-wing monster.

He knew better than anyone else that this wasn't about 'ethics in video game journalism' and gave the punters what they wanted: column after column putting pro-diversity 'elites' in the crosshairs, with his first column titled 'Feminist Bullies Tearing the Video Game Industry Apart'.

If anyone wants to study how a conflagration such as the one on Capitol Hill in January 2021 builds, it might be useful to track the way language swiftly becomes physical violence under the right conditions.

The essential grievance of the Gamergate fallout was treated as a shocking flare-up in online hostilities and not, as it was, the inevitable consequence of an unedifying social refusal to deal with male violence against women.

The mountain moves in pieces. Stone by stone, apparently 'reasonable' people in mainstream media organisations began throwing around terms like 'social justice warrior' and 'virtue signalling' as a convenient shorthand for people who care about trivial things like violence against women and human dignity. It was deployed not just by extremists but laundered through the slightly more palatable mouths of opinion columnists and conservative networks like Fox News – and even, once similar terms gained traction, in more centre-right outlets and publications in the United Kingdom and Australia.

At the heart of this grotesque performance was perhaps a belief that language itself could never actualise the danger contained in the words. In the worst cases, however, those pundits and far-right actors wielding the words knew exactly what could come of it.

They just didn't care.

And so this project of shifting the tone of 'de Overton window of what is acceptable – greased t Trump's campaign for presidency. It allowed his v

Once that happened, the man himself became the ultimate proof that it is possible not just to survive while disregarding almost every decent convention of modern society but to become *President of the United States of America*.

Enabled at every turn, Trump spent four years stoking racist hearts and poisoned minds, having already bragged about sexually assaulting women and getting away with it. With each utterance and each failure to be penalised, his supporters grew bolder.

Yes, women stormed the Capitol. Yes, some people of colour have been among Trump's most ardent loyalists. We have seen throughout civilisation the complex psychology of people who have been drafted to act against their own interests. We have seen, too, the refusal of members of otherwise disenfranchised minority groups to deal with hatred if they do so from a position of power. The 'I got mine' state of mind is a powerful one. But it is true, too, to say that there are those who have grown up in a world so steeped in the rituals of everyday woman-hating and an innate white supremacy that these people can't or won't see the yoke of their own captivity.

Gamergate is just one expression of this atmosphere. And, obviously, not all video gamers are fascist coup enthusiasts. I spent most of my childhood and early twenties playing console games like Metal Gear Solid and Battlefield. But there, in the Capitol and standing next to a Mr Tumnus look-a-like in a horned helmet, was a man with a tattoo on his hand from the video game Dishonored. He sports the 'mark of the outsider', which in the game appears on characters who have been chosen by the Outsider himself. Curiously, the storyline involves a corrupt leader who has presided over a deadly pandemic and is eventually overthrown … in a coup.

The Capitol Hill rioters, whether the rest even knew about this game or not, truly believed they were working to take back a 'stolen election'. And who might possibly have given them that idea? Narcissus himself.

In mid-January, the United States House Judiciary Committee released a report in support of a resolution to impeach 'Donald John Trump, President of the United States, for high crimes and misdemeanours'.

The report says:

> Members of this mob also made clear that they attacked the Capitol because they believed the President had directed them to. One, individual, Jacob Chansley, who wore a 'bearskin headdress' and 'carried a spear, approximately 6 feet in length,' later told police that he came as part of a group effort at the request of the President.
>
> Another, Derrick Evans, had posted on social media at 12:08 AM on January 6th that he was going to D.C. to '#StopTheSteal,' in response to the President's tweet. Similarly, a livestream video from inside the Capitol revealed an insurrectionist explaining, '[o]ur president wants us here … We wait and take orders from our president'.

So what we have here now is a far-right or alt-right nationalist movement taking orders from a man who has admitted to sexually assaulting women. These two things are not a coincidence.

Take this May 2019 report from the Organisation for Security and Cooperation in Europe (OSCE) that notes that the terms 'alt-right' or 'alternative right' are a 'contemporary description of white supremacy and white nationalism'. These movements are also, OSCE says, 'often misogynist'.

'Both men and women who are part of them hold the belief that women should primarily stay at home, raise children and care for the family,' the report says. 'Women may perform the role of "wife with a purpose" or that of "tradwives".'

The OSCE cites studies from the International Centre for Counterterrorism, the UN Office of Counterterrorism and the Council of Europe, which all show that one of the causes that leads to violent extremism is 'liberal societies with higher gender equality in which men feel intimidated by women's independence, as exemplified by the "involuntary celibacy" (Incel) movement'.

Incels are men who quite literally believe they cannot get sex from women because the world has given the latter too much power. More colloquially, this is 'blue balls' as a radicalising force.

Mull that over for a second. Some men have gone to war over their lack of sex. In April 2018, Alek Minassian drove a van into a crowd of mostly female pedestrians in Toronto, killing ten people. Before his act of fatal rage, he declared an 'Incel rebellion' and praised the 22-year-old mass murderer Elliot Rodger who killed six people in a 2014 shooting rampage in California.

Rodger was a virgin and he was angry about it.

Remember, the dangerous fury that fed Gamergate started with a man who felt aggrieved that Zoë Quinn, a casual partner, had allegedly slept with another man. A whole ocean of pain and misery was formed because Eron Gjoni felt that Quinn belonged to him.

The fingerprints of this malicious entitlement are the same that crop up again and again in family violence matters. Intimate partner abuse, as it happens, is also a reliable predictor of terrorism and extremism.

Misogyny is its own closed ecosystem, supporting the everyday m-of-the-food-chain diminishment of women all the way to x predators' radical violence.

19, journalist and author Jess Hill published the most Australian book of the past decade. Resulting from a five-year study, *See What You Made Me Do* is an unnerving but deeply real portrait of domestic abuse in Australia and around the world. Hill is methodical in peeling back the many layers of abuse, none quite so alarming to me as the conditioning of boys to reject femininity in all its forms. This becomes not just a disease for men but, as Hill writes, the 'ghost in the machine of our culture'.

In it, she quotes family therapist and masculinity expert Terrence Real, who says the principal medium of the message is shame.

The way we turn boys into men, so to speak, 'is through injury', according to Real. 'We pull them away from their own expressiveness, from their feelings, from sensitivity to others,' he is quoted as saying. 'Disconnection is not fallout from traditional masculinity. Disconnection is masculinity.'

As Hill establishes prior to this quote, female laughter at the male is terrifying to men not because they can't overpower women physically – that is a lesson taught to them in their bones – but because it makes them look weak in front of other men. And in a world where traditional masculinity rules, this is a very dangerous place to be.

The balance needs to be reset. In return, the anger meted out is righteous.

It is also so hopelessly pathetic when confronted.

Jacob Chansley, the most recognisable of the Capitol Hill terrorists with his bearskin shawl and horned helmet, was detained in custody after the riot. His mother, Martha Chansley, told ABC15 news that her son hadn't been fed his organic food diet since the arrest.

'He gets very sick if he doesn't eat organic food – literally will get physically sick,' she said.

*

In Melbourne, there is a house with some of my favourite people in it and it is to this house I make a pilgrimage whenever I am in town. The men who live there are all from regional New South Wales and they are all young and heterosexual, which seems a strange thing upon which to remark at all these days. They date women, but the gentle affection usually reserved for romance between men and women is unguarded here, allowed to roam free. It's really quite beautiful.

When I visit and the door to their home is opened, I am smothered with hugs and kisses. We kiss on the cheek, on the lips. We hug for longer than commonly held convention would allow, plus another five seconds for good measure.

In *Dear Friends: American Photographs of Men Together 1840–1918*, David Deitcher writes: '[In the late Victorian period] men posed for photographers holding hands, entwining limbs, or resting in the shelter of each other's accommodating bodies, innocent of the suspicion that such behaviour would later arouse.'

Viewing these photos is like watching the final footage of the thylacine. It sparks the acute sense this is a marvel of the past not easily reintroduced, if at all. It conjures a melancholy that this pure, decent thing was lost to successive generations. That suffering these men of the past endured in loneliness, cut off from the joy of male companionship, has happened and will never be undone.

There are things we learn in that desolation.

One of the Melbourne boys, a dear friend of mine I'm going

[illegible] was in Sydney while I was writing this chapter and

[illegible] er a few beers at the Vic on the Park Hotel

[illegible]

[illegible] You need to write it.'

[illegible] proceeded to tell me about the relationship he

[illegible] ical father, which was built on a foundation of

ambient physical terror and the tension of unpredictable tempers. On one occasion in his teenage years, as Logan had begun to become stronger, he began firmly telling his father about the hurt his numerous affairs had caused both himself and the family. Logan's grandfather was there, too.

'You could see Dad just getting angrier and angrier,' Logan told me. 'His face was straining and red and I could see my pop looking at him to get him to calm down and looking at me to make me stop. He was trying to say, "Stop, he's gonna fucken kill you," but I didn't. And my dad just grabbed me by the throat and lifted me over the balcony railing and held me there. I was screaming at him, "Just fucken do it, go on and fucken do it."'

Logan's grandfather knew well what he was dealing with because he had, in his own way in a different time, instilled that same male rage in *his* son.

'Pop told me about my dad's eighteenth birthday party. Dad had a bunch of his mates around to the farmhouse and they got fucked up. They were on a rampage and Dad thought this was the moment he was finally going to shape up to his old man,' Logan said.

As he describes it, his youthful father was lean but rippling with muscle. He was drunk out of his skull and led the charge against his father.

'Pop told me he thought he was going to die that night,' Logan told me.

Logan has emerged from this kind of childhood teeming with big ideas about love and gentleness. He's a musician and singer. On one of my visits to the Melbourne house he showed me his notebook, where he writes down snatches of lyrics and ideas for songs. He'd only ever shown three other people.

Here was a young man, then only twenty-one, who was justifiably at a loss when trying to figure his way through all the emotion and feeling of being so young. That is the price we children pay for the aberrations of fatherhood; we are left alone in a wilderness of spite and anger that can never bring us into the world, only away from it.

In John Williams's novel *Stoner*, he describes the observations of the main character, a university professor, during World War Two:

> He saw the classrooms emptied of their young men, he saw the haunted looks upon those who remained behind, and saw in those looks the slow death of the heart, the bitter attrition of feeling and care.

War is a singular experience, I believe, but Williams could just as easily be describing the trajectory of many young men who are spat into the cauldron of the world alive to none of its beauty, primed for its rejection of them.

Either way, the death toll mounts.

I do wish I could grab some of these more severe men and make them understand what I have had to discover by cutting away the confected, infected, parts of myself.

The work has happened slowly over the years but more consciously in the course of writing this book. It is difficult, of course, to confront the notion that many of these behaviours and artifices are hoarded for an imagined future. This is an illness and, like hoarders of stuff, all we have to show for it is a pile of rubbish, which offers no help, only harm. The collection serves only to obscure the person we are, underneath it all, and to keep others at bay.

I want to shake my former colleagues of this misery and tell them that it is worth the deconstruction. Everything else is bleak, and dangerous.

It is so easy for me now to cast my mind back and look afresh upon the disconnection that held my life together, like a single strand of spider's web cut loose from its moorings on a gentle breeze. There was a period of about ten years there during which I didn't cry at all. Not at my grandfather's funeral, nor at any point in high school or the year after when everything felt so strange and uncertain. When I finally did cry, in my third year of university, it was explosive.

During the pandemic lockdown I was on a video call with my friend Candice, ruminating on the unique terrors of mind-bending isolation. I'm not sure how it came up, but as the conversation turned to emotional coping mechanisms I yelled at her through my phone screen: 'You ever seen a man try and push a tear back into its duct? Welcome to the Morton family!'

When I wrote about them in my first book, I broke their number-one rule. By 'them' I mean the men, because they controlled everything. That rule is this: never, ever, ever show signs of weakness. That includes doing any number of 'weak' things. Dad, for instance, wore only olive green or brown jeans on the cattle station. Blue jeans, according to his honestly quite opaque logic, were for poofters. For formal events such as a race meet or rodeo (yes, formal), he would break out the dental-white moleskins which apparently did not feature on his jeans-Kinsey scale. To appear strong, one must also be willing to prove it by fighting other men, cattle (when provoked) and nature more broadly. Most significantly of all, however, the Morton categorical imperative dictated that we should never admit to having emotional problems. In fact, it was preferable to have no emotions at all. Except anger, which was the pig of emotions. It could be pork, bacon, ham, whatever the circumstances required.

I broke the rule when writing my book, but I didn't do it to provoke anger. I felt a profound sense of loss for these men. Even the ones who hurt me.

Having since surrounded myself with better role models, the grief is all the more real.

'The greatest strength I have ever witnessed is gentleness,' Séamus told me once. He's right, of course, and he has modelled this way of being for as long as I've known him.

In the animal kingdom, exposing our soft underbellies is often a sure path to death or injury. Some animals do it deliberately, however, to indicate submission. This, too, is a measure of the instincts coded in us. Softness is weakness. Actual death, social death – it's all the same. We fear it.

The problem, especially for men, is that the rigid avoidance of this pain of exposure is itself a death and perhaps the worst one of all because it means you cannot *live.*

Not all vulnerabilities will be received well by all people. Some will be exploited. You may show your most true self to someone and be laughed at or met with disdain.

Still, choose to do this. There is liberty in it.

It struck me, while writing this book, that expressing myself and being open to the world was an inoculation. Suddenly, I didn't care what other people thought about me. To be more precise, I didn't care to the same crippling degree as before. The more of us who do it, the safer we are; a kind of herd immunity for the mind. There is a point, not too far down this path, where you will be greeted with the kind of knowledge that could move

one else is the same as you.

spend all their allotted time on this planet that freedom might feel like.

Loneliness

I broke earlier than I thought I would, in a doctor's clinic beneath the Tokyo Tower, after an eventful morning when I suddenly realised I'd left my anti-anxiety medication back in Australia.

Friends and fellow travellers had warned me that Japan was a country that not only nursed a sense of isolation, but actively provoked it. Tokyo, especially. But I was nonplussed. I had grown up so close to loneliness in my waking life that the feeling was more akin to friendship. What could a city that split its people into atoms teach me about the art of being alone?

To be perfectly frank, my main fear about the trip was that I would not feel this promised sense of detachment at all, that I would end up moving through the city as I had through my own life: alone, certainly, but not always lonely.

And then, to reward my sweet idiocy, the universe arranged a few things to aid my cause. I flew into Tokyo during what I then believed to be the middle – how wrong I was – of a coronavirus epidemic that was sweeping the world.

I was sick. People in the airport looked at me the way characters in a B-grade horror film react to a friend the moment after said friend has been bitten by a zombie. They know there's no coming back from that. And the sweat pouring from the victim is not to do with the zombie fever; it's that the victim knows it, too. Deep down.

I had just finished writing an article about Covid-19. I knew the score. While waiting in the airport queue for an hour to collect my Japan Rail pass, I wondered who in the line would be strong enough to do what the group required, which was to take a crowbar and cave my skull in. My eyes settled on a small, stumpy Asian woman who reminded me a lot of my mum, Deb, and I knew it would be her. It's never the ones you first expect; people tend not to factor in the tactical physical advantage of having a low centre of gravity.

If you are after an isolating, awkward or plain lonely entree to a city, then I've yet to discover a better one than my introduction to Tokyo that morning. The illness was so debilitating, I didn't realise that first day that I had left my antidepressants back in Sydney. But the next morning, when I went to leave my hotel on the park by Tokyo's Shiodome railway station, I walked straight into a wall.

Five years after starting on the medication, I was convinced I didn't really need to be on it anymore. Staying with the dosage turned out to be far easier than trying to get off it, however.

Did you know that trying to get off my type of antidepressant can lead you to having thoughts of wanting to kill yourself? Spoiler alert! I found this mildly amusing when my GP first told me about it, as is my wont, because to me it seemed like being sold a home alarm system that, when you try to uninstall it, sends individual text messages to known house burglars with your address and location of valuables.

Give me back my money!

Before these dire side-effects kick in, however, missing even a day's dose can be pretty whacky. My record prior to Japan was three days, after which my brain felt like it was about to melt. On day two in Tokyo, the world had shifted almost (but not quite!) imperceptibly along its horizon so not only was I now aware I had left my entire prescription back home, but also I felt like I was on a cruise ship for my troubles. And not a *fun* cruise ship, but one of those ones you recognise from grainy closed-circuit TV security recordings of a ship venturing into a dangerous tropical storm. Usually there is a pleasantly holiday-themed older person sliding across a varnished floor and into a grand piano, or a tray of mojitos exploding on to the pool deck. Fun to watch, not amazing to live.

Maybe, I thought calmly, this would be a good way to come down from the high dose that had been in my system for half a decade? And, besides, navigating the Australian health system was almost beyond my reach; what hope did I have in Japan? So I went about my day, making a beeline for the absolutely nuts Shimbashi railway station so I could jump a train to Shibuya and explore. There was a moment, deep within the catacombs-like underbelly of the station, with the Japanese salarymen dissecting my path at every turn that I realised how fucked I truly was.

My brain lost the ability to smooth-track through fast-walking subjects. The commuters in their mid-morning haste turned into elongated blurs. I was completely incapable of judging the distance between each one, getting caught by their glancing blows as they moved through the crowd like laser beams. It was, quite literally, a spin out.

I'm not going to last the rest of this trip without medication, I thought.

Still, I'm a rock-bottom type guy. I need to know the worst has arrived before attempting remediation work. And so I blundered through Shibuya like a Roomba without an algorithm before hitting the worthless clay soil of my own lowest point.

On the recommendation of an acquaintance from social media, I found myself at the Tokyo Medical and Surgical Clinic underneath the candy-cane-coloured Tokyo Tower, where a doctor with a startling English accent asked me what I was doing in Japan in the first place.

'I'm writing a book about love and vulnerability. And loneliness,' I offered, through the increasing static of my brain.

I might have imagined this, but I recall the young doctor in that moment doing a theatrical slow swivel towards me in his chair before looking me directly in the eyes and saying: 'Well, you've certainly come to the right place for that.'

There was a hint of melancholy in his voice and, right then, I wanted him to hug me. Here was somebody who understood my pain and maybe I could provide some solace for his.

Yes, this particular moment was loneliness. The bite of it is bone-crushing in the way solitude isn't.

Solitude is a sort of mistake in our programming. Loneliness is the correct code, from a survival perspective. It exists for the same reason as physical pain: to warn us.

Of course we are not meant to be alone. In pre-history, that meant certain death. And as we've already established, pre-history is the very basis for our brain. I have enjoyed so many stretches of solitude in my life, the way they seemed totally borderless and plump with nothing. But there is always an invisible line that divides elixir and poison.

Loneliness is a disease, like cancer, and certainly deadlier than the coronavirus, which at that point was starting to shut air travel between China and countries like Singapore. Loneliness might even be more fatal than smoking, which is doubly bad news for me. Apparently sitting is also, medically, as bad as both smoking and loneliness, which at the time of writing this book gives me the kind of trifecta I could never manage on the Melbourne Cup.

You know that feeling, though, don't you? When your solitude morphs from guilty pleasure into the searing failure of loneliness? Social creatures like us have all experienced the bleed from one state to the other, like water turning into gas under heat.

Solitude is wind or water, so beautiful and necessary. Loneliness is what happens when the wind or water become so persistent they erode the substance around them. It is erosion. When does wind or water become a force that can wear down the face of granite? Not today or tomorrow, or next Tuesday. But it will.

After the doctor gave me my new prescription for the drugs I'd left back in Australia, I took my dose and went to sleep for seven hours and then another ten while my brain recalibrated.

Although it is surely insufferable, I awoke from that restorative slumber with a new mission in mind: to go to the bar where they filmed *Lost in Translation* and wait for deliverance, whether that be in the form of Bill Murray or Scarlett Johansson.

Nobody tells you, until you are that high up and can see it for yourself, that every high-rise in Tokyo has blinking red lights at their highest points. I imagine it's an air traffic control thing, though I've never noticed it in any other city before. It feels unique and, because I've seen it nowhere else before, it seems to reinforce the loneliness of the vista.

Being fifty-two floors above the largest metropolis on earth is its own kind of psychic realignment. In the months before my trip to Japan, my friend Bridie introduced me to the writing of Australian academic Jill Ker Conway; in her beloved memoir *The Road from Coorain*, she describes the landscape of outback Australia as the 'annihilation of self'. Having grown up under that same vast skies, I read that passage and thought: *Yes, yes, yes! That's it!* Though I now know that you can get the same experience at the New York Bar at the top of the Park Hyatt in Shinjuku.

Up there, I ceased to exist. There was a five-piece jazz band and windows that stretched across two floors with views out on to the expanse of Tokyo beyond, and there was the bar with the angular lamps where Bill Murray met Scarlett Johansson and where I now sat. At either end of the space were floor-high murals by Italian artist Valerio Adami, which themselves were enough to make a person feel small, bright as they were. The room was an absence more than it was a presence, and that allowed the city to rush in at you. The city and all of its people, all of those constituent parts, refracted by the light and yet as one.

After recovering from the early low point of my trip to the doctor, I was enthralled. This dance between the two states of mere solitude and the messier work of loneliness was more familiar territory for me. To drift along the imaginary plane between them felt real, like nothing else had in recent memory.

If only there was a way to stay there, at that precise moment, for eternity. If only there was a way to make it stable, whatever that chemical reaction was. I liked it.

Before my trip, I had lunch with a sex worker called Mischa Maxwell in Sydney's Kings Cross district to pick her brains about this book and the city she knows on a deeper level than many tourists. Much of her clientele is in Japan; the 'loneliest men on the planet' as she calls them. Theirs is a cultural malaise far deeper than my shallow performance as a solitary tourist.

'When you're working the life of a salaryman, which is 9 am to 9 pm, then you have to go out drinking with the boss for two or three hours,' Maxwell told me. 'You don't want to go home drunk, so you'll typically stay in a capsule hotel.'

The ubiquitous 711s or Lawson's mini-marts and convenience stores on every corner of Tokyo's streets are for this very reason stocked with entire work outfits for men. You can roll in drunk or hungover and walk out with a crisp white shirt, underwear, pants and socks.

The expectation imposed on the Japanese salaryman is to give over the child-rearing and home-management to his wife, to such a degree that he is provided a small stipend by her with which to go about his day. By the time the average family has its second kid, the wife and children have moved into the second bedroom to leave their working husband and father to his diminishing role as cog in machine.

There are no winners in the stultifying existence of the honour-bound Japanese family. Both women and men suffer, for different reasons no doubt, but the suffering has often defied categorisation.

'So, at age forty-five, you're getting no sex, you have no money to divorce,' Maxwell told me. 'So, the children of that generation are seeing how unhappy their parents are and are opting not to marry. They are opting not to marry at all because it is miserable; it's a miserable lifestyle.'

Enter the sex industry, a sector as old as civilisation itself but honed to such an astonishing degree of efficiency and specificity in Japan, its single point of precision can peel open the most bizarre or fetid desires of a single person and sate them.

I consider myself especially open-minded, which is no small achievement for a kid from outback Queensland with heavy Protestant and Catholic influences, but the array of services for sexual fetishes, kink and garden-variety horniness in Japan is paralysing.

Sure, you can go to a blowjob bar where sex workers attend to you below while you're being served drinks above the table, but what struck me about the myriad options on offer is that so many of them are more about providing attention than sexual release.

'For single women, there are things called host bars where you go and buy drinks,' Maxwell told me, 'but there are hot blokes around that will flirt with you and encourage you to buy more and more and more drinks. And they get a cut of the drinks that they encourage you to buy. At a hostess bar, same thing. I'll flirt with you outrageously, tell you how amazing you are and convince you to buy drinks. I'll be drinking water, by the way; you'll be drinking vodka or sake.

'So that's enough emotional interaction for you and then you're happy to go home.'

If the going gets really tough, a tired salaryman can always duck into a Don Quijote mega-mart in Tokyo and pick up a six-pack of Tenga eggs for $30. A Tenga egg is essentially a single-use, lubed-up penis pocket – a Kinder Surprise for adults starved of affection.

Another option for release is to visit a *sōpu*, or soapland, a form of brothel that sprang up across Japan after prostitution was made illegal in the 1950s. Here the cover for sex services is a modern public bathhouse, where patrons can sit on chairs with holes in them – *Sukebe Isu* – and be washed top to bottom by attendants. If a client manages to reach climax under such trying circumstances, then that is just an unfortunate accident of biology.

Maxwell told me you can also opt for some 'delivery health' – health being sexual stimulation in this particular Japanese context – where a nurse will come to your apartment, take your temperature, give you the once over and then, if you pay her properly, go further.

You'd be forgiven for thinking Japan is a wonderland of sexual freedom, but its proliferation of kink happened in spite of a moralistic neoconservatism, not because its people are loose by design.

I don't mean conservativism in the repressed Christian-right manner of speaking. Japanese people seek out this bewildering spectacle of sexual services precisely because they have been told over and over again by custom or decree that vulnerability is weakness, and love – the kind that can be fulfilling and beautiful in and outside of marriage – is only a species of duty. In such a culture, it becomes shameful to seek the reassurances of tenderness or affection with those you know. So, it is outsourced.

A further reason Japanese people have become so inflamed with loneliness and its terrifying dimensions is the same reason it has turned to a constellation of sexual enterprise: a crippling prudishness of the state. The sex industry is not a cure, per se, it is a symptom. That said, in lieu of a cure it is a terrifically necessary part of Japanese life.

The labyrinthine network of sex services in Japan is, in its strange way, the very thing keeping the charade of honour-bound men and women from falling apart completely.

If this natural human desire had nowhere else to live, the system would implode.

Now, teaching Japanese children sex education without assiduously avoiding the naughty bits (like showing penises and vaginas in the textbook for eight- to ten-year-olds in the curriculum that covers the headline 'As the body approaches adulthood') would help overcome some of the prudishness.

But I can hardly complain, having been on the receiving end of a Queensland state school sex education program as a young gay man, which is rather like being taught how to swim by a man who has already drowned.

You can see how these eddies of sexual conservatism turn into geysers of abandon among certain people. The great preoccupation with any kind of sex but especially gay sex – and *particularly* men who have sex with men – by the religious moral crusaders always scanned as morbid curiosity to me.

It is a titillation for them, a way to approach the fatal boundaries of an interesting sex life without tipping head first into moral destruction. I mean, good grief, at least the rest of us have the decency to be honest about it.

Anyway, this is a long (but sexy) way of making what I see as an essential point: I see no true love or genuine company in the spirit of our friendly neighbourhood moral crusaders. This is not meant as a nasty criticism for the sake of it. I see only destitution in their eyes, a light that burns so dimly and then only because the performance of absolutism throws out the occasional spark from the friction of weapons-grade cognitive dissonance.

To configure our true selves based on external whim is a tragedy.

And isn't that, after all, the surest path to loneliness?

One of my most excruciating lonely moments came in the company of friends I professed to love and who on paper loved me too, but to whom I was utterly incapable of giving access.

I wish I had known then the cause of that ethereal distance. I had built the walls, how was it possible to be ignorant of their existence?

We make mistakes of authorship when we ascribe motives to other minds. In the throes of a dark, furious despair half a decade ago, I was told by a wise therapist, through a somewhat elaborate series of questions about the arrival of the First Fleet, that I was 'colonising other peoples' minds'.

It was me. I was turning up unannounced in their heads and f[illegible] on them my customs and beliefs without any regard for [illegible]ight have been there before. And then I turned that work [illegible]elf and imagined, or totally fabricated, their view of me.

The evidence of their alleged indifference or disdain towards me was planted. And I was the one who planted it.

I think this is how we become lonely. Certainly, those of us who have known loneliness have likely also experienced rejection and spite, apathy or indifference; the many vagaries of another person's response to a sliver of our own vulnerability that disappoints us in ways we cannot quite define.

Perhaps we were greeted with too much emotion or not enough, or the tenor of their voice sounded accusatory or sarcastic, or there was too little reciprocity in the sharing of weakness, or we read our own shame on their words as they hung in the air between us.

It must be universal, this misalignment of our shame and its reception in others. We should not be deterred by it. For the five or ten people who for whatever reason are unable or unwilling to meet your shame – your peculiar underbelly of truth – there will be at least one who understands its measure. And this above all is an antidote to loneliness.

Though it works best at full participation. So many horrors of modern society could be softened, if not entirely banished, with a full-throated willingness to be open to the world. My mind here keeps coming back to politics and how few within its ranks can admit being wrong. I'm not naive. I know the system reinforces this blundering state of affairs that locks us into policy prescriptions that, sometimes, even public proponents concede privately will not work. Most of us punish error and ignore personal growth. Outside of the realm of power, imagine how many garden-variety bullies might find healing if we were all trained to respond to injustice and pain in good faith. It is a lesson I try, and fail, to learn every day. It is no easy thing to show a teetering world your open palm.

Back in Japan, the poison of cultural loneliness has been so pervasive that a whole category of the population – those who die alone – have had a word coined in their honour.

Kodokushi, quite literally 'lonely death', is not solely a Japanese phenomenon but it is one they have named.

'A single-minded focus on economic growth, followed by painful economic stagnation over the past generation, had frayed families and communities, leaving them trapped in a demographic crucible of increasing age and declining births,' Norimitsu Onishi wrote in the *New York Times* in 2017. 'The extreme isolation of elderly Japanese is so common that an entire industry has emerged around it.'

When a person dies alone in Japan, employees from specialised cleaning companies are called in to wipe grime and dirt, the smell of death, from the apartment. These cleaners will also organise the mementos and belongings of the lonely death, *kodokushi*, partly because it needs to be done. They are compelled, also, by the idea that it is particularly intolerable for a human life to end without remark or memorial. Sorting the stuff of a life, then, is one way to honour the dead.

In the survey of Japan's Changing Societal Structure and Support by Families and Communities (reporting in 2017), it emerged that in any two-week period 15 per cent of elderly men who lived alone spoke to someone else just once or even *never*. Almost 9 per cent of younger men who lived alone met the same criteria, two spurs in the data that are jarringly disproportionate. More than 30 per cent of elderly men who lived alone noted they had no 'reliable person' who could provide them with 'a little help'.

Diagnosing the terra-forming nature of great economic upheaval – both on the way up and when it comes crashing back down – is only part of the story. I do worry about the ones who seem to think an economy is something that exists outside people, made only from raw numbers and adhesive tape. People are an economy. And just as they can shape it, economic forces can bend entire populations or groups to fit prevailing trends, the way trees grow almost horizontal in perpetually windswept valleys or plains.

At least one major bump in the graph for *kodokushi* happened after the collapse of the economy in the late 1980s when many senior Japanese salarymen were forced to retire early. Having given up on their families or jettisoned the idea of starting one entirely, these men managed to sacrifice themselves on the altar of corporate dominance.

If your god is fair and just, perhaps you could argue the trade-off. The great corporate deities in Japan, however, were capricious and beyond entreaty. Like Communist Romania's dictatorial quest for dominance at the expense of the individual, Japan's capitalist blood thirst came at enormous social and personal cost.

The case of *kodokushi* that catapulted the issue on to the national stage was that of a 69-year-old man who was found in the year 2000, having been dead for three years. As the *New York Times* reported, his rent and electricity had been paid directly from his bank account until his savings ran out. It was this that alerted the authorities who discovered a skeleton near the kitchen, just a metre or so away from the next-door neighbours. The bones had been picked clean by maggots and beetles.

As the economy railroaded entire generations, people like this man were increasingly isolated. Some families were forced to warehouse their elderly, or forget them entirely, and many men died alone because they prioritised work above all else.

Dark, I suppose, that this poor wretch was not alone in this kind of death. Not even in Japan.

In 2006, the skeletal remains of 38-year-old Joyce Carol Vincent were found in her north London bedsit. She had died in December 2003 in her kitchen, not far from the Christmas presents she had wrapped but never had the chance to deliver.

Vincent's death was ultimately anything but private, becoming a national media sensation that sparked a docudrama series and even a poem in Joel Sadler-Puckering's debut collection *I Know Why the Gay Man Dances.*

She did have family, however. By all accounts they were a nice family that loved her, but Vincent had also been the subject of domestic violence, and for reasons we will never truly understand she chose to gulp down the attendant shame on her own.

I use the word shame here advisedly because there ought to be none where a person has been targeted for violence or oppression. I can't speak for Vincent, though from my own experience I crafted shame throughout my life from legion tiny insults and outrages, each one too small to prick me but which cumulatively became an insurgency of pain and embarrassment.

Each instance of pain was, for me, as they have been for countless others throughout history, another indication of how to measure worth.

This way loneliness lies.

I have been wondering about this complex intersection of shame and loneliness for longer than I care to admit. You'll find no claim to wisdom here, just an extrapolation of the self. Intriguing research is beginning to emerge, at least as far as alcohol dependency and social deficits are concerned. Certainly, it's no stretch to say that people who are serious alcoholics didn't just fall into the habit out of casual curiosity. Having once been there myself and seen the scattered lives of others who know the terrain of drunken stupor well, it is as if they required alcohol above all else.

Leo Tolstoy had a similar notion, writing in his 1890 essay 'Why Do Men Stupefy Themselves?', that alcohol – and other mind-altering substances – are employed to obscure cataclysmic fissures of the soul.

> The diversions which might distract attention from the consciousness of this discord are insufficient, or have become stale, and so in order to be able to live on, disregarding the indications conscience gives of the wrongness of their life people (by poisoning it temporarily) stop the activity of the organ through which conscience manifests itself, as a man by covering his eyes hides from himself what he does not wish to see.
>
> When a man is sober he is ashamed of what seems all right when he is drunk.

Over a hundred years after Tolstoy's observations, Stanford University School of Medicine researcher Anne Pascale Le Berre published a paper in the journal *Neuropsychology*, in which she examined the potential causal links between heavy drinking and stunted personal skills.

Individuals with alcohol use disorder can suffer from emotional and social cognition defects that distort social interactions. The problem, Le Berre says, is that they do not have any 'real insight' or accurate metacognition as to the origins of these problems. Alcohol use, then, may be relied upon as a coping mechanism. They drink to 'relieve the emotional and social burden, feeding the vicious cycle of addiction'.

We do not yet know, however, whether these deficits *lead* to alcoholism or whether it is the drinking itself that causes them. Currently, evidence can be found to support both theses.

Le Berre's analysis looks at specific conditions such as alexithymia, which is often associated with poor wellbeing including low levels of happiness and life satisfaction. For a person with alexithymia, it means they have trouble identifying their own feelings in the self and separating those from the physical sensation of emotional arousal. They also have difficulty being able to describe their feelings to others and possess 'restricted imaginative processes featured by limited fantasy life and an externally oriented style of thinking'.

Her paper also explores more general emotion decoding deficits in alcohol-dependent people and those with a faulty or misfiring theory of mind, which, when so damaged, makes it hard or impossible to 'predict, anticipate, and interpret the behavior of others and facilitate appropriate social interactions'.

Loneliness creeps in through these shoddy building codes. Yes, there are other forces at play, such as demographic shifts in older age that compound the stratification of families, especially in the Western world, but the explanatory power of shame is compelling here.

In 2018, my then boss asked me to write a feature for the weekend paper about Britain's decision to appoint the world's first minister for loneliness. (It became something of a joke in the office as my amused colleagues pantomimed the thought-process of the commissioning editor who had to select perhaps the loneliest person in the building for the job.)

The ministry was created after the execution-style killing of British Labour MP Jo Cox by a right-wing extremist in the lead-up to Brexit. As it happened, Cox had just established a commission on loneliness.

In the end, her family acknowledged the fingerprints of loneliness across the life of Cox's killer.

'We feel nothing but pity for him that his life was so devoid of love and filled with hatred, his only way of finding meaning was to attack a woman who represented all that was good about the country in an act of supreme cowardice,' Cox's husband, Brendan, said at the time.

The theologian John O'Donohue evokes this fortress of hatred, or fear, in his book *Eternal Echoes*:

> The way you think about your life can turn your soul into a haunted room. You are afraid to risk going in there anymore. Your fantasy peoples this room of the heart with sad presences which ultimately become disturbing and sinister. The haunted room in the mind installs a lonesome one at the heart of your life.
>
> It would be devastating in the autumn of your life to look back and recognise that you had created a series of haunted rooms in your heart.

Loneliness is a form of mourning and loss, a quiet temple in which contemplations are performed without end or audience.

In the grief of our singular privation, we are left with the outline of things we once knew. I think this is where the difference between loneliness and solitude reveals itself: in the quality of the shading of that outline. In solitude we have knowledge of, and access to, the thing that is temporarily missing. It turns on an axis of choice. Imagine a bridge that you have chosen not to cross because you are happy on your riverbank. That's solitude. Loneliness is a washed-away bridge in front of the woman who can no longer remember what the other side of the river looks like.

Certainly there were moments during my cognitive and social isolation in Japan when I wondered where that bridge had gone – desperate as I was for a way back to the other side – but it was largely a tour of the rest stops on the highway outside of loneliness itself.

I found myself transfixed by the lights, an unsettling diorama that I knew to contain the most number of people living anywhere in one place that I had ever visited – and yet I felt more alone there than even on the 1000-square-kilometre cattle station I once called home and shared with just three other people.

In her book *The Lonely City*, Olivia Laing captures this jarring inversion of expectation, the way the lighted windows of other people's lives can move you to dissonance. She writes:

> You can see them, but you can't reach them and so this commonplace urban phenomenon, available in any city of the world on any night, conveys to even the most social a tremor of loneliness, its uneasy combination of separation and exposure.
>
> You can be lonely anywhere, but there is a particular flavour to the loneliness that comes from living in a city, surrounded by millions of people.

At the opposite end of the age spectrum in Japan, an alternative reality of loneliness has been developing for decades, first described by clinicians in 1978 as a type of 'withdrawal neurosis'.

A few years later the term *hikikomori* was coined to describe these voluntary shut-ins, almost always children or young adults, who turned their backs on society and remained living in their parents' basements or spare rooms for years at a time. Even indefinitely.

A 2010 paper in the *Journal of Nervous and Mental Disease* by University of California researchers Alan Teo and Albert Gaw recounted the empirical evidence thus far. While the majority of so-called *hikikomori* cases actually had well-defined mental conditions already known to science, the researchers found that 'a notable subset of cases with substantial psychopathology do not meet criteria for any existing psychiatric disorder'. They suggest *hikikomori* is a culture-bound syndrome that may warrant classification as a totally new psychiatric disorder.

The paper includes the case study of a fourteen-year-old Japanese boy who decided, without warning nor apparent cause, that he no longer wanted to attend school. He had normal results on a battery of laboratory tests, a mid-range IQ score and no medical history of note.

The boy left home just once a week, each Sunday, to rent a DVD with his father at the local video store.

> This living situation continued for two years. Then, at the time of entrance into high school, the patient suddenly reported that he wanted to return to school. He entered a vocational school specialising in design and since then has regularly attended classes.

The psychiatrist providing therapy to the patient reported that the boy's decision happened gradually, although it appeared sudden. The patient spent two years in social withdrawal and apparently spent much of that time interrogating the conditions of his life and what he might want to achieve in the future.

Estimates for the condition, which is recognised by the nation's ministry at least as a mysterious phenomenon if not a defined illness, range from 0.9 to 3.8 per cent of the population having some history of *hikikomori*. Other studies suggest as many as 14,000 cases are recorded in any given year.

These curious cases have been likened to modern hermits, and they are only counted officially if they stay away from society – including no longer maintaining their own friendships and outside connections – for six months or more.

What would possess you?

I once thought I was made for a life in the hermitage, on account of having grown up somewhere west of elsewhere on a broad sweep of land that approached Luxembourg in size.

But what I actually wanted, at my core, was to feel the pulse of compatibility with others and, frustrated by my inability to make it so, the purgatory of being alone seemed as good a way as any to save face.

The information that finally killed off my notion of hermitude was reading the story of Christopher Thomas Knight, a man who disappeared from normal society sometime after the Chernobyl nuclear power station blew its core through the roof and sent radiation over half of Europe.

Knight lived in the woods around Maine in the United States for almost thirty years, neither speaking to nor interacting with a single human soul. When I read the account of his astonishing disappearance in *GQ Magazine* in 2014, the thing that struck me almost immediately was that, later, Knight could not, at all, explain why he did it.

The closest he came was conceding to a long period of self-reflection.

'I did examine myself,' he told the writer Michael Finkel. 'Solitude did increase my perception. But here's the tricky thing – when I applied my increased perception to myself, I lost my identity. With no audience, no one to perform for, I was just there. There was no need to define myself; I became irrelevant. The moon was the minute hand, the seasons the hour hand. I didn't even have a name. I never felt lonely. To put it romantically: I was completely free.'

Knight suffered for his decades lost to the world, but not because he was gone. Only because, eventually, he was found, arrested and dragged to jail for the years he spent stealing food and other items with which to sustain himself in the wilderness.

He had always vowed to spend the rest of his life as a single, inconsequential element against the backdrop of everything. Instead, the world dragged him back.

I've never been one to speak ill of modern society – apart from frequent and half-serious detours into condemning the Agrarian Revolution as the worst act of folly in human history – but I will do so here.

Part of the uneasiness of being really, truly lonely, I think, is the gap between the expectations we have for ourselves and the reality of our achievements. This shortfall, as we often perceive it even if we argue otherwise, is the fuel for inadequacies that contribute to our feeling of shame and lead to us distancing ourselves from others.

Sure, some people handle this better than others. And I don't believe it's the billionaires or world-renowned artists or champion dog breeders (probably especially not them), but rather people like Christopher Knight. There are those who know enough to shut out as much of the noise as possible, like Odysseus's sailors who were commanded to plug their ears with beeswax as they approached the legendary but deadly Sirens.

What we could do and be and have has never been bigger or more accessible. To an overwhelming extent we are required to participate in this infinite regress and, dear reader, I do not say this from a position of practised enlightenment.

I am more ensnared by the apparatus of modernity than almost anyone else I can think of, save for the poor souls who must, for obscenely low pay, watch videos and images of war, torture, paedophilia and countless other acts of depravity in order to remove them from social media websites. But as a day-to-day proposition, my life is wired into the electric everything of this existence and, essentially without pause, its stimuli are slingshot into my brain like one of those fish cannons that shoot salmon over dam walls.

To move through the world like this is as disorienting for me as I suspect it is for the poor salmon who find themselves sucked into what looks like a pneumatic tube but which is actually just a big, enclosed waterslide.

To the salmon, it would appear very much as if they were at one moment in their living room and, the next, being shot into the sun.

I saw one fish get put into the cannon upside down so that its pink little belly pointed towards the ceiling of the tube in what must have been an experience rather like the night I 'lost' my virginity; a vignette that was at once harrowing and bizarre, although with slightly more legs.

I told you I could joke about it.

Discombobulating is both the appropriate word to describe this salmon-tube sensation and also, as it turns out, onomatopoeic for the sound of the process.

Exposure to *all this, all day* has a tendency to distort the dimensions of our reality to the point where we have almost, without even knowing it, created a hyper-networked version of the Total Perspective Vortex machine in Douglas Adams's *Hitchhiker's Guide to the Galaxy*.

Keen students of the series will remember that a man, Trin Tragula, built the machine as a way of finally getting back at his wife who constantly grilled him about spending his time dithering and dreaming. 'Have a sense of proportion,' she told him as many as thirty-eight times a day.

> And so he built the Total Perspective Vortex – just to show her. And into one end he plugged the whole of reality as extrapolated from a piece of fairy cake, and into the other end he plugged his wife: so that when he turned it on she saw in one instant the whole infinity of creation and herself in relation to it.

> To Trin Tragula's horror, the shock completely annihilated her brain; but to his satisfaction he realised that he had proved conclusively that if life is going to exist in a Universe of this size, then the one thing it cannot afford to have is a sense of proportion.

Of course the only being to ever survive the machine, Zaphod Beeblebrox, did so because when he entered the machine he was, in fact, the most important thing alive in the universe at that point and the power of perspective simply confirmed his own already impressive ego.

We cannot hope to be Zaphod, in the grand scheme of our own actuality.

I'd venture that it would be foolish to try it out and yet, here we are, day after day and hour after hour, plugged into the totality of us through social media and we are drunk with the insanity of it.

Please know that when I say all of this I do so with the knowledge that, in many ways, the internet and in particular social media has made me a better person. In the vacuum that was my youth and early adulthood – a void made so by poverty and a cultural barrenness that was obvious to everyone else except myself – networking sites with real people from all around the world have granted me an education that otherwise simply was not there.

However, I've never been one for moderation.

I participate in platforms like Facebook and Twitter, Instagram and (once upon a time) Tumblr – or in flashes of particular desperation, TikTok and Snapchat – the way I once drank, played the pokies and routinely visited the local KFC in Surfers Paradise. All in.

That can't be good for the head.

I mean, think about it. Our brains are not substantially different to the ones our ancestors hauled around in their skulls and all they had to do with theirs was fashion some tools, maintain a baseline level of social grace with the rest of a small tribe and avoid death, an end about which they were aware but only dimly.

Go further back with essentially the same neural architecture and they didn't even have to contemplate inevitable nothingness. We were once, like every other animal, in a state of blissful ignorance about our certain demise.

In 2009, the neuroscientist David Eagleman published his slim book *Sum* in which he offered forty short stories about possible afterlives, one of which has stayed with me for the decade since I first read it.

In the story 'Metamorphosis', Eagleman writes:

> There are three deaths. Now the first is when the body ceases to function, of course. And the second is when the body is consigned, or you know, put in the grave. The third is that moment sometime in the future when your name is spoken for the last time.

Eagleman imagines a sort of lobby where people who have died are kept in a holding pattern until the last person with any knowledge or link to you on earth speaks your name and there are no more people to remember you.

Depending on a person's stature or family networks, this [illegible] quick process – perhaps within a generation [illegible] retch on for centuries.

[illegible] this story it felt like a gut punch because it [illegible] until then ill-defined, that I longed to leave a [illegible] and it wasn't clear at all what that would be.

Not as a vehicle for ego, though I suppose the desire to exist is an extreme act of arrogance, but as a final push against being forgotten and the loneliness that springs from that fertile soil. After my mum, sister and brother are gone from this plane of existence, who would or could speak my name? I had no children (and the prospect still seems unlikely for reasons of biology and poor organisational skills) and no *thing* that would commend my name to others.

The average person alive today has access to more information about the cosmos and people's lives than the sum total of all human beings alive in, say, the 600s AD had access to. Our power, as individuals, to *change* anything about that state of affairs, however, has grown marginally and nowhere near at the pace of the uplift in our cognition.

To possess information without power is to wander the streets of Tokyo, or any big city, and to feel utterly, inexplicably alone against the fact of those overwhelming numbers, those unknowable lives behind illuminated panes of glass.

On any given day, in the forest of social media interactions to which I have become almost ritually ordained, I can view a mind-boggling slice of humanity at its best and worst. Here's just a taste of what I've recently seen: thousands of my countrymen and women banding together to help people during the hellish bushfire season of 2019–20; arguments about whether Australians ought to spell it 'maths' or 'math' and whether the latter is treasonous; a dog, interviewed on TikTok, that breathes air heavily into a microphone in rapid bursts; a series of increasingly absurd memes riffing on dancing Ghanaian funeral directors as a portent of death; a poet who tweeted, in a moment of discovery, that 'hold your horses' might in fact mean 'be stable'; political malcontents accusing every politician of being corrupt except the ones from their own tribe; an actual convicted paedophile winning plaudits for his own partisan tweeting; a man shamed on the internet into not dancing because he was overweight and then being invited to a dance party with a thousand people so that he could feel free to express himself; people advocating for the death of the elderly in a pandemic; and any manner of wry commentary about the granular detail of ordinary life that makes you stop and say, 'Hey, I do that, too.'

This is not an argument one way or the other for the inherent goodness or badness of social media. It's the sheer onslaught of *stuff* that makes us lonely. And if you even dip a toe in the puddle of that world, which increasing numbers of us do, it is difficult to avoid being inundated by it.

If there were any doubt about this thesis, certainly in my world, it was laid to rest when the coronavirus pandemic reached Australia's shores with force just days after I returned home from my trip to New York.

As the nation was put into lockdown, Séamus and I adhered to even stricter rules. While other people in New South Wales were meeting a friend for a socially distanced walk and visiting family members for carefully spaced picnics, there was a period of five weeks when I wasn't in close proximity to anyone except Séamus.

Thanks to his job as an intensive care nurse, our world became incredibly small. Even with the proliferation of video calls and the same social media infrastructure we enjoyed pre-pandemic, the world shrank. I had essentially the same access to all those lives and all those people I had before, but the loneliness descended like an especially plump turkey on the end of a fishing rod. I was confused. I did not want it and it scared me.

Just a week into the worst of it, when fear still cut through the air like a loosed arrow, I tweeted to no one in particular: 'Happy Wednesday everyone! It's like I can feel each individual synapse of my brain misfire as it happens in real time, as if I'm walking over a frayed rope bridge in a jungle and watching the fibres snap.'

In my case at least, the feeling came because I was forced to confront who I was, really, at my most elemental.

This is another way to see loneliness: it is who we are when the world falls away and we are left as a single point in infinite space, scrubbed of all edifice. This was all well and good for Christopher Thomas Knight, who deliberately turned his back on society, but for those of us who have yet to adapt – or who are thrust suddenly into a pared-back version of reality from which we hope to rebound – our diminishment can be a source of terror.

It's not as simple as saying I am bad at being on my own. I prefer it most often on most days. The mandatory shut-in of 2020, however, made me realise that solitude was only a preference after (or perhaps because) I had already had my weekly or daily fill of social contact.

The abject pleasure I took in my own quiet nothingness was possible only because it was mine to embrace.

Having the removalist of isolation turn up and acquire all of my distractions – the travel, the work trips, festivals, speaking engagements, visits to the pub, dinner parties, brunches; hell, even the gym – made me understand, against my will, how empty my life seemed below the surface.

The contentment I thought I was cultivating was an illusion.

It was a booking system, actually – a way to delay further examination of the heart and mind while staying so occupied it was almost impossible to discover the deceit. At least, as long as the pyramid scheme of my own happiness kept growing.

My hope, then, was a great fraud that revealed itself only when the world and I stopped moving.

I'm not sure if we are meant to break the fourth wall of our writing, but my publisher Catherine Milne sent a little snippet from a *Vanity Fair* interview with US poet laureate Joy Harjo, after we discussed the delicate matter of my having finally understood what was expected of me in writing this manuscript and becoming completely frozen in fear.

Harjo told *Vanity Fair* that 'you wind up sitting there at the kitchen table with your demons who have haunted you and harassed you from day one. You're confined, so you either have to make friends with them or continue the fight.'

Yes, I thought, *that is precisely what is happening*. Social distancing be damned, I was holding a cocktail party for my demons. A carousing, ebullient knees-up from which we would emerge as friends or continue in bitter enmity.

The hyper-connection of my online life did not salve this loneliness, it reinforced it. Whatever hits of relief the chaos of being *extremely online* offered were ephemeral, its lashes and psychological whiplash longer lasting, more internally divisive and ultimately corrupting.

I even gave up on the direct video calls with groups of friends, in the end. Mostly because the angles involved kinked my neck, but partly on account of the slipperiness of the encounters; they never felt quite real. Writing in *The Conversation* in May 2020, Bond University assistant professor in organisational psychology Libby Sander and school of psychology assistant professor Oliver Bauman explain that this is because we miss the most important part of social interaction.

'We need to work harder to process non-verbal cues. Paying more attention to these consumes a lot of energy,' they write.

Moreover, they say, silence provides a 'natural rhythm' in real-life conversations but online we can never be quite sure if it is intended or a glitch in the service.

What these video sessions could never re-create, what I longed for most, was the calm togetherness you feel with close friends, where neither feels the need to talk but you can sunbake in their company nonetheless, even at opposite ends of a table or lounge. Those are the moments that pass as the most true.

There is no performance, no urgent need for the trade of information or stories. Just you and them, the sight of their skin and knowing that it would be warm to the touch – and then reaching over and confirming it. Nothing between you but a palpable love, the kind you could stretch around your shoulders like a coat when the chill sets in.

Kindness

It was a deceptively cold blue-sky day in New York City at the close of winter, wind biting into me as I walked with no particular destination in mind from the Empire State Building towards lower Manhattan.

What I wanted was shelter, and potentially a burrito. Instead, I happened upon the Museum of Sex, which announced itself with a large, silver sign but was otherwise housed in a nondescript building on Fifth Avenue that beckoned nobody.

In a past life, I would have been too embarrassed to walk in. My family are half Catholic and half Protestant, a heady combination of shame and prudishness that has produced within me a perpetual motion machine powered by the tension between furious guilt and the heat produced by sexual repression.

On this day, though, my face was ice and I thought the history of silent-era pornography – or 'stag' films as they were known – would at least warm part of me up. The gallery space was filled with grainy old footage of people having sex at comically high frame rates, which was good for a laugh, but I was unprepared for what I would discover on the floor above.

The museum had recently begun a move away from kitsch pornographic amusement (although not entirely) and, at the time I visited, featured a photographic exhibit by Laia Abril that loosely charted the history of abortion in different countries.

From panels of photographs I learned about the 1915 criminal case of Maria R., an unmarried Catholic servant girl in Austria, who attempted to abort her unwanted pregnancy by lying down with an eighteen-kilogram stone positioned on her abdomen. She did this over several evenings and after her fourth attempt, she started bleeding. A few days later, as the exhibit panel explained, the foetus was 'expelled'. The court found that the stone had caused the termination of her pregnancy.

There was also the story of Samita, a 35-year-old woman in India, who inserted a grapevine stalk into her uterus to induce heavy bleeding. She almost died.

The wire coat hanger also made an appearance in the exhibition – its use is experiencing a resurgence in the United States because access to safe, legal abortion is becoming more difficult – as did stories of women who sought to ingest poison in a bid to end their pregnancies.

Each framed photograph and its accompanying information panel made up a catalogue of a bitter war on women, often perpetrated by men in an attempt to keep their own 'mistakes' private, but also by men in general who colonised not just the sex lives of the women with whom they consorted but their wombs as well.

In 1928, a 22-year-old Brazilian schoolteacher called Philomena wrote to her boyfriend, Romeu, informing him that she was about to have an illegal abortion and that she may not survive.

'I did what you advised me to do and what I should do,' she wrote. 'I ask you to forgive [my] numerous mistakes; of love alone, I committed them.'

Philomena did not survive the abortion.

In the end, the story that floored me was of an unnamed woman – featured in a large black-and-white photograph – who performed about 5000 abortions on women in France and across Europe between 1973 and 1992.

'It was always the same,' she was quoted as saying. 'A woman would lend her home to four or five or ten women to perform the abortions on the kitchen table. In France, Italy and Spain, women came to us with different situations and problems, with or without children, with or without money. Who was I to choose?

'We decided to take them all, as long as their pregnancies had not passed twelve weeks.'

Alongside her photo was a story that jagged my heart. She described a particular woman, who came 'all alone and sad' to one of the host's houses for her abortion. Imagine the terror of that moment. While this woman waited her turn, a friend of the host – a man – began talking to her before suddenly leaving the room. When he returned, he held a single rose which he gave to her. 'When it is her turn for the abortion,' the woman who performed the abortion was quoted as saying, 'he began to play the piano.'

Perhaps it was the singular frost of that day, or the weariness of travelling or because I hadn't eaten lunch yet, but the idea of that moment made me cry. It was beautiful. It was *kind* in the truest way we know of kindness: sincere, and unadulterated by transaction. It served, in the poor soul so afraid in that room, to elevate her condition above its miserable present.

'What I regret most in my life are failures of kindness,' author George Saunders once wrote. 'Those moments when another human being was there, in front of me, suffering, and I responded … sensibly. Reservedly. Mildly.'

He's right. We all remember them in our own lives, too. Portions of the one life we get have been spent in cool detachment when someone was hurting or needed help. Malice is not required. Villains are not indifferent, but indifference can be harmful.

I recall those moments of studied inattention, like Saunders did, and they make me recoil. What is it, I have often thought, that stops us from engaging more readily in the heady wonder of benevolence? And what was it that made that man play the piano for that frightened woman, about to go through a medical procedure on a kitchen table? Did he know what it must have meant to her?

I mean, it feels *good* to perform even the smallest act of kindness.

I spent much of my early twenties reckoning with this apparent moral twist: is there any way to be kind without receiving something in return?

Is there a way to be truly, wholly selfless and, if there is, does it matter?

For all my mental contortions on the subject, George Price did it worse.

The American evolutionary biologist, who derived a single formula explaining Darwin's natural selection, tried to repeat his career success by attempting to discover the perfect mathematical framework for human altruism.

Specifically, he became obsessed with whether it was possible to be truly selfless or whether every dose of magnanimity came with even the smallest expectation of perks. Great thinkers since Darwin had wondered about this because animals and humans alike have been known to sacrifice themselves for the apparent greater good, creating a thorny problem for the very notion that evolution must prompt each individual to survive and replicate its genes at all costs.

This was all the more difficult a question because it wasn't always obvious whether the animal, strictly speaking, had any control over their martyrdom. Like, if a bear crashed a picnic and everyone ran away but I was the slowest so got killed, I could imagine researchers being so appalled at my lack of athleticism that their only conclusion could have been: *he must have done that deliberately.*

Price's search would drive him mad and contribute – alongside the religious delusions he began suffering, potentially because of a thyroid condition – to his suicide.

Look, I didn't say there were easy answers. The genius, who himself had abandoned his wife and children and moved to London in his quest for good (couldn't see the trees for the forest, I suppose), eventually began taking homeless people into his own house and giving away every last item in his possession. Often, he would wander over to the railway stations of Euston and King's Cross and give people whatever they asked for. Money, clothes, food. Nothing was too much.

When the lease on his house ran out, he became homeless himself. This was a short-lived rush and, by the close of 1974, George Price had nothing left to give. In early January the next year, he killed himself in a cold Euston squat house with a pair of nail scissors.

There were a few currents that swirled together in Price's desperate search, but the original spark came from the family he abandoned. What were human families *for*, he wondered. Specifically, what is the point of fatherhood?

In my honest opinion, he took the concept a bit too far. If you have to ask, you can't afford it. You know the drill.

In a way, George Price failed his experiment of giving without purpose because he had set out to prove something – and proof, we know, can be a kind of reward for the faithless. Sometimes we demand absolute certainty in things because we cannot be satisfied with mere belief. Not necessarily in a religious or spiritual sense, but in matters of the heart nonetheless.

In her poem 'Kindness', Naomi Shihab Nye teaches us that sorrow is so often an entree to the deep wellspring of kindness. We must wake up every day with sorrow, she says, and test its dimensions by speaking it out loud. In doing so, we are made aware of all sorrows. We are given access to the true state of things – all that hurt – and asked to be gentle with it.

I think this understanding of sorrow is where the best form of such generosity is born.

There are those of us who, however imperfectly, seek to brandish good will because they have looked into the mouth of the world and found it a place of gnashing cruelty, certain pain and overbearing discomfort. Sorrow is a universal entitlement of our species. None, living or dead, have managed to avoid it. Some feel it more keenly than others, however. These are the people who have been abused or discarded, found despair when they went searching for love; the ones who met injustice with a hyper-individualistic justice they knew would never cover the cloth but pressed on anyway because covering some of it is better than leaving a blank space. They are the chronically ill, the terminally ill and the students of assorted distress. We find kindness, too, among the poor and the dispossessed who, in having nothing, know in their bones that the distance between happiness and hopelessness can be a single crack of light.

In my experience, the kindest people it is possible to meet are those who have been, or still are, in the dirt.

Again, it's Steinbeck's *The Grapes of Wrath* that breathed life into the concept for me. In the closing pages, as the Joad family is pulled deeper into false promises and desperation, Ma encounters a man at a general store who has been made to work there for a pittance. Nevertheless, he provides a ten-cent loan for some much-needed sugar.

'Thanks to you, I'm learnin' one thing good,' Ma says. 'Learnin' it all a time, ever' day. If you're in trouble or hurt or need – go to poor people. They're the only ones that'll help – the only ones.'

In early 2020 I took myself to New York, that fabled city I had longed to visit, to do research for this book. And it was there, in that place where the schism between rich and poor is repulsive and unavoidable, that the guilt of my own frolic with a newly minted book advance in my pocket took hold.

To be clear, this was a lot of money for someone like me. More than I had ever known at any one time. And I was spending it, like an absolute wanker. If ever there were a Venn diagram of punchable offences, I'd be at the centre.

Still, I was there in the skin of a boy who knew the precise volume of poverty; how much space it can take up inside a person. My family toured its edge of oblivion like it was the crater of an active volcano.

I understood perfectly well the relative value of the American bank notes in my wallet to me and to the man or woman on the street. This is a particular talent of the poor, I think. It is not exclusive to them, but you'd be forgiven for thinking so.

When I'd given away all of the actual cash in my wallet to the rough sleepers and other beggers, I came across one particular homeless man called Cardell Jackson who had lost his job four months before and was out begging for scraps to feed his family, temporarily holed up in a shelter from which they would soon have to move.

'Man, I don't have any cash on me,' I explained, 'but let me take you somewhere to get some food.'

'Sir, I'm just looking for a little extra for my wife and kids,' he said.

'That's fine,' I said. 'Pick anywhere around here and we'll dine in and order more to go.'

Cardell, bless him, picked a fancy new place that had only recently opened. The clientele were well-to-do folk on a night out with their partners and friends.

When we walked through the door, a hush descended on the room. It was like stepping into the vacuum of space, I imagine, except it was the other diners' eyes being sucked out of their skulls, not ours. Cardell was carrying a piece of tarpaulin he used as an umbrella and an oversized backpack in which he kept a baffling array of what could only have been pots, judging by the clanking sound they made.

Because it used to be the case all the time, I still get nervous when I walk into a store that has any item priced above $50, assuming the staff will shortly ask me to leave. But I placed my credit card on the counter and waited for the server to come over. When she did, she made eyes at me that seemed to enquire: *Are you in trouble, sir? Do I need to call anyone?*

I ordered a rum and coke for me and a vodka fire-engine for Cardell, who was now studying the menu. He pretended he could not see properly, though I soon discovered he could not read.

'Does it look like I give a fuck?' I asked him. And it was true. I didn't want him to think this had become an exercise in pity, because my own mum had always taught us people did not require it. We had come for dignity, or nothing at all.

Cardell ordered a take-away lobster bake, spaghetti bolognese and onion rings for his family, and a steak for himself. While we ate, we talked about the grind of living, wearing the half-horrified glances of the other diners like medals. The two of us talked for an hour over another round of drinks and parted ways close to midnight. I eventually lost sight of Cardell in a plume of steam rising through a grate from beneath the road.

And then I sat with myself at an Irish pub and wondered what it was that I felt.

'People who come from your place, they always want to protect the underdog,' my therapist said to me, a few months later, during one of our regular sessions in Sydney. 'Because it is kind of a way of protecting ourselves. Random acts of kindness are a way of healing, it's a corrective emotional experience and I tell everybody to do that even if they don't need to.'

One cannot be kind if we do not first start by being generous with ourselves.

I don't want this to come off like some new-age 'live your truth' mantra because, let's face it, that's how we got anti-5G conspiracy theories and an anti-vaccination movement whose members would rather their children get measles than read a peer-reviewed scientific paper. Nor is this a version of the overwrought trope of 'self care' which has a kernel of worthiness at its core that is too often strangled or repurposed as middle-class luxury.

The self-directed kindness I speak of here isn't a bubble bath or lanolin face mask, though I have been known to use both liberally. It is far more rudimentary in its way, and more difficult to pull off. What we must give ourselves is a rigorous compassion, the kind that doesn't absolve wrongdoing or poor behaviour but allows us to meet both from a place of understanding.

Writer and essayist Esmé Weijun Wang told a short story recently about how it ought to work. When Wang was in middle school, a student broke a beaker in science class and Wang sprang into action, cleaning up the broken glass with her bare hands. She was only twelve but, she said, back then, 'I thought that was my job to be good, that was my job.' Now Wang is an adult and her best friend has a saying borrowed from that distant memory, which is deployed whenever Wang hurts herself in the service of becoming the Good Girl:

> Don't pick up the glass with your bare hands.

In her story, Wang went on to say: 'I don't know who needs to hear this but: don't pick up the glass with your bare hands.'

Kindness to others can only come when you have paid deep attention to your own flaws and accepted them anyway. Yes, it springs from sorrow, but only when we have made peace with the hurt that dwells inside us. Such a detente is necessary not only for yourself, but for others. If you feed that hurt so much, it outgrows you and it must find somewhere else to go.

That's the simple arithmetic of it.

Personally, I don't think there is a way to be kind without experiencing at least a murmur of goodness. I also don't think that it matters.

As I have been writing this book, I have returned time and again to this piece from David Whyte on vulnerability, a perfect medium through which kindness can travel.

> The only choice we have as we mature is how we inhabit our vulnerability, how we become larger and more courageous and more compassionate through our intimacy with disappearance. Our choice is to inhabit vulnerability as generous citizens of loss, robustly and fully, or conversely, as misers and complainers, reluctant and fearful, always at the gates of existence, but never bravely and completely attempting to enter, never wanting to risk ourselves, never walking fully through the door.

There are benefits to what feels like bravery in that first choice. Performing random acts of kindness makes us *happier*, according to a recent experiment from researchers at Oxford University.

The study of 683 people by Lee Rowland and Oliver Scott Curry asked what none before them had yet considered: did it matter if the target of your spontaneous goodwill was family, someone you barely knew, yourself or a complete stranger?

In short, no. Happiness increased for people in every group.

But get this. Even paying active attention to someone else being kind is enough to get that juicy hit of cheer. I can vouch for this approach. You don't even have to be there in person. Just queue up a video compilation of kindness and go to town.

Sometimes when I've had a bad day or if I'm procrastinating in the shadow of a larger task or, if I'm perfectly honest, just migrating between various instances of intellectual paralysis, I will seek out these feel-good videos or stories.

There is a school of thought that these entries in the kindness canon are mawkish or, at a minimum, insubstantial in the face of a more systemic cruelty. But isn't that type of thinking part of the problem?

I've been riddled with that cynicism myself, depending on the phase of the moon, and it tends to be counterproductive. Getting muddled about the utility of small gestures when there is a bigger picture ignores the fact there is no beach without each grain of sand.

In biology, and the study of other complex systems, there is a property known as 'emergence', which describes behaviours of an entity that only appear at a larger level and which could not have been achieved by the constituent parts on their own.

Life itself is the best example. How did we go from elemental particles of matter that themselves are totally lifeless to breathing, thinking, *doing* organisms? How did they organise themselves in the first place to even get to a stage where some threshold was crossed to breathe life into them? We have ideas about this, but right now we just do not know.

In this same way, the institutions that govern us emerge from us. If you want systemic change, feed it from the core. Start with kindness.

It's worth noting that, although kindness can make you happier, this is not a manifesto to live *happily*. Fuck that noise.

I cannot count the number of times someone has intimated that I should just be happier, as if this state of being could be ordered from a menu. 'Why don't you just get the Big Mac?' they might as well ask.

Happiness as a goal is a rort. If you don't believe me, stare into the eyes of one of those wellness influencers and see if the experience doesn't immediately give you a panic attack.

Look, I've been there. On the rebound from one of my many all-consuming lows, it is often difficult to pinpoint whether the new feeling I have is happiness or a mania dressed in the wrong clothes. Here, you might find me speaking at twice the usual rate of words while declaring that I am, indeed, a 'new man' and going on grand adventures. Maybe I'll learn piano, or French! Maybe I'll start hosting grand dinner parties where I invite interesting people over and then talk about nothing but Chekhov, thereby recreating the plays of Chekhov in which the characters always end up talking to the wrong people.

These things are never happiness, however, and believing that they might be is a worrisome thing. Let's be very clear about this. Happiness exists as a counterpoint to grief, loss and the many fluctuations of ordinary life. Its sails cannot be hoisted inside a bottle, like a replica ship, and stored for all time on the mantlepiece. We do not deliberately come into its possession, nor consciously maintain it when we do. It happens to us, when the conditions are right. We should stand ready to receive it.

For moments, or entire stretches of time that ache with the sensation of permanency, I have felt desperately sad, such that nothing could penetrate the atmosphere of my own longing. I do not imagine I am alone in this, even among people who would not typically be considered depressed.

You are allowed to be sad. Sometimes, in this state, the very notion that we *should* be feeling any other way contributes to the longevity of that darkness. If it were always as easy as simply turning on the light, we would have built electricity substations for our own emotions.

We need not wait for kindness, however. It is not a state of being but a thing of doing, and it is perhaps at its most potent when all around is sorrow. There is no need to attach strings or conditions. These amount to nothing more than arbitrary control in search of moral validation. Like forgiveness, kindness should not be mediated through the prism of what you want or expect. Telling a homeless person, for example, that you'll give them cash as long as they don't spend it on drugs or booze is not kind. That is an act designed to validate your own moral framework. It is the unhelpful result of a saviour complex with you at its centre.

While at university, my school friend Matthew used to play us one of his favourite tracks by the now obscure musical project Lazyboy, called 'Underwear Goes Inside the Pants'. There was one section of the song in particular that guided my thinking then and which I have never since forgotten. I'm not sure how advisable it is to divine philosophical positions from a stand-up comedian and former band member of noted musical group Aqua, but we discover inspiration wherever it may fall.

Lazyboy asks us to consider what a homeless person might *do* with the money other than salve their predicament? They don't have a house. It's not like you'll be giving them enough for med school.

Of course, a homeless person might use it on accommodation or shelter. Or booze. Or some clothes. The point is, an act of kindness can do much for the soul and perhaps not a lot for the structural conditions of a life. It is worth asking how we expect anyone to survive long enough for those systemic forces to change, if they ever do. Maybe the test of our generosity is how willing we are to get them through that waiting.

A few years ago I met a young bloke in Redfern who asked for some money as I was walking back across the park with my groceries. I fished $50 out of my wallet and he proceeded to explain that $100 would secure him accommodation for a few nights.

His name was Matt and he was insistent that the money was for shelter. I told him time and time again that I didn't care, he could do whatever made him safest or most comfortable. How could I possibly know what that looked like for him? It was clear in his manner that he had been browbeaten before. Matt was used to fielding questions about what he would do with the money, which is another way of saying his worth as an individual was always up for appraisal.

I offered him another $50 and he looked to be genuinely in shock, staring at it for a beat too long before looking into my eyes.

'Can I give you a hug?' he asked.

'Of course, man.'

It was one of those lingering hugs, the kind that creates its own atmosphere, and I realised while we were embraced that I must have needed it as much as he seemed to.

One of the great innovations of the human brain is the ability to time-travel mentally, to imagine a thousand or more different future scenarios in which we might be stuck in this job or dating that person, winning the lotto or losing it all. We use this ability to process decisions in the here and now and we can project it onto other people, too. Babies don't appear to be born with such a skill, though they develop it within a few years.

In some experiments, researchers test a toddler's ability by placing an object in a box while an adult volunteer is in the room. When the adult leaves the room, the researcher swaps the object to a different box. The toddler watches this happen and they are then asked to identify which box *the adult* thinks the object will be in when they return to the room. The child knows where it actually is but that is not the question.

To answer it successfully they must be able to see the world with the inputs and assumptions of the other; to know that this adult can justifiably believe something that is simply no longer true.

This is the beginning of empathy.

Kindness, then, is allowing these concessions for others as we may sometimes allow them for ourselves. It means granting the complexity of life to strangers that we figure into our own thinking. And it involves the use of that mental time-travel to understand, in the marrow of us, that our own circumstances might also one day be different. It need not matter if we have suffered before, though this of course may heighten the instinct to be kind. It matters only that we can imagine it.

The righteous are simply defective in this manner. They see in themselves a string of correct decisions, even in adversity, that were made judiciously and with the full force of reason: a set of choices that could never have been influenced by the prickly impersonality of fate.

Nobody, myself included, is immune from the blunt inaccuracy of this righteousness. It swaddles us and makes a mockery of good judgement. To be fair and just is an exercise in voluminous accounting: the ledger of our past should include not only the moments when we were right but the many, conveniently forgotten, in which we were marginally, totally or even cataclysmically wrong. When the past is audited in this way, kindness follows.

We have all displayed these episodes of suffocating moral virtue. They are difficult to admit, of course, but unfortunately in some cases, they are lifelong afflictions. I cannot count the number of times I've heard of a hard-right or conservative American politician – usually a man – preaching the 'crimes' of homosexuality only to be found months or years later sucking dick underneath an airport bathroom stall.

Pastor Tom Brock, for example, left the Evangelical Lutheran Church in America because they allowed 'practising homosexuals' to be ordained. Brock even went so far as to say God sent a tornado to the Minneapolis Convention Center during a conference where the matter was being debated, which, frankly, marks the supreme being as something of a disappointing micromanager.

Brock, it turns out, was gay. He even admitted to giving in to 'temptation' during a trip to Slovakia.

One-time mayor of Mississippi town Southaven, Greg Davis, took a similarly hard line against same-sex marriage and queer issues. Davis, you will not be surprised to learn, is gay. His charade faltered when he purchased $67 worth of toys from a gay sex shop in Canada and charged them to taxpayers in what can only be described as a cock-up. He's not the first, nor the last, to be brought down by an errant dildo or its likeness.

In 2019, former Republican lawmaker Aaron Schock was photographed shirtless with his hands down the pants of another bloke who he was also kissing, otherwise known as the 'gay trifecta'. This did not happen in private, but at the celebrity-heavy music festival Coachella.

Schock, in his time as a lawmaker, voted against adding LGBTQ people to federal hate crime protections; against the repeal of Don't Ask, Don't Tell (an armed forces policy that demanded military members erase their homosexuality under threat of being kicked out); and *for* a constitutional amendment banning same-sex marriage.

'What I had to share was unwelcome news to every single person in my family,' Schock wrote on Instagram, after the pictures were published and he came out to his relatives. 'I can live openly now as a gay man because of the extraordinary, brave people who had the courage to fight for our rights when I did not.'

We haven't even come to those leaders of gay conversion therapy who have either come out as gay or, worse, been caught sexually abusing their so-called 'patients'.

In September 2019, McKrae Game, the founder of the Hope for Wholeness Network – a conversion 'therapy' program that promised 'freedom from homosexuality through Jesus Christ' – renounced everything he had ever taught after coming out as gay himself.

'I was a religious zealot that hurt people,' Game told the *Post and Courier* in an interview. 'People said they attempted suicide over me and the things I said to them. People, I know, are in therapy because of me. Why would I want that to continue?'

That same month, I tweeted a link to another article about Game and included my brief thoughts: 'Annual reminder that conversion therapy is psychological torture.'

What followed was an intriguing, delicate exchange between myself and a woman that tapped something difficult to grasp within myself.

'I'm straight and I'm furious with him. The damage he has inflicted on others,' she commented.

The race to condemnation is often swift in such morally contemptible cases, but I wasn't so sure it was helpful.

'I'm torn,' I replied. 'I certainly think he is a victim of the religious bigotry that used him as much as he used that to ensnare others. It's a tragedy.'

My acquaintance thought the man's contrition was convenient and wrote that it 'smacks a bit' of 'I was only following orders'.

It's a fair claim, though I thought it more vexed than a craven Nuremberg defence.

'Yeah,' I replied, 'although I think this has a lot more to do with brainwashing/indoctrination from a very young age which skews my reaction. Fury is justified, I just hope it moves beyond him to the real culprits. I'm glad he was honest.'

I mention this not to admonish anyone who feels they cannot exercise kindness towards people like Game – though I'd like to think I would – but to prove an earlier point. If just one of these men (they are mostly but not always men) had been able to be gentle with themselves first we wouldn't be here now.

It is true, also, that they did not themselves form in a vacuum, nor did the people in their atmosphere who let hatred curdle. What if – hear me out here – they, too, were inwardly kind first?

And so on and so on.

Look, I know this all sounds so anodyne. In this moment I am struggling with an occasional instinct for cynicism which threatens to white-ant my thinking. It is very easy to be dismissive without doing the intellectual work of self-directed inquisition.

We owe ourselves the generosity of such understanding.

Dysfunction

At a certain point, if your notions of love are so rigid as to be inflexible, the very idea of it snaps in the mind of the bearer like kindling underfoot.

A concept of love can be built with such an uncompromising attention to detail that it breaks. The splinters of this once unbending thing can burrow beneath skin.

Some declare that all love is fealty and are ruined when they encounter the passionately disloyal. Others have claimed it honours only distance and they are brought to their knees when the loneliness inevitably comes.

Depending on the account, love is either an excess or a threadbare thing. The holder of either view is wounded by the gap between their estimation of it and the quantity received; too little or too much. Mistakes are made in practice, too. Ought it be proved through action or word, perhaps a chemically balanced mix of the two? And how might the other interpret this equation if they have settled on a rigidity of thought all their own?

Love, in one view, is a deficit. All give, no take. Or the other way around. These fundamentalists are neither happy when they meet their opposite nor when they become entangled with their equal.

People who are afraid think love is not for them. The fear drives them to avoid it at all costs. In some cases, this deformed understanding of love compels them to seize it, as if it were a natural resource or the spoils of war. Many commit acts of violence and abuse, in isolation or systematically, because they believe love is a monster and they its purest expression, products of a broken love who know only how to break.

We see the name of love invoked where really there is nothing but terror and control.

Fyodor Dostoyevsky maintained that true hell is the 'suffering of being unable to love'. I think I know something of that place and my boy Dostoyevsky is on the money.

Let's do this by way of comparison.

Even if we have not known it for ourselves, it is likely there are people in our lives who have been visited by warmth and emotional intimacy. In them, it is possible to see the fertile soil of the heart and how it might sustain a life. To know this is to understand, even dimly, that the missing thing may be just as powerful a force as its presence.

Look for the outlines.

I once reported on a town in Queensland called Acland, which had been slowly bought up and shipped away by a coal mine just a few hundred metres from its border. It had been a small but thriving little place with a general store, community hall, a few churches. It's all gone now, of course. The mine wanted it that way, so in 2008 they moved people's houses to different locations and demolished what nobody was willing to take.

The satellite images of the town make for curious viewing because there is just the skeleton of it – blocks of divided land now overgrown and cut across by a familiar grid of streets and roads that no longer service the thing they once contained. Even if you looked at these images without knowing the story behind them, you would think to yourself immediately: *there used to be a town here.*

So it is for love. You can peer into someone's eyes and without pause think to yourself: *there used to be love here.* You can see this in broken people, the haunted or dysfunctional. People who are in jail or mired so fully in the embrace of drug addiction. Children from shattered families and adults with strange afflictions of the heart or mind.

It is not that these poor souls have refused to love, though they may now have given up, but that they *had* loved before and now they don't. Maybe it was even a long time before now, back in the ink of their past. Further back, still, in the ruined lives of their forebears.

Almost always there will be a person or a few people who failed to love them and in so doing wound the mainspring of their clockwork existence.

This is the secret knowledge of anyone who has suffered trauma, especially when they were young. Oh, everyone's talking about it now. Trauma-informed this, trauma-aware that. We must be aware of trauma the way a zookeeper is aware of the lion: knowing that the cage is sometimes more dangerous than the thing it keeps, that it often pays to be wary of both.

The eyes can glaze over. Mine certainly do, despite a cellular understanding of how the emptiness of the thing that came before it can score a person. I am not a diagnosis, though knowing the name for what has happened to me has a beneficial explanatory power all its own. Complex PTSD feels like such a new thing in the Australian context, even though it has been solidified as a recognised condition globally since the mid-1990s.

Psychiatrist Bessel van der Kolk says the person with trauma is a 'living memorial' to the horror of their past, carrying it around with them in their flesh and bones.

'This is not about something you think or something you figure out,' he told *On Being* host Krista Tippett in an interview in 2013. 'This is about your body, your organism, having been reset to interpret the world as a terrifying place and yourself as being unsafe. And it has nothing to do with cognition.'

The particular kind of developmental trauma that marked my early life did not involve sexual abuse, though psychologists have learned now that the distinction between types of abuse is not important. The physical scars may heal or disappear entirely, but in each case it's the visceral impact that matters, the emotional damage inflicted by a powerful breach of trust. When this happens, a void is opened up that disturbs a delicate equilibrium. A space is created for all the hurt in the world to rush in.

It's a funny word, trust, because we use it so casually. Corporations talk about trust all the time, but what they typically mean is unearned loyalty. We remark to our friends when they've done something quintessentially *them*: 'Trust you to do that!' Some of us take part in trust exercises on workplace retreats, falling backwards into the arms of Susan in Accounts. Older brothers ask you to 'trust them' when they propose a new adventure that will, you know in your heart, result in the axle of the motorbike snapping in two when you run it at full speed into a gully.

Such usage has a way of masking the total, absolute and clarifying grip trust has on us when we ask another person – implicitly or otherwise – to hold our emotional safety in their hands and to please, *please*, not crush it.

Whatever else comes of the various abuses, there is this and this alone that marks us as the walking wounded.

I have moved through the world since childhood almost universally incapable of recovering the thing stolen from me – and here's the thing: when you lose it once, a spark goes out. The light that once revealed the complex footwork of trust between two people is gone and, in the dark, you struggle to discover it anew each time. How did it go again? Left foot, right foot.

The slow seep of this realisation eventually ends with the hidden code of our lives revealing itself fully. I see it now wherever I turn.

Hurt people, shuffling in the dark, hurting themselves and others. I am one of them. Game recognises game.

It is this broken love I see at the foot of most mistakes and errors; the Atlas on whose shoulders rest our fallen hopes.

The problem with what can sometimes be a single instance of abused trust is that it echoes across the years.

Some researchers have noted the near complete similarity between subjects with complex trauma and those who have suffered actual torture as political prisoners at the hands of government agencies or, worse, terrorist organisations.

Torture syndrome, as it is called, 'is marked by existential dilemma, guilt, shame, distrust, attachment problems, damage to beliefs about safety and justice, and somatisation', Griffith University's Angela Ebert and Murray J. Dyck wrote in a 2004 paper published in the *Clinical Psychology Review*.

Somatisation, where severe psychological distress manifests as physical symptoms such as excruciating stomach pains or sudden hair loss, is testament to the power of the embattled mind.

At the end of such a process, the researchers say, there is a kind of 'mental death' that takes place regardless of whether the torture was political or domestic, such as a child might experience at the hands of an abusive parent or caregiver.

Generally, Ebert and Dyck say in their paper, torture has much in common with other profound, multiple and extended personal traumas. The common characteristics include a feeling of entrapment in a bad situation owing to human action (as opposed to natural causes) and specifically arising from intentional harm, rather than accidental harm. 'Dehumanising' processes are used to disassemble the victim's identity.

Reading the list of symptoms is a strange experience because, quite necessarily, I have never dwelled too long on the idea that these might be the strings to which I am attached.

There is another hallmark of the trauma survivor. They see the world as something that happens *to* them, over which they have little or no control. That is the ultimate mental death, really. Structurally, such a view is no different to the intellectual understanding that the universe may well be pre-determined in its outcome.

In this knowledge we gain a sense of why destructive behaviours are so common across the life of the child who grew around their rotten experiences. Substance abuse, for example, might blunt the sharp tip of pain, but more fundamentally – in a world where we have decided control is illusory – what's the point of resisting? The more we cling to this frame of reference, the more evidence we are provided that it might just be true.

'Mental defeat is most likely to occur when a victim is unable to escape continuous threats and violent treatment by other humans, such that the victim experiences helplessness, powerlessness, and uncontrollability,' Ebert and Dyck say.

We begin to see the near invisible strand of spider's web glint in the light of this truth. Absence begets absence. The doing is both the only available option and, eventually, the proof of your unworthiness.

If you remove love from the equation, nothing makes sense.

I'm still controlling the self-destructive impulses that arise from this defeat. On the outside at least, I appear to be an extremely well put together human being. This is a well-crafted ruse. It's as if I was built by an apprentice in God's workshop who was very good at sewing on the outfits but forgot to tend to the inside. On the inside, it's a mess in there. I imagine my innards resemble a dropped tart. Perhaps you can see what they used to be, though dessert has been cancelled all the same.

In such a life, as in mine, an astonishing amount of effort must be poured like concrete into the void just to stop it filling up with other nonsense. This is not a long-term solution, and it will weigh you down all the same, but better that something largely inert, like work, is stuffed in the cracks than something actively harmful.

Though you may believe otherwise, the apparatus of mental health care is so often completely blind to the presence of trauma. How is that even possible, I hear you ask, when we seem to be talking about it all the time? Well, for a start, we cannot change what we do not see.

A 2018 review by researchers at Cardiff University and the University of Bristol found that undetected post-traumatic stress disorder was present in almost 30 per cent of people using specialist mental health services in the United States of America, Australia, the United Kingdom, Germany and the Netherlands. It also included a smaller number of results from South Africa, Spain and Turkey.

Although PTSD screening was high in examined cases, the rate at which these obvious symptoms were actually *recorded* as being PTSD in clinical records was low. In the majority of cases, the authors say, mental health clinicians simply failed to identify PTSD in their patients despite those same patients meeting the criteria. 'Furthermore, given how common PTSD was on screening, the failure of clinical recognition of this disorder was one that potentially affected a substantial proportion of all patients under the care of specialist mental health services,' the paper, published in the *British Journal of Psychiatry*, says.

In other words, clinicians just didn't know what they were looking at. According to this study, mental health services checked for PTSD at entry but rarely recorded it as a distinct condition. You cannot treat what you can't name.

I was one of these patients. Not in this study, but there I am in the data nonetheless. My own symptoms always felt worse than the generalised anxiety disorder and depression identified in the original diagnosis; but, once made, clinicians never bothered to quibble with it.

Nor did I, for that matter. Largely this was due to an overwhelming fight to not kill myself and partly because I really didn't know anything at all about the condition I thought I had. Maybe this was just how bad these illnesses could get, I thought while ignoring the pulse of foreboding from somewhere inside my rib cage.

The authors of the paper further note that it is possible some patients were being treated for conditions such as obsessive-compulsive disorder, addiction or psychosis when these were not the main event in a clinical sense. They ought to have been receiving treatment for PTSD. Failing to treat the primary condition – PTSD – can actually lead to worse clinical outcomes in treatment for the secondary disorders like OCD. The paper says:

> This is avoidable, as PTSD is a treatable disorder.

Avoidable.

That word is like lightning to me. It contains aborted possibility and thwarted potential. To have avoided, in this context, is to have minimised or missed entirely the soul-rattling struggle of mental ill-health. For years, the real-world symptoms of my trauma stalked me through different rounds of therapy with different therapists, as it does for tens of thousands of others, and I could not treat it because I did not know it had a name.

You'd think I might have cottoned on when I started writing my previous book about the trauma that snaked its way through my family across the generations. I had every reason to reflect on whether this was the root of my own troubles, but I did not. Trauma is what happens to other people, after all.

The New South Wales government has spent some time, through actuarial work, in making sense of trauma's insidious breeding grounds using the data it collects across the portfolios of health, mental health, education, justice and the child protection system. This is a data set many orders of magnitude more fine-grained than those available at the federal level, though the analysis incorporated various welfare payments, too.

Statistics for more than 3.1 million children and young people (aged under twenty-five as at June 2017) were included in the work, which estimates the future cost to various government services of an individual's health and social care over their lifetime.

The headline figures are notable – the total cost is estimated at almost half a trillion dollars between now and when each person turns forty – but of less interest to me than some of the smaller numbers.

Take children with 'exposure to mental illness' as an example. Kids are considered to be in this group if they themselves have had to access a mental health service or if their parents or guardians have had to. These children account for less than 8 per cent of everyone in the data but exactly 17 per cent of the total future cost. Over their lifetimes, they will use approximately $300,000 each in government services and payments, more than twice the average.

Other groups are higher as individuals: young mothers under the age of twenty-one have an estimated cost of more than $900,000 each, which is 6.3 times higher than the typical Australian resident.

When you begin to chart the way these different groups jump into and out of each other's way, you end up with a sketch for the places love might have been but wasn't. It's not that people from these backgrounds do not love their children – indeed, many I've met have loved more furiously than anyone else in the country – but that their lack of resources establishes more points of failure than other people will ever have to deal with.

The children affected by mental illness, whether personally or by witnessing it in their caregivers, are almost six times more likely to end up in out-of-home care at least once.

Now, even one placement in the foster care system can be enough to freeze a child in time, the way trauma has a habit of doing. It need only be a matter of days or weeks. The infinite terror of that loneliness lasts a lifetime.

Say some of those children who end up in placements become young mothers with brittle support networks but a desperate desire to love their baby more than they were loved themselves. If we fail them, and we so often do, things become bleak.

This group is *fifteen* times more likely than the typical person to have their children end up in out-of-home care and they end up in custody or jail four times as often on average.

Any young person aged between sixteen and eighteen who has had at least one 'interaction' with the justice system, or who as a child has been the subject of a 'risk of significant harm' notice and accompanying assessment in the child protection system, is more than fifty times more likely than others to end up in care, twelve times more likely to have their own children taken by child services and 8.1 times more likely to spend time behind bars at least once.

The footnotes define the breadth of parental risk factors in such cases.

> There are five parental risk factors that flag interaction with the justice system, AOD (alcohol or drug) issues, domestic violence, or mental illness.
>
> They include parent in custody, parent interaction with justice, proven AOD related offence or AOD hospital admission, and proven domestic violence related offence or victim of domestic violence and treatment for mental health in NSW hospital or ambulatory services.

And so we have this daisy chain of heartbreak that has as its defining feature an absence of love. I mean this in the widest possible view. These are real people behind these statistics, yet so often our systems, by design, see them as numbers stripped of human dignity. Our institutions struggle to account for the reasons people might end up in these positions – trauma, malnourished love – and they are overwhelmed by the scale of the damage.

If managers of these programs and portfolios ever have time to pause and reflect on the nature of this widespread rot, it might jam their brains as it does mine. When you've learned to see the background code of trauma in the lives of others, it is impossible to ignore the way one set of loveless mishaps complements another, and how these two in concert help ensure yet another, totally different, instance of pain and suffering.

I've taken the time to step through it here, for those who may not have the special goggles of insight, to make a case for more love, not less.

That's how we got into this mess.

Can we even teach an institution to love? What would it mean, say, to have a welfare system that peers beyond its economic outgoings to examine the hearts and minds of its – and please forgive me for using this word – clients.

Well may you laugh. On another day I would be similarly tempted, but cynicism won't pick this lock.

I do think the whole forms from its parts and, much like our efforts with kindness, we don't begin to turn this tide from the top. You must have noticed it, this seething inhumanity that is chewing through the veneer of civilisation. It is more obvious in some places than others. For example, it is difficult anywhere online to find the full portrait of a human being. There are snatches of conversations and monologues attached to social media accounts that may or may not be people, who can say? These online projections of ourselves are never complete and, though they may be curated, lack the totality of our physical selves. So much about who we are as a species is contingent on being able to look someone in the eye when we do and say things to them.

There have got to be consequences when we give that up.

We have coarsened ourselves in the race for digital literacy. But this isn't some anti-technology screed. I'm not making the argument we should never have discovered, or put to use, electromagnetism and then developed the internet. That alone would have ruined much of my childhood attempts at jimmying open a window to the world outside my regional Queensland home. It doesn't do to dwell on who, precisely, I would be without the character-building tension of using the dial-up modem to connect to a porn site during high school when you're on the family computer and everyone else is in bed. Scientists have measured the loudest sound in the world and it is the *ka-klang ka-klang* of a dial-up modem when you're a horny teenager.

This is to say, my life has been shaped at all the right milestones by these seemingly exponential leaps in our capacity to be severely online. Even as my time has become more beset with projects and interventions of one kind or another, I am addicted to social media.

To borrow from David Chalmers's philosophical zombie argument that I referenced way back in the chapter titled The Self (that it is impossible to know if another human being is genuinely conscious) there is yet another level to the uncertainty. We approach this additional layer online.

No matter our intuition, nor even the actual knowledge that another human is right there on a keyboard on the other side of that social media account, we may never see them as truly real. A diminished simulacrum, perhaps. A caricature. And they will do the same for me because at this point the self has been filtered twice, first outside my skull and then through the machinery of modern life.

In his *Quarterly Essay* 'Net Loss', the art critic Sebastian Smee wrestles with the remarkable problem of the 'inner life', which he says is 'rich, complex and often obscure, even to ourselves, but essential to who we are'.

> It is a part of us we neglect at our peril.
>
> I am interested in it because of my sense that, as we live more and more of our lives online and attached to our phones, and as we are battered and buffeted by all the informational, corporate and political surges of contemporary life, this notion of an elusive but somehow sustaining inner self is eroding.

> I think this may be a bigger change, with more serious ramifications, than we realise. Once nurtured in secret, protected by norms of discretion or a presumption of mystery, this 'inner' self today feels harshly illuminated and remorselessly externalised, and at the same time flattened, constricted and quantified.

We do that to ourselves. Just rest the mind on what we'd be willing to do to others playing the same game.

A couple of years ago, when I was living in Melbourne, my best friend's younger sister, who is much like a sister to me, came to visit.

Alice – the youngest in her family – is a ray of light. But for murky reasons perhaps known only by those destined to fill the final place on the family ticket, she is acutely aware of how she measures up against the rest of her family.

Sadly, she often finds herself lacking, without a shred of evidence to build the case.

Alice has an astounding emotional intelligence and is variously regarded within her family as the one with the sharpest judgement of character in people. She can pick a fraud or a disloyal person the way some cats can apparently sniff out cancer. But online, the usual markers and signposts on which her evaluations depend, vanish. She is adrift without these cues.

During her visit, we indulged our usual mutual pastime of taking photographs on adventure-seeking walks before mainlining chardonnay while uploading our pics to Instagram. I had just liked one of her photos and was about to add a comment when I noticed the post had disappeared.

'Where did the photo go?' I asked her.

She was frazzled and a little upset.

'It didn't get enough likes so I deleted it,' she told me.

The picture had only been online for three minutes.

It was 2010 before I had a proper inkling that the disease of depersonalisation was moving out from the dusty corners of internet forums and blog comments to the mainstream. I was working for the women's website Mamamia when the publisher Mia Freedman (also my boss) did a guest appearance on the *Today Show* and host Karl Stefanovic asked her to join him in standing up and singing the Australian national anthem for the Tour de France winner Cadel Evans. (I know, what even is that sentence.)

Mia refused. Her reason was that Evans, a cyclist, was not a hero and she just didn't see why he deserved a standing ovation on breakfast television. Maybe I'm just an out-of-touch leftie, but of all the things Mamamia had published or that had been said by our publisher in the course of my time working there, this one didn't ring any alarm bells.

The rape and death threats she received lasted for a week.

The people who sent these frankly horrific messages did so on Twitter and Facebook and over email. They never bothered to hide their faces, names or businesses. More than one threatened to rape Mia's children.

I had never seen anything like it.

Mia didn't look at her emails or accounts for a week, but my colleagues and I did. We saw it all. Hundreds and hundreds of deranged and sick comments from ostensibly normal people.

As my world has expanded I have come to see versions of this bile again and again. Crusaders against same-sex marriage dealt it during the national postal vote on human rights while others copped (and still cop) vitriol purely on account of their race. Where ethnicity is involved, the taunts and threats are always worse. So it goes for women.

It's not the same as real life, it's frequently worse.

I'll use my own experience because I feel it more keenly. Yes, having 'faggot' yelled at you from a passing Datsun in country Queensland is a visceral experience. It always comes with that frisson of potential violence, the immediacy of which is never quite replicated on the internet. But, in almost every case, these drive-by aggressions were done by people who must have known I could never figure out who they were.

Online, they do it in full view. These people have stripped *themselves* of personhood, almost as if they too are only avatars in a game.

That's telling.

It is no coincidence that depersonalisation is a feature of mental ill-health. When it is not showing up as a symptom of other conditions, it has its own titular disorder. It is closely related to dissociation, a key behaviour documented in complex post-traumatic stress disorder.

In both cases, the person feels a total disconnection from their thoughts and feelings. As this progresses, they become disconnected from their very identity. Ego, in the psychological sense, melts away and it is as if reality itself has ceased to function.

Stress has something to do with this phenomenon in the most literal sense. Being constantly online induces 'situational demands' that far outstrip our ability to cope with them.

In a December 2020 journal paper published in *Human Communication Research*, a German team led by Anna Freytag found that it is not so much how much we do online – especially when it comes to sending and receiving messages – but how we are permanently aware of the world in our phones and computers even when we are not using them.

After three rigorous experiments, the researchers found:

> The inclusion of one's online environment in cognitive structures may vary between people and situations, but increases the overall complexity in daily life since users now operate simultaneously in multiple online and offline contexts and need to process information that would not be salient (or similarly obtrusive) in a purely offline setting.

It is this online vigilance that increases stress, the researchers say. As a general rule, human beings are not known for their wise decision-making under the influence of high or even ambient stress.

One of the survival tactics for people in extreme distress is to create shortcuts online to pare back the information that needs to be processed. In order to cope, we might turn all of those real people in our phones into mere effigies; an adaptation made at the point of crisis that then becomes preserved in amber, like the big mosquito from *Jurassic Park*. That people might unknowingly, or deliberately, weaponise depersonalisation online is not necessarily an indicator of mental illness, though I admit the similarities have piqued my curiosity.

One is a coping mechanism to endure torment, the other a tool to inflict it. Maybe I'm being naive. It wouldn't be the first time.

(When I was a kid I always assumed the *Jurassic Park* sequels would have to, even superficially, deal with the clear fact that the park concept's founder and perhaps key backers would need to be jailed for corporate manslaughter or something. You know, after five people were eaten by velociraptors, a T. rex and a dilophosaur. But no! That's not how the world works *at all*. Turns out, if you have enough money, most laws become guidelines. Four people died on a ride at Dreamworld on the Gold Coast, for example, and the management just paid some lowball fines, dismantled the river rapids and reopened the park.)

I guess it is possible some people are just so irredeemably awful the fourth wall of the internet theatre / pleasure dome means nothing at all to them. I suspect, however, that the screen between them and the world does something crucial and yet intangible to the self.

To be clear, I'm guilty of this myself. I have said and written things online, across the course of my life, that now provoke shame in me. In high school and early university, many of those comments were the fruit of anger, flung out into the ether because it felt better and easier to make the world angry alongside me. In my twenties, the acid was still there in smatterings across the internet – and, yes, still drips from my tongue on occasion now, though I hope my mistakes these days are ones of human frailty and not malice.

We have to do better. If we cannot or will not guard ourselves and others against the erosion of self – if we can't express even a modicum of love for our condition, our *wholeness* – then what chance the state?

So much about us is already invisible, not least of all the trauma we carry around like an unexploded World War Two grenade in our back pocket.

It's for protection, we yell at no one in particular. *It helped once!*

Those of us who have been there and survived that can see it all quite clearly: the catalogue of horrors we call *experience* shows up over and over again in the eyes of everyone else. And all the while, we have outsourced our humanity to social media moderators and hoped that the small part we play in the modern discourse couldn't possibly be stitched together and used to inform oh, I don't know, everything else.

Listen, if you can get to Kevin Bacon in six degrees then it is more than likely what you do matters. It really, really does. And, sure, who the hell is going to read this book and change their mind? Probably not anyone you know. Maybe the idea will ferment in some poor sod's brain for half a decade. Maybe this will radicalise someone in the wrong way and a bunch of fascists will dox me, but even that is asking a bit much of the writing.

But, to be honest, I'm tired of being cynical. I am exhausted by the carousel of hurt and pain that passes my eyes every day. I don't want the secret code of trauma, nor the reminders of how so small an error can destroy a whole person for decades, if not the rest of their life.

Still, if I could turn back the clock I'd probably have RSI by now.

One of my all-time favourite books was first lent to me by my beautiful pal Mitchell Bingemann. That book is Kurt Vonnegut's *Sirens of Titan.*

On 14 June 2016 I messaged Mitchell on Facebook and transcribed the nineteen passages I had underlined in the book's pages as I was reading.

I saved the best for last.

> It took us that long to realise that a purpose of human life, no matter who is controlling it, is to love whoever is around to be loved.

And then I wrote to Mitchell:

> That's the bit where I cried. I embarked on a little experiment last year, my year of living vulnerably, and it has had mixed success I must say but I feel a bit freer for it and I think this part made me happy sad.

Happy sad.

It becomes, I think, the landmark emotion of anyone who has travelled the road out from trauma and seen the way the landscape changes gradually. From desert to native grasses and eventually fields of green.

Solace is a destination.

Doubt

School plays, like droughts and colonoscopies, must simply be endured. A little fidelity to the original subject matter is expected, however, especially when you're attempting an adaptation of the Bible.

After moving from an extremely isolated cattle station to a real school with real students in it, I had discovered for the first time the richness of Catholic mass. Mum had always been a Catholic, but my entry to the faith came through this powerful allure of candles and pageantry. Here was an institution that spoke to my blunt yearning for costumes and singing and rituals. Faith and fashion are not born of the same spring, to be frank, but a little 'Him and hymn' arrangement – a marriage, if you will – was just the thing for both of us.

My favourite hymn was 'All the Ends of the Earth', which had a lovely lilt, and I would spend most of mass dreaming about the mysteries of the tabernacle, which looked for all the world like a Dalek at a fancy-dress party. I wanted the keys to that little vessel. It was like a Holden Barina for God.

This fascination transmogrified into a sense of religious duty, which is how I came to throw my hat into the ring to play the lead role of Jesus in my Catholic primary school's Easter play. I could not face having some of the less enthusiastic students mangle their performances and risk, in this small act, unravelling millennia of church doctrine and respect. This burden was mine to carry and I wore the crown heavily.

I also wore my own figure heavily on account of the meat pies I had used to replace both a balanced diet and my father. This was a dilemma because although I knew I had to give this role my all, I would also be giving the crowd all my rolls the moment my shirt came off for the crucifixion. I would play the Son of God but he would be played, for perhaps the first time in history, as Fat Jesus.

What were the rulings on such a matter? To my incomplete knowledge I was not aware of any pronouncements in Vatican II that might have barred the casting of a fuller-figured Jesus. A kindly teacher offered me the choice of performing the character with a shirt on, but this seemed an unreasonable concession. It would be akin to playing Don Vito Corleone with a Cornish accent.

My concerns were compounded by the structural integrity of the crucifix itself. It was one of those two-bit jobs held together by string and was surprisingly dense. And it was here, strung up loosely by my hands with my gut hanging over the school-issued Jesus shorts, that I imagined various catastrophes. In one, the string snapped and the structure collapsed and I went plummeting to the ground like a fleshy and over-ripened fruit. There, on the ground, I would persevere with the lines, surrounded by shattered timber like an overly dramatic pirate after a broadside.

'Forgive them, for they know not what they do!'

While my tiny arms began shaking under the stress of both the imaginary and real-world acting crucifixion, I found a moment to pity the audience. There was sobbing somewhere, but it was not clear whether it was coming from Mary Magdalene (a girl called Samantha, brown pigtails) or the assistant principal (religious education) who had come for the Lord but been given *Lord of the Flies*.

Never have I been so happy to be placed in a tomb, which in this case was a sports equipment shed with a roller door. I wondered what Jesus would have done in there with some plastic wickets and an exercise ball – from Pontius Pilate to conscious Pilates. And when it was time for my resurrection I did not want to come out of my tomb, which had become my corrugated protection against the barbs of the amateur theatre critics outside.

There hasn't been a more uneasy exit from a cave since Plato's prisoners made a bid for freedom.

Thankfully, one of the key tenets of Christianity is forgiveness. My heart was pure, if a little fatty.

Whatever religious life I might have led never made it much further than the pantomime of the Church. For example, I stayed on the Saturday night reading roster all through high school even though I had stopped believing in an omnipotent God. The church was the only place in my home town where I could take to a lectern (or pulpit, in this case) and do the public speaking in which I had become so interested. I read aloud the Gospels of Matthew, Mark, Luke and John, letters from Paul to the Corinthians, prayers of the faithful. Greedily, I read anything that was given to me because it gave me a chance to practise my speaking voice to a crowd.

I used to get annoyed when others performed the same service in their monotones, stumbling over the sentences or failing completely to acknowledge the clear existence of punctuation in the paragraphs.

What God would allow this? I wondered.

My participation in religion, such that it was, became a sort of play in itself. It fed a desire to be on stage and the only stage in town was the church. I wasn't a confident child. Speaking publicly would send me into a state of paralysis beforehand and result in hours-long headaches afterwards. But a pure thrill existed for just a few minutes right in the middle. It felt rather how I imagine street luge feels at the X-Games: terrifying, with the potential for death.

I guess that might be the broad umbrella under which much of religion as an organised structure sits, only here the death is guaranteed, eventually.

The finer details of religion never made much sense to me.

Nathanael West's 1933 novella, the masterpiece *Miss Lonelyhearts*, deals with this intrigue through the story of a newspaper advice columnist who is weighed down by the reams and reams of letters he receives from readers who are suffering in one way or another.

He thinks the answer to his despondency might lie in Christ, though his editor mocks him for it at every turn. As do his friends.

In a local speakeasy, where he often goes to drink (and occasionally get physically assaulted), his friends engage in ideological deconstructions.

'Well, that's the trouble with his approach to God. It's too damn literary – plain song, Latin poetry, medieval painting, Huysmans, stained-glass windows and crap like that,' one says. 'Even if he were to have a genuine religious experience, it would be personal and so meaningless, except to a psychologist.'

West's novel is a vindication of doubt, I think. In the closing pages, Miss Lonelyhearts is possessed by a religious certainty so severe that it becomes a threat to his life.

He'd have been better off struggling to hold the faith; I've always found that to be far more interesting than bookish rectitude anyhow.

The first religious instruction I ever had came via Sister Anne Maree Jensen, a Catholic nun who taught herself to fly planes and then took over the aerial ministry for the church based out of Longreach in central Queensland.

I was just a small boy on a cattle station who knew the particular buzz of her aircraft the way some animals know the call of their young. At the airfield in Longreach, she would jump into the four-seat Cessna 172N and spend weeks of the year visiting cattle and sheep stations dotted around an area of Queensland the size of a regular European nation. She came for tea and biscuits, mostly, but for the Catholic faithful she would say a remote mass with communion and wine.

My mum, Deb, was about the age I am now and I remember watching her partake in this apparently solemn ritual. The bowed head, the crossing of the chest and heart; secret signals. If you want to engage the interest of a fledgling young gay boy, you'd be hard-pressed to find a more effective medium. Sister Anne Maree didn't wear a habit or anything traditional, which was disappointing, but she always came to celebrate mass with the requisite urns and vessels, candles and fabrics.

I figured if the church ever gave up too much of its centuries-old theatre, then I wouldn't get visits from the nun at all. She'd just fly overhead and push some unleavened bread out of an open plane door and be on her way. Apart from Mum, she was the only adult company in my life that I actually enjoyed in those young years. Everyone else was either a jackaroo, a station cook or a truck driver, and I had less in common with those figures.

Sister Anne Maree would bring me picture books to read. They were Bible stories, but I didn't really know what the Bible was.

Seemed to have a lot of gore and death in it, which corroborated my experience of life so far.

The one I remember best was about Samson and Delilah, ultimately a cautionary tale against haircuts and treacherous women. I was too young to know that the Bible was filled with such *dangerous women* (imagine I am saying that in a spooky ghost voice), but had I understood it then I might have tested the water a little more carefully.

By the time we had moved to Boonah, a small country town southwest of Brisbane, I had missed out on the next intake for confirmation in the Church. Baptism, apparently, is only step one in a long list of hurdles required by tradition to maintain your position in the club.

The tiny Catholic primary school I attended was attached to the church in town, and it was here that I was obliged to attend mass with my classmates who had, almost all of them, been confirmed and thus admitted to the sacred art of wine drinking and communion-having. They all got to line up in the middle of mass and have a go.

I was jealous of them. Why not me? I, too, wanted the tongue bread.

It was these urges, and not the desire for any closer union with God, that drove me to commit to the church later in primary school. I volunteered to do my confirmation, five years after my peers, because I wanted to be fully immersed in what was, until that point in my life, the gayest thing I knew.

In 2018, when life was marginally more simple than it is today, the internet became obsessed with Knickers, the large steer whose photo, showing him standing in a West Australian field next to his cow buddies, went global on account of his heft.

I want to be very clear: Knickers is a big unit. He is 1.94 metres tall at the shoulder and, in the photo that went viral, he is twice as high as his fellow cows. The image was a sensation. My friends and I loved Knickers the big boy.

Now, when you google 'the large steer' (as I just did, to remind myself of the details), there is a list of other related searches people have done which, if I am being totally honest, has brought me genuine and total joy.

'Why is knickers the cow so big,' one search term reads. People actually searched this. I endorse their effort. Another, my favourite, asks: 'Is the giant cow real?'

This is all to say that when I did my communion I looked like Knickers the steer. Twice as tall as the little Year 2 kids and with a face that said to the congregation: *This is as awkward for me as it is for you*.

If I ever thought there was a God, he deserted me that day. I went to the church dressed in cream pants and a bright orange Hawaiian shirt. The costume, for that is what it was, made me look like a 45-year-old dad coming to pick his son up on his alternate custody weekend.

Mum took photos on the night, back when we still used film cameras, so I didn't get to see what they looked like for weeks. I think the way I saw myself reflected back in those prints (not good) is much like the interplay of religion and society. In many cases it has become a representation of us and, in many cases, we cast our eyes upon it and think, *Is that really who we are?*

I went through a very boring phase of hating everything about religion, a year or so before coming out as gay and for quite a few years after. At its peak it was an intense and childish pursuit. When Mum gently asked if I wanted to come to Saturday night mass, I'd launch into uninvited monologues about the embarrassment of believing something so silly. I mocked the very system that had supported her at the bedrock of our family struggle and, worse, I ridiculed her for seeking refuge in it.

I'm so ashamed of that young man. Looking back, I think I was mourning not just the treatment of queer people (and women, and children) but the gradual loss of my ability to believe in anything at all. How desperate I was to experience what I assumed was the comfort of a religious scaffold.

They call it faith for a reason, I suppose. But I've had faith in lots of things before and since. I believed in Mum, for starters, and that she would do everything she could to keep us safe. I also had a conviction that, all things considered, the structures in society existed to protect us. Police, courts, hospitals. Even Centrelink.

I had literally no evidence to support these wild theories and, in some cases, there was an abundance of fact to establish the precise opposite. I heard Mum on the phone to Centrelink, for crying out loud. Like Mum, though, I needed to believe these things were true. Everything else in my life was chaos and uncertainty – *Would we still have a house? Would the lights stay on? Would we have to pretend Christmas didn't matter so Mum could breathe a little easier?* – the hallmarks of which were the gradual erosion of my strength and resolve. It's like being in a bouncing castle for more than two minutes with a dozen other kids and then trying to get out. You have to constantly assess the angle and momentum of the bounces if you are to even flirt with staying on your feet, and even then the physics can outwit you. The longer you fight to escape, the harder it becomes. Your muscles burn with exertion.

The equations are not simple, nor the effort insignificant.

And so I wanted to acquire stability wherever possible.

The death of my personal faith felt like the end of curiosity itself, and that was devastating. It was also a mistake.

I realise now that my newfound atheism had driven curiosity from the field, at least when it came to questions of the *why*. However, to me, the realm of the natural world and the cosmos has given me more joy and wonder than anything else. It's not that I thought religion itself provided these open mysteries for the benefit of inquiry. But in crushing even the consideration of it, I swapped what I viewed as an 'unacceptable doubt' for something even worse: an answer.

Look, I can say now that I do not believe in a 'God'. That is true. But there is something unsettling about the ease with which some people, my younger self included, declare that they *know* there is no God. Boring – next!

The great physicist Richard Feynman attempted to unravel these great challenges and came to the view that it is quite possible to be a scientist and believe in a God from religion, though the manner in which we must get there cannot be through absolutes.

'It is imperative in science to doubt; it is absolutely necessary, for progress in science, to have uncertainty as a fundamental part of your inner nature,' he says in a compendium of his short works, *The Pleasure of Finding Things Out.*

> To make progress in understanding, we must remain modest and allow that we do not know. Nothing is certain or proved beyond all doubt.
>
> You investigate for curiosity, because it is *unknown*, not because you know the answer. And as you develop more information in the sciences, it is not that you are finding out the truth, but that you are finding out that this or that is more or less likely.

Truth is not a destination at which we should ever hope to arrive.

In 2014, I was invited back by my alma mater (I like using the fancy term for it because no one ever seems to do that for their public high school) in Boonah to give an address to all the students at their end-of-year awards night.

It was a custom to bring back school leaders a decade after they have graduated to impart advice. Here is some of what I said to the crowd in the hall that night.

> All those years ago, when I was where you are, I remember thinking the person who gave this speech was so *old.* And so *together.*
>
> Lies, all of it. Nobody knows what they are doing. Not your politicians, not your lawyers, not your journalists, not your teachers.
>
> The trick to growing up, I've found, is to not grow up. It is an appalling denial of childhood spirit that we quietly expect people to lose their sense of childhood wonder, joy and laughter by the sheer act of becoming an adult. Don't do that.

I'm aware of the irony of the circumstances. I was twenty-seven. My adult brain had literally only finished pruning out Pokemon references and cheat codes for *Grand Theft Auto* in favour of the raw processing power needed to hide the fact that I was a smoker from real-estate agents at rental inspections. What could this kid possibly know about the vicissitudes of adulthood?

And yet I haven't resiled from that position in the six years since the speech night. If anything, circumstance has intervened to reinforce the message I tried to impart that night. There is a pressure, I think, to adopt modes of thinking about the world as we grow older that conform with the very silly idea that adults know anything at all about the state of things.

Civilisation is largely guesswork. Where we do meet discovery, such as through science, it is never the end of the matter. There are always more questions. It's not like Einstein untangled the mysteries of gravity with his General Theory of Relativity and then went partying in Ibiza. There was more work to do and, a century later, we're still looking for gravitons and other elementary particles.

For the same reason that I spurned the certainty of some religious adherents, I eventually came to reject the absolutes of my frankly very annoying atheism. I don't think it is at all likely there is a God, but it is not interesting (or accurate) to say I know for sure.

Confidence is unappealing in such matters. It can also be dangerous. Doubt, on the other hand, is a constellation of possibilities. There is a freedom in it that we are taught to abhor.

'Fundamentalism does not converse or explore,' poet and theologian John O'Donohue writes in *Eternal Echoes*. 'It presents truth. It is essentially non-cognitive. This false certainty can only endure through believing that everyone else is wrong.

'It is not surprising that such fundamentalism desires power in order to implement its vision and force others to do as prescribed. There is neither acceptance nor generosity in its differences with the world.'

I've always separated the structures of religion from the common people of faith. This has been particularly necessary when I consider the church of my upbringing, which incubated a profound dissonance in me throughout my time in it.

The people of this church are fiendishly practical in the face of obtuse leadership and still almost pathologically committed to the assumed splendour of top-down complexity. The same rituals that captivated me as a child feel so barren before the drama of real, messy life.

I know the Church has changed. Is changing. Though it is frequently rather late to the party. Imagine getting a reflex test at a GP clinic and waiting 400 years for the nerve to kick.

Among the congregation that I knew, faith was not ostentatious. It had a utility about it, like the earth on which we walked. Things grew in that faith, blossomed even, but it was not an adornment. It was the thing itself. It was living, not a performance. And it was a faith riddled with the essential doubt of being in the world.

In *Damascus*, Christos Tsiolkas adds a gut-wrenching twist to the Bible story of 'Doubting Thomas' – the disciple who did not believe Jesus had risen from the dead. In one of the final confrontations between Thomas and Saul, Tsiolkas has crafted a caustic meditation on the subject of doubt. Thomas tells Saul that death is a fact and it has happened to their beloved Jesus.

> Saul sits back on the tiled floor. 'You are lost, brother. That is why the Saviour does not come to you. You doubt and so all you have is this world. May it be enough for you.'
>
> And with that he turns his back to Thomas. To combat doubt he must make his heart stone.

When *Damascus* was released, I sat down with Tsiolkas in a Surry Hills park and chain-smoked with him as we discussed its theme. It was a dream commission because he had written a book about the very things with which I had struggled for so long. I happen to adore his writing, too, though had never met him before that morning. I was actually outside his hotel googling profiles of him to see if he was a smoker – I had a sneaking suspicion he was – because I thought our chat would be more free-flowing and fun if we could both be at peace with our vices. I had just found a line in an article that confirmed Tsiolkas was a smoker when I looked to my left and saw him sitting on a bench having a fag. Maybe God had smiled on me.

Damascus, his retelling of the birth of Christianity after the death of Jesus, is fiction but, to my eye, closer to an accurate reading of what must have taken place in those dark days.

Tsiolkas told me he had a similar 'agony' of faith to my own, when he was fifteen and 'couldn't reconcile sexuality and Christian ethics'. He read the letters of Saint Paul (as I had, standing at the pulpit in church) and thought them an unambiguous rejection of people like him. And, on the surface at least, the novel is a story about religious conviction, though Tsiolkas says the exploration of essential truths goes much further.

'I think there is a difference between people's faith and belief. And we all struggle – even if you're an atheist you struggle with political belief, you struggle with political ideals and social, cultural questions,' he tells me on that morning on the bench. He said he worries sometimes that readers now want the world in the novel 'to reflect what we are, what we want and what we think, what we believe is true, which is to damn the whole of literature and philosophy and history'.

Doubt and questioning, in Tsiolkas's view, are important for writers of fiction.

'I used to really be suspicious of doubting myself,' he said, 'and I know that doubt can also be lacerating, that sometimes political activism requires a certainty, but if I've learned anything in my life it is that doubt is really important. That doubt is also that thing that stops you being a monster, condemning swathes of people.'

Zealotry of any stripe gives him pause, especially in politics, and I can't help but find echoes of my own experience in this assessment. We saw the perfect form of this idea during the pandemic that swept through Victoria in its second wave. In a bid to overcorrect some one-eyed reporting in the media, hundreds of super Dan Andrews fans banded together to become its opposite force. In doing so, however, both sides of hard-right and nominally left voices became the same thing: a fact-free celebration of certainty. First, the genuine public health criticisms of the Victorian response were lashed as a media conspiracy. This had to be broadened out to a deeper plot when the ombudsman slammed human rights abuses in the public housing tower lockdown and when eminent epidemiologists noted that contact tracing in the state was so thoroughly depleted it could never have stopped the seeding of the virus in its second wave. An independent inquiry led by a respected judge teased out the many failures. Even when the government itself announced reforms and changes on the fly to boost this capacity, the strongest supporters of Daniel Andrews refused to acknowledge mistakes had been made. They lived in a world where they believed in their leader and that belief was enough to bend reality itself.

My problem with this frankly terrifying episode of blinkered fervour – this was a public health crisis! – is not that people support Labor or Liberal but that the mere fact of this support is often the end of curiosity.

While professional reactionaries demonstrated the same all-in approach to Donald Trump, even when he vowed to dismantle the very idea of democracy and the United States, many of these were acting in bad faith. This was their job, to stir the anger and division. They were dangerous because of it.

In Victoria, I don't think people were deliberate in the same way. And, certainly, it pales in comparison to the deadly force of far-right groupthink. My chief concern – and I mean this genuinely, it keeps me up at night – is that we don't get to split these issues into Left and Right. When we forsake facts in order to 'win' an argument for our own team this is not done in isolation. It is an act of aversion to truth that leads us increasingly into a world where nothing means anything.

What will the worst kinds of people do with that friction-less state of things?

I've often joked that the only books in our house were *Goosebumps* and the romance novels of Danielle Steele. That's largely true, although Mum also had a fun side hustle in true crime and borrowed the latest Mary Higgins Clark from the local library whenever they came in.

As my world has expanded with age, most of the people I've met – friends or otherwise – have come from homes where ideas were discussed and the great works of literature, philosophy and journalism were on hand to study. Not all children are taught what to think by their parents, though of course many are. Not every child is presented with the nomenclature of ideology and systems of thought from which they might form their worldview, though of course some are.

To the extent that I had any organising principles bequeathed to me at all, they were scant and confined to the realm of morality: be honest, pay your debts, work hard. That was the sum total of my worldly education.

You might think this is heading in an awkward direction. The last thing I want is for anyone to imagine I am blaming my mum for not knowing enough about Kant, post-modernism or late-stage capitalism (although as I understand it there are a lot of Kants in both).

Mum taught me one thing that trumps all of the above: curiosity.

Deb is much like the little hobbits from Tolkien's *Lord of the Rings* in both temperament and stature; though she might have wished for a similarly comfortable life as them, having had adversity thrust upon her was an education in itself.

None of the difficulties she faced dimmed her child-like sense of wonder, even in the guts of our family's misery. She taught us to notice the birdlife in the garden, the stars at night and the way people treated each other. There was so much wisdom in her inquiry, none of it scraped from the 'right' books or journals. It was a pure, vital interrogation of everything that was real.

And so, when the time came, I entered the world as a vacant plot of land. Without the requisite confidence of class or comfort, it would be some time before I could see the value in arriving at my own thoughts completely anew. In the presence of others, I felt dumb and unworthy. *How can I possibly understand what it means to live a life if I haven't read Nabokov?* I thought to myself, after someone name-dropped him in conversation. Turns out, you can do just fine never having read *Lolita* for yourself. In fact, it might be for the best.

This isn't a low-ball bid for the offcuts of anti-intellectualism. It's an argument for *thinking*. After all, doubt is only as useful as the attendant inquisition. If this thing I thought I knew isn't so, what might be? Doubt ought to propel us outwards into the cosmos of ideas and, when done properly, it can become an inexhaustible resource in aid of discovery.

It wasn't until my very late twenties that I came to believe I had anything of use to add to conversations apart from the odd quip, bad pun or requests for a drink order. To be fair, this suited my nature anyhow. It was often easier to observe people in full flight and run through the merits in my head. That's why I prefer writing as a form of thinking; the ideas clarify themselves. Writing, to me, is an act of extraction. It's the Gina Rinehart of my intuition.

Perhaps this is because I have a short attention span and have been known to forget to do something within half a second of being reminded to do it. Still, it is a more deliberate process. I'm not relying on my episodic or long-term memory to regurgitate facts. I'm trying to identify the connective tissue that might hold them together: a narrative or schema, I suppose.

Doubt is the engine of this project.

In my very early twenties, I found myself accidentally working for a state government education minister in Queensland, having stumbled into a job in the department responding to media requests.

It wasn't explicitly mentioned, but there was an expectation I would become a member of the Labor Party in the process. That was never on my radar and, to be perfectly honest, I knew as much about politics as I did about chemical engineering. There's always been a natural suspicion in my family of joining groups, although I'm honestly not sure how that came to pass. Maybe a distant cousin had been mugged by girl guides? Perhaps a childcare working bee went dangerously off the rails? I cannot say. I do know that I refused to join the Labor Party because, in my mind, I was there to provide media advice and I didn't think it particularly mattered whether I was 'one of them'.

That didn't stop the barrage of requests. I remember thinking how odd it was that even the youngest members of the office would drop off pre-filled membership forms for their local branch. Then there were those who asked which faction I would be joining, although it was really more of an elaborate suggestion. Join the right! No, the left! What about Old Guard? (To this day, I couldn't tell you what the fuck Old Guard is. It's apparently a Queensland thing; read into that what you will.)

What was most alarming about these entreaties was the tribalism that generated them. Everything was viewed through the prism of not just overarching political rivalry, but rivalry within the same damned party. There was a time for argument in these factions, of course, when platforms came up for debate, but even then these policy grudge matches happened at the level of leadership. Ordinary members were bound by these initial positions even before they were bound by the final outcome. It was conceivable, then, that you could disagree first with your faction's position and subsequently with the final position of the party. And still you'd have to suck it up and pretend you believed it. I understand the concept, but watching it in action in the minds of the young staffers and apparatchiks in the office was mind-boggling. The cognitive dissonance was so palpable it crawled out of their eyes. Some of them argued for things they knew could not be true, or helpful, because that was the position other people had decided for them.

I'd sooner try my luck with Nabokov.

I never did join the party, though the experience there added ballast to a nascent idea that there was something very off-putting about regulation faith.

The American writer, and practising Catholic, Mary Gordon told journalist Bill Moyers that the 'ability to question, the ability to take a sceptical position, is absolutely central to my understanding of myself. Faith without doubt is just either nostalgia or a kind of addiction.'

It worries me that this perfectly reasonable approach in religion and politics has been weaponised by conspiracy theorists everywhere. Most recently the particularly energised conspiracy-heads have taken to burning down, or blowing up, 5G mobile phone towers because they believe that these communications towers: are used to control human microchips; cause cancer owing to an excess in 'radiation' (non-ionising, but whatever); or are the source of the novel coronavirus, a virus noted for sharing literally zero per cent of its RNA with cell towers.

Here, these disparate groups have used a centuries-old lynchpin of scientific endeavour – doubt – as a fig leaf for the kind of ignorance you'd really have to try very hard to sustain. By their argument, they are the true heirs to scientific scepticism.

This is not doubt. For starters, there is evidence that much of the recent uptick in angst about 5G towers (for crying out loud, we've already had 3G and 4G) has something to do with foreign disinformation campaigns. But those campaigns only work because there is a nugget of fear in ordinary individuals who are convinced something *very* nefarious is afoot.

And this is why they do not exercise doubt in any common understanding of the word. They start convinced and retrofit the 'evidence' as they come across it, no matter how outlandish or frankly absurd the claim.

Honestly, certitude left unchecked will get us all killed. Overconfidence twinned with arrogance will take us there quicker.

In one form or another, starting with the hardcore anti-vaccination crowd, I've been reporting on this phenomenon of reality rejection for a decade now, and for much of that time the movement's king rat has been the science of climate change. I don't think it's useful to revisit some of the arguments used to counter climate change warnings, but it helps to know they often are prosecuted by people who would prefer the planet die than admit they don't know how to read a temperature chart. It's not nice, but it has to be said.

Do we find room within the framework of *actual* science to update our assessments of how bad (or good) things might be under different scenarios? Yes. That is precisely the mechanism we have been operating under since Sir Francis Bacon put on one of those weird concertina collars at the turn of the seventeenth century and codified the scientific method.

Doubt, used correctly, provides an avenue through which we may discover the most truly difficult of truths: that we may have been wrong. And that is a powerful thing.

Often wrong, never in doubt. That was almost a maxim in daily newspaper journalism at the end of a so-called glory age, when people paid for news, businesses advertised around it and the technology allowing direct feedback from consumers was scarcely a step up from whatever it was the Phoenicians used.

In the years that followed, uncertainty seemed a difficult burden of changing times. Editors underestimated the concern of readers, who suddenly represented a tangible mass of people. Oh, the humanity. Slowly, and then suddenly, working journalists everywhere had to re-evaluate what it meant to be certain enough to print something, or put it to air. The *Daily Mail*'s catch-cry in the internet age became *Never wrong for long*, though it is hard to say whether this came from a genuine desire for accuracy (unlikely) or just from the legal threats. For anyone who truly cared about the work, doubt bloomed into a heightened awareness. They say homing pigeons might be able to sense changes in the earth's magnetic field and, in a similar way, I became good at triangulating sources of doubt. My colleague and friend Justine Ferrari called herself a 'professional sceptic', which I liked, even though the phrase had become co-opted by people who thought loss of surface ice on the planet was the result of overly ambitious solar flares.

Finding the space to be wrong is a liberating thing, even though it can take some convincing and a cavalier approach to personal pride. There is an unfolding righteousness going on around the world right now. Everyone is right about everything, all of the time, or so it seems. Statistically speaking, this simply cannot be true.

The problem, as I see it, is that the need for rectitude has become caught up in an evolutionary arms race. Each of us feels compelled to be more right, more certain, than the last person. And so on until the results become absurd. Correctness, then, is like a bird that has grown a hopelessly over-the-top, Liberace-style plumage to attract a mate, but in doing so has made itself the worst hide-and-seek contestant in the animal kingdom.

One of my favourite cartoons on the subject, source unknown, features a giraffe and an acacia tree in Africa. Both start out small, the giraffe resembling a stunted horse. The tree then grows taller to escape the prying tongue of the animal and, in the next panel, the giraffe's neck has caught up. This cycle repeats itself until the final panel when the giraffe, now with a comically long neck, again meets the eyeline of the acacia tree.

The tree, looking annoyed, says to the giraffe: 'Dude, fuck off!'

We can't stop being right – about climate change, about equality, about religion – because what if the other side persists in saying the opposite? Our concessions might be made alone. How do we survive if the acacia tree keeps growing and we give up?

I don't know the answer. I don't know anything, really. But I have a sneaking suspicion we've lost something bigger than ourselves in the pursuit of certainty.

Maybe good can come from such a future of round-the-clock exactitude. But I doubt it.

Next

About two weeks after this manuscript was due, a deadline I had already missed more than twice, I started dating someone.

I had never dated anyone before so, in the 33-year-long printout of my life, this news was big. It stood out like a tiny rocky island in a lonely ocean of avoidance. Imagine, for example, that you adopt an orphaned mountain gorilla and raise it without incident for one-third of a century and then, one day – without warning – the animal turns to you and says calmly and in perfect English: 'I don't like this house.' That's how big a departure from ordinary life this was for me.

I've lost count of the number of wildlife rescue videos I've seen where an abandoned seal pup, squirrel or stork are shown in montages growing up with their new carer before the audience is told that they can never return to their natural habitat because 'they wouldn't know how to survive'.

Yes, I thought while watching each one, *that sounds very familiar*. Here I was now ejecting thirty-three years of status quo and beginning to date a man whose company I enjoyed and to whom I was attracted. You might argue that a baby seal raised in captivity would have at least *some* instinct for hunting and thriving in the wild; and you might similarly argue that I must have had some inkling of how to conduct myself on this new terrain.

Reader, I did not.

'You know everything about what it means to be vulnerable,' my therapist said to me in early August when I was struggling with the concept of involving another human being in my life. 'But can *you* be vulnerable?'

The thought was indeed terrifying. I had conquered all of the minor vulnerability bosses of general love and kindness, forgiveness and beauty. There had been successes in ventures of solitude and reckoning with loneliness, victories of touch and, I hoped, open thinking. Ultimately, though, these were all limbs of a grander mission. A synecdoche.

Fear has a tight grip on the years, however, and the work from its release is exhausting. I was still afraid.

'You have a false self at times, which you know you wear to protect you. I'm wondering about that false self,' the therapist said. His lime-green motorcycle helmet was perched on the bench next to him. His shirt sleeves were rolled up, revealing tattoos down his arms. A less open version of myself would have wondered if I should really be taking advice from this man.

'How eroded is it so that your true self is showing through now?' he asked me.

'That's a good question,' I said.

He responded: 'I know.'

Dating someone, anyone really, was something I had totally forbidden. It's not just that I didn't consider it. I took active steps to extricate myself from situations that might lead to it or that had, despite my hyper-vigilance, already crossed silently from friendship into proto-dates. They never lasted beyond this embryonic stage because I didn't let them.

Let's not over-egg the backstory, though. If I'm honest, there also just weren't that many of these occasions that needed my strategic escape. For the most part, I recognised nothing in anyone else that might have approached interest in me. I was one of those subatomic particles, a neutrino, that has no electrical charge and almost no mass, flitting across the universe and interacting with precious little. Such particles are incredibly hard to detect because, almost every single time, they will pass right through matter. They just slip *through* the earth. About 100 trillion will pass through our bodies every second.

In romantic terms, I was a wee baby neutrino going about my affairs largely undetected.

I met *him* at a house party in the middle of February, in a time I'm going to call pre-coronavirus (PC), although technically the contagion was already being detected in returned travellers to Australia. Nothing had shut down yet. Life seemed normal and brimming with possibility. It rained ever so gently that night, so the street in Sydney's inner west had a colourful sheen of light like a second star-flecked sky. It was late summer and the atmosphere was still sticky.

In the stifling closeness of the slim terrace house and modest courtyard, we all rubbed shoulders and apologised politely as we moved slowly past one another to get another drink, or head out for a smoke. I look back on that evening with a disgusted fondness: *We were touching each other all the time! Haven't you heard about zoonotic viruses and just how much damage one of them is about to do to everything in your otherwise constant world?*

Anyway, it was my first party in a long time, so I drank too much in the excitement and started talking to a man I had never met before. I knew about half the people there but had never come across him – online or off – and though I found him to be cute and intelligent, it never once entered my mind that anything might come of this encounter.

I remember nothing of what I said to him that night, though recall engaging my nervous habit of saying whatever comes to mind in rapid-fire succession. I had 'given up' smoking since my recent return from Japan, and had switched to a heated tobacco vape I bought from a Don Quijote store in Shibuya. The little machine superheats – but doesn't actually burn – miniature versions of a cigarette and produces almost no smoke. But my supply of the tobacco sticks was exhausted halfway through the evening and, not wanting to go without, I began lighting them as if they were actual cigarettes and smoking them anyway.

To a very large degree, the whole display was unedifying. People asked me what I was working on, in the way I always imagined writers were asked about their projects at louche cocktail parties, and I fumbled with lighting the stub of a compact tobacco stick while attempting a homily about love and vulnerability.

I didn't look like the kind of guy from whom you might ordinarily take such advice. For reasons that remain opaque, the man took a shine to me and I to him, and we met up for a drink a week later. And then the country was locked down. A national angst set in, the economy tanked and I barely left my apartment for more than two months.

Somehow, after years of arguing privately to myself that 'now was not a good time to figure out dating', I decided the moment to break with a lifetime's convention was during the most significant public health crisis in more than a century. Whether the circumstances made it easier or not is still hard to gauge.

'It's very normal to feel nervous,' my therapist told me, 'but not for a 33-year-old.'

I was like, alright mate, I get it! It has taken an exceptionally long time to make the most incremental of moves.

When I was in the final year of high school, Mum attempted to teach me how to drive in her manual car while on a deserted dirt road that we took to visit Grandma in a nursing home. It did not go well. In fact, not only did Mum give up within half an hour – 'Rick, I can't do this,' she said in exasperation – but the whole episode appears to have been so traumatising that Mum wiped from her memory the fact she ever even drove a manual car.

When my sister, Lauryn, and I raised this simple fact only recently, Deb was insistent she had never driven a manual. She told us that very same Toyota Seca, which she drove from 1995 to circa 2009, was automatic.

'Mum, I didn't get my manual licence because that car was manual and I couldn't drive it, remember?' I said to her.

When Mum does or says something silly, I try to be reassuring, but Lauryn has a habit of going for the jugular.

'Good God, woman! You're losing your mind,' she said.

But I know Mum had suctioned out the memory from her brain on account of that single, abortive lesson. I know this because by the time I started full-time work on the Gold Coast, I had to pay for my own driving lessons (in an automatic) and I am pretty sure the driving instructor actively hated me.

If you're wondering how any of this relates to dating in your thirties, bear with me, I promise there is a point at which I'll soon be arriving in my dual-control Toyota Yaris. The instructor's name was Mark or Steve or something similarly driving-instructor-like. Whenever he arrived for one of our lessons, I could see his face through the windshield as he rolled to a stop. Every time, the look that had settled on his features was one you might see on a man of a certain vintage who has just discovered his favourite football player is gay.

And, to be fair, I think he hated me because I was a danger to him and everyone else on the road. The longer I delayed the lessons, the more afraid I became of the everyday mechanics of actually driving a car. And fear, as we surely all know by now, is the god of error.

So what I'm saying is that I waited two years before learning to drive and it almost stopped me from getting across the line. In one actual test, I drove the wrong way up a turning lane onto a major road and then had the gall to ask if that meant I had failed.

The longer I delayed getting my licence, the stronger the chance was that I would annoy my driving instructor by allegedly going 'too fast' the 'wrong way' on a 'busy road'. Or, as it happens, the more I resisted getting behind the wheel at all. The same applies with my reticence to being fully vulnerable with a person I actually like.

That I even made it as far as four dates with my pandemic man is startling to me, though of course it does little to change the fact I still, in the end, ran away. Or, at least, I think I did. It was more of a commando roll, off a bed and out into the night, in any case. That was the end; a sudden severance.

And I'm telling you this, I suppose, because it would not be helpful for anyone to believe this is a book written by someone who has *figured it out.* I think there are laws about that. Insecurities fraud, perhaps.

This isn't a revelation, though it never ceases to amaze how many people will happily tell you that they have stumbled on to the secret code of living more fully and passionately.

I wonder, too, what the utility of such premature epiphany is. Some of these people are in their thirties! What on earth are you supposed to do for the rest of your life if you're done *figuring*? Rest? Sleep a full eight hours? Get day drunk? Honestly, it sounds exhausting.

If you do even a pinch of homework, most of these full-throttle completists (as in, *I have finished myself*) turn out to be billionaires, the children of billionaires or in some way billionaire-adjacent. By which I mean, people with vast means at their disposal easily mistake the accrual of extreme wealth for lasting self-actualisation.

The rest of us will simply have to settle for doing the work, which is pretty much the capitalist model under which our labour allows the plutocrats to erroneously make claims of holy achievement.

Forgive me for being crass but, bitch, *you* didn't figure anything out. You've just got staff.

So, really, you and I are where we are. What I've tried to present over the course of this book is not a sense of finality but progress. And, more importantly, a method. A way of being more open to the breadth of goodness in the world. It's not meant to be hokey. I'm an optimist by birth and a cynic in my work. These methods of revival are not contracts I've entered into lightly, or even willingly at times. But they have succeeded, in combination or in isolation, in tinkering with the mess of cords and wires that I've come to fondly refer to as 'my brain'.

A nudge here and there can become momentum.

'There is still the little boy inside there who still has insecurities,' my therapist told me in our August session.

When I got home I joked about that little boy with my flatmate Séamus. 'My therapist told me I need to kill a seven-year-old boy,' I told him, just to see the reaction on his face.

There is still so much fear in me, nesting somewhere in the recesses of my mind. Less of it than there was a decade ago, when my body was 73 per cent fear and 12 per cent rum and 20 per cent failed mathematics classes.

'I'm afraid that if I let my guard down, I undo thirty-three years of good work,' I told the therapist. 'I feel like, if I get into a relationship and it doesn't last —'

He cut me off here and chided me. 'That's called avoidance,' he said.

'I know, I'm just trying to be honest with you,' I told him.

'So am I,' he said, before letting it go and urging me to continue.

He wanted me to shade the outline of my fear. What is it that I'm afraid of, he asked. He knew what it was, he told me, but he was waiting for me to tell him, which, frankly, made him sound like one of those boys in primary school who boasts about knowing how to get money out of phone boxes but can't tell you the secret until you show him your way of doing it.

'It's fear that, uh, well, I mean fear that it won't last,' I told him. 'Fear that, once I've done it, I've opened Pandora's Box and I can't go back to my previous life of being OK-ish. It's more like, if anything, if it didn't last it would be easier for me.'

Look, I'll be honest with you. Maybe I am writing this book for myself. It's a message in a bottle written during stolen glimpses of clarity to a man who, I know from experience, is prone to crab-walking away from revelation. One of my favourite tropes in fiction and on the screen is the character who, knowing they will forget or have their memory wiped, must find a way to ensure their future self rediscovers important knowledge. In *The Sirens of Titan*, Kurt Vonnegut has a mind-controlled soldier on Mars called Unk perform this very act of rebellion. Over a series of memory erasures, Unk grows steadily more aware of his situation with the help of a mystery 'hero' he imagines as a god. But the strange letters he receives are from a past self:

> Unk had written the letter to himself before having his memory cleaned out. It was literature in its finest sense, since it made Unk courageous, watchful, and secretly free. It made him his own hero in very trying times.

Oftentimes, being your own provocation for change can be littered with hurt: in Unk's case, literally, as the Martian soldiers were controlled with antennae that deliver electric shocks if they stray from regulation activity such as looking in one direction or another.

'The more pain I train myself to stand, the more I learn,' Unk has written to himself in the letter. 'You are afraid of pain now, Unk, but you won't learn anything if you don't invite the pain. And the more you learn, the gladder you will be to stand the pain.'

In the same way – if I could reach him – I might write to the me of my early twenties, or to the me I was before I became a teenager. It does not preoccupy me as much as it used to, this knowledge that those were wasted years, but occasionally the recall of what might have been stings.

Perhaps I would send both those previous selves this book. I mean, we'd have to be careful. If the eight-year-old version of me knew that he really did grow up to become a writer, in the face of *all* of what lay before him, he might have an aneurysm or, worse, turn into an intolerable dickhead.

I have a friend whose son is named Max. But as she explained to me one day: 'It's Max really but I named him Maximillian on his birth certificate in case he grew up to be a cunt and needed options.'

It's fun to imagine having all the answers and shortcuts when you needed them, though that defeats the purpose of the pain. The only advice I could or would give my younger selves is the same advice I am trying to slip into my food and drink now, like unwanted medication for the cat: *Don't avoid.*

Bertrand Russell called the outcome: 'Of all forms of caution, caution in love is perhaps the most fatal to true happiness.'

It is *hard* to really understand the cost of shrinking yourself to escape pain. This is at the heart of my diagnosis of complex post-traumatic stress disorder. When I was still so small, the worst possible things happened. These atrocities of the mind and body were excruciating in the moment, but more vicious still in how they fundamentally altered my future.

How is it that decades of a life that hasn't been lived yet can be warped in a single, present moment? Perhaps our lives stretch before us like the netting of space–time itself.

I distinctly remember hearing the announcement in February 2016 that the Laser Interferometer Gravitational-Wave Observatory (LIGO) detectors had confirmed for the first time in human history the measurement of gravitational waves. LIGO is a truly elegant observatory. There are two of them, actually, separated by 3000 kilometres on the mainland United States of America and operated in unison. Each has four-kilometre-long vacuum tubes, or 'arms', filled with the most precise mirror measurement system ever developed. The idea is simple: if gravitational waves exist they will tear through space and time, distorting the very fabric of the world around us. When they pass through these LIGO observatories – first one and then, in a fraction of a second, the other – the experimental arms will measure the contraction of space. In the data we would see the moment our physical environment wobbled back and forth with the arrival of these cosmic currents.

The waves first detected formed more than one billion years ago in the final fraction of a second of a violent merger between two spinning black holes, about twenty-nine and thirty-six times the size of our sun. Bam. And for one billion years since, these ripples in the fabric of space and time have raced outwards in all directions in the universe. At the speed of light, they pass through entire galaxies and mind-meltingly empty stretches of ink-black space. They are still out there shooting through the unknown when life on earth consisted only of just single-celled organisms or, at best, a few cells hung together like washing on a city high-rise balcony. Half a billion years ago, when life here exploded into more intricate forms and the groundwork was laid for the dinosaurs that would follow, the waves from this single collision were halfway to earth.

We didn't exist yet, of course.

In 1915, these wobbles in our physical reality were just one hundred years away from earth when Albert Einstein first predicted their existence, in general. He didn't know that, when the time and the money and the technology were right, these specific waves would arrive at the LIGO detector, just one week after it was switched back on following major upgrades.

For all that cosmic effort, and what must have been a screaming cataclysm that birthed it, the twin arms of the LIGO experiment warped in space and time by a size 10,000 times *smaller* than the nucleus of an atom.

In the most material of ways, our verified reality changed in 2015 (detected then, and announced to the world in early 2016) on account of something shocking that happened one billion light years away – one billion *years* ago. Like gravity waves, the force of early trauma does diminish over time, though it has a very long tail. I can almost feel the distortions of space and time as these disturbances roll through the years from that moment when I first confronted my dad about the affair I had witnessed him having with our governess. There is a contraction of love; as if the very substance of it is being squeezed through a tube. At first, the effects of this early and repeated hurt were stitched into my brain as coping mechanisms.

The heat of that first night – spent alone on a 1000-square-kilometre cattle station fourteen hours from my mother, brother and sister – sticks in my memory and on my skin. In my mind, it is as if I could walk across the polished wooden floorboards and collect that boy in my arms. He is still so real to me. Tangible.

He is frozen in fear, I can see that now. He didn't know that then, and he wouldn't understand it for more than two decades. The paralysis of that moment is a survival instinct that he took with him into adulthood, but one we both no longer need.

A way of looking at complex PTSD that makes the most sense to me is this: that boy is a ghost with unfinished business, hanging around the corridors of my soul, banging on my interior with desperate warnings about imagined future hurt, extrapolated from those torturous days and nights of years before.

He is a boy out of time, applying lessons that are no longer relevant to scenarios he has never visited.

Complex PTSD is a psychic cold war; an intercontinental ballistic missile warning system that has been calibrated to sense the most fluffy, delicate down feather falling to earth on a gentle current of air. All fear and destruction.

It's Nena's '99 Luftballons': a bunch of harmless red balloons that start a war between the animalistic part of the mind and the you that is, at least theoretically, in control of the rest of it.

George Saunders tells the story of a whole graveyard of ghosts in his novel *Lincoln in the Bardo*. They have convinced themselves that they are not dead, though of course they are. It is one of the most beautiful, life-affirming novels I have ever read, despite the subject matter – or perhaps because of it. Grief can be beautiful, if we learn to grow with it. It has to be so. Near the end of the book, Saunders recounts the decision of the various graveyard ghosts to finally leave the earthly plane, having accepted that they long ago left the world of the living. These little vignettes are heart-stopping in their profundity.

One spirit, roger bevins iii, is among the last to go in a loud crack of light and thunder.

> It is nearly noon and you must decide; you have seen what you have seen, and it has wounded you, and it seems you only have one choice left.
>
> None of it was real; nothing was real. Everything was real, inconceivably real, infinitely dear.
>
> These and all things started as nothing, latent with a vast energy-broth, but then we named them, and loved them, and, in this way, brought them forth.

And then he is gone.

So it is that I must convince the haunting child that his time here is done; that his protection has served me well when we most needed it but that his persistence since has done us harm. This isn't meant to sound melodramatic; I am being as precise as I can with the language. If I am to embrace the future I have already worked so hard to call forth, then I must let that boy rest.

He is tired, can't you see that? He fought so hard. We survived, because of him. He can enjoy his valour from the bleachers, free from pain.

If you think deeply enough about what it means to rewire a brain from a trauma that has frozen parts of it in time, there is an inescapable conclusion.

To undo that lasting code, you are in effect removing the last real-world form of a distant and threatened self. In my case, there really was a ghost in the machine and his name was Rick.

How funny, in its coal-black way, that farewells are sometimes the way we get better. I must unwrap his little fists from the cords of my amygdala and cut him loose.

Thank you, I might say, unsure if this is truly an end or just a beginning.

Beginnings

'I don't even have a reason to cry anymore,' Mum said with genuine surprise. 'There's nothing to cry about!'

That wasn't strictly true, but it was as far as we allowed hope to fly into the Morton household. Hope was like a chicken; it could become airborne briefly, but it was ultimately a ground-dwelling thing.

At the time of Mum's curious announcement, the Queensland–New South Wales border had been more or less closed for four months, save for a small window, which I had missed. And, yes, Deb had saved up for a holiday of her own to Cairns, which she was due to take in May 2020 with an old friend from Adelaide, but that had to be postponed to September. As that date approached, it had to be put off again.

Having saved some money for the now aborted holiday, she attempted to spend it on other things but was thwarted here, too.

'I tried to buy a new bra from Big Girls Don't Cry,' she tells me during one of our regular phone chats. 'But they won't accept my email on the site, so I can't get it! I've never had any money, and now that I do I can't fucking spend it.'

My role here, as advisor and court jester, was to soothe. I admit it was a struggle, given the specificity of the information she had just provided.

'Well, apparently big girls do cry,' I tell her.

And we laugh and laugh.

I do not think either she, my sister or I were natural-born funny people. We were certainly bent in that direction by life, however. Humour is a tonic. The darker our lives became across the years, the more we worked to develop a kind of bolt-on system of jokes and laughter, often directed at our own struggle.

Like laughing at an electricity substation during a violent storm, we discovered that making fun of our predicament caused the dire circumstances to lose some of their power.

That, I think, ought to be the final lesson.

It is not as if we sat down as a family and decided to be funny in the face of being well and truly fucked. It rose from the ashes of our existence like a deficient phoenix, covered in soot and looking suspiciously like one of Mum's chickens.

Some time would pass before I discovered the crisp and, at first, confronting philosophy of Albert Camus, especially as he presented it in *Le Mythe de Sisyphe.* Here was an account of the natural absurdity that had coursed through the gutters that ringed our life. Camus gives voice to the smoker's chesty wheeze laugh of our almost comical survival.

The boulder goes up, it goes down. Up, down, up, down.

Wry observation, if not quite happiness, is a radical political act.

'Happiness and the absurd are two sons of the same earth. They are inseparable,' Camus writes. 'The struggle itself toward the heights is enough to fill a man's heart. One must imagine Sisyphus happy.'

Camus traverses impressive territory in his quest to answer the question of whether we should kill ourselves. The answer – no – is not so easily arrived at as it may seem. But it is the correct answer, precisely because the mission is absurd.

'The human heart has a tiresome tendency to label as fate only what crushes it,' he writes. 'But happiness likewise, in its way, is without reason, since it is inevitable.'

Vulnerability, then, is nearer to the Aristotelian concept of a life well lived. Nearer, still, to Nietzsche in its direct call for us to witness the full breadth of human tragedy and success and decide to live anyway. It is here, feet planted in the trembling earth, that we find solace.

It is impossible to finish this book without further reference to the pandemic that shuttered whole countries – the world, even – and livelihoods. It is difficult to ignore the far-reaching consequences of that deadly pathogen as it infected tens of millions of people, killing more than 1.7 million at the time of writing.

To be frank, 2020 feels like some kind of fever dream. It has the scale of a Hollywood blockbuster and, simultaneously, the strange hyper-local manifestation that makes it difficult to tell the difference between the two.

When my brother, Toby, arrived home just before things began to unravel nationally, and in time to build the chook shed, Mum was anxious. One can hardly blame her, given her experience of the last seven or more years trying to ward off drug-addled hangers-on in between the occasional stabbing (one) or axe chase (also singular).

Toby had kicked a psychotic and dangerous meth habit, but his prospects were dim and fading by the day.

'Did you hear the news that the government is going to double the dole?' I said to her down the phone, knowing that Toby was on this very payment.

Mum paused and then replied: 'Don't tell your brother.'

I cackled at the crispness of the phrasing, its direct route from brain to meaning. The layers of it spoke a secret language known only to the few of us, a whole cosmos of understanding in four words. That Toby was in debt so deep he will likely never rescue himself from it, even though he is almost thirty-six and still has time for things to right themselves. That, even though he is living back home again, he will more than likely pay no board, so what's the use in being the first with the news about more money? That more money, in his very specific case, was not necessarily helpful.

We joked because to do otherwise seemed threadbare and slim. *Not again*, we thought on his return, before settling back into the rhythm we knew to be ours. Not long after he had come home, the somewhat new police officer in town pulled Toby over for a licence check. He was riding a different motorcycle almost every other week with no explanation for where he was getting them. When the officer saw Toby's name on the licence, he said: 'Oh, I read your brother's book. It was really good.'

That book, which in part detailed Toby's extensive criminal history and addiction to all sorts of drugs, was Toby's pride and joy even though I suspect he still has not read it.

He rode around town the rest of the day, stoked that he was something of a minor celebrity in his home town. He too, perhaps better than the rest of his immediate family, has learned that things are the way they are and overthinking them can be a curse.

I don't think being funny about difficult situations is defeatist, by the way. It is the opposite of laying down arms. Humour deployed against adversity is a very particular *fuck you* to those circumstances, one that shows up only as a faint blur on enemy radar. It is hard to grip, more trying still to counter.

It is a thing that makes even death insignificant.

When my Uncle Mick died, the funeral was held just outside Dalby. He and his wife – my mum's sister Annie, who went before him – were mad golfers. They lived in a tiny half-tin house that backed onto the golf course at Bell on the Darling Downs, and it was here that their marriage became a type of satire about a working-class couple and a game dominated by preening masochists.

Annie was even smaller than my mum, but she had the kind of density of spirit you might find in a coked-up chihuahua. Mick was borderline mute, or at least that is how he appeared to me when I was a kid. He made eyes at you that indicated either surprise or resignation, and one gets the sense that this, too, is how he dealt with the love of his life.

Mick was the kind of man who learned to exercise his Miranda rights early and it largely served him well.

There was also the pub, which was located a short buggy ride from their home and the golf course, and within this Bermuda triangle much of their best comedy was written.

God, I loved them.

On one night, Mick failed to appear for dinner, so Annie called the pub and asked if her husband was drinking. He was, the bartender said.

With an efficiency only made possible by her diminutive frame, Annie glided to the car in rage and drove to the pub. Here, she stormed inside and confronted Mick and each of his friends individually.

'You're an arsehole, you're an arsehole and you're an arsehole. You're all fucken arseholes,' she yelled at them, before dragging her husband outside.

In a moment of apparent regret, Annie turned on her heel and popped her head back inside the pub.

'Not you, Terry; I'm sorry, you're not an arsehole,' she said.

And that was that.

As the mourners gathered for Mick's funeral and I sat in a pew hurriedly finishing writing my eulogy to him, my usual demeanour blotted with anxiety and grief, cousin Heidi told Mum, my sister and I of the now abandoned plan for his casket.

As she spoke, she handed us a few golf tees.

'These are to throw on the coffin when he goes down,' she said with a calm exactness. 'We thought about throwing golf balls in but thought better of it because they'd all come bouncing back out.'

It's hard to escape the fact that laughing at grisly things is, in itself, sometimes just very funny.

At the wake in Dalby RSL that evening, we all got a little bit drunk and one of Mum's shoes broke. She had to walk through the club with one bare foot to get to the car, and she laughed so hard from the embarrassment she did a little wee. Yes, we were that family. There are those who consider any kind of jape or mockery at a funeral to cross the boundaries of good taste, but those are the people we need to worry about the most. Would you want to go to a funeral with them?

At a certain point, rigidity becomes a safety hazard. The chief structural engineer of the 828-metre 'supertall' Burj Khalifa tower in Dubai says the building moves back and forth some two metres at the very top.

Structural engineer Bill Baker has a term for the art of building tolerance for eddies and whirlpools of air into these structures: it's a matter of 'confusing the wind', he says.

To various degrees, all skyscrapers around the world must move. To be unbendable, in the end, is to shatter. All that commitment to unyielding strength will only take a building, or a person, so far.

I like the poetry of that notion. Vulnerability is a design feature that allows us to confuse the wind. If we take our cues from Camus – and we could do a lot worse, to be frank – the stinging blows of an otherwise meaningless world can be absorbed.

It is not folly or uncaring, neither distasteful nor silly. To make ourselves fully alive we must disrobe before it all.

In his book *Nuptials*, published in 1938, Camus writes:

> I love this life with abandon and wish to speak of it boldly: it makes me proud of my human condition.
>
> Yet people have often told me: there's nothing to be proud of. Yes, there is: this sun, this sea, my heart leaping with youth, the salt taste of my body and this vast landscape in which tenderness and glory merge in blue and yellow.
>
> It is to conquer this that I need my strength and my resources. Everything here leaves me intact, I surrender nothing of myself, and don no mask: learning patiently and arduously how to live is enough for me, well worth all their arts of living.

I am not old. By the time this book becomes a real thing, I will have turned thirty-four.

While I was writing this, stuck in lockdown with my flatmate Séamus, we watched *The Young Pope* in all its gaudy sacrilege. In such escapism, I was not expecting to have the wind knocked out of me when Jude Law's Pope is told: 'Holy Father. You're so young and yet you have such old ideas.'

The line he delivers in response contains a universe: 'You're wrong about that. I'm an orphan. And orphans are never young.'

You'll find no orphan here, though Law's character says a person need not lose their mother and father to become one. In this sense, he uses the word as a catch-all for suffering. Suffering is a wound clock, skipping forward through time.

Yes, of course, I thought. How often we have observed timelessness in the eyes of people who have been hurt. I've seen enough of it myself to know how it leaks out of a person, the way it announces itself behind any mask. There are no right or wrong ways to deal with such collected pain. You might lean into it, as I did for a time, until it has had its spell. It may never leave you. You might leave deliberately on account of it. Lord knows I have been consumed with such notions before; there may still come a time when I am again, such is the nature of things.

All of these approaches may feel true for different people and at different moments. It is the obsidian character of distress that makes it so inscrutable.

But I am here, now, and I have seen with my own twin peepers and more than a segment of my own heart a lifetime's worth of jagged neglect and all that bitter dying and crying, the beast heart of self-loathing and the endless mouth of regret. My siblings and I have laughed at most of it – even in the lower colon of despair – and felt the pale sensations of harm and humour curl around our bodies like enlivened vines. For years, under the bough-rocking grace of Deb Morton, we endured the ache of uncertainty; we moved with the elements because we had to.

We confused the wind.

And I'm damned if I am done with that bamboozling. Throughout, there were pockets of grace and light. Sometimes it was enough to see it only as morning broke, cleaving yesterday from the present. If only for a moment, even thick with the scent of not knowing, it was there. A shimmer of the world as it ought to be.

Oh, it was absurd alright. Unspeakably silly. And unfair! Yes, it was that, too. Anger sometimes broke through like a geyser of boiling water from the earth. I wondered if even the smallest part of a tear on a cheek ever made it back into the atmosphere, so that it might become better acquainted with its life-giving cousins in the clouds. Maybe these were the two sides, I thought,

But mostly, we laughed and turned into the wind and confounded it.

That is what love is, I think. It is turning into the world. Love is taking the soft hide of our selves and handing it over so that we might feel everything. When next you have the chance, go outside at night. Find a quiet spot, if you can, and even better if it is tucked away from the incursions of man-made light.

Tilt your head, as you must, and look at the night sky. You've seen it before, no doubt. But now I want you to take the time to notice every single point of carbonated fizz in the sky. Every last bubble of blazing fire beamed directly to you. Don't skim or skip. Attend to each of them.

Odds are that you alone will focus on one in that precise moment that no other soul on earth is looking at.

It will be as if it were created just for you.

That is love. The everything sent from without and the turning to face it, the feeling of it on a naked patch of very human skin.

It is the overwhelming notion that it was there all along.

Acknowledgements

I love the acknowledgement section of a book. It always feels like such a special glimpse into the real emotional hinterland of the author, more informal than the rigour of the pages before it.

Sorry if this disappoints.

To my mum, Deb, thank you as ever for your irrepressible curiosity and love. You taught us how to see the world. Lauryn, the funniest of us, you make me laugh every day. And Toby, who still finds it within himself to be excited for these books I am sure he has not read; I love that.

My dear Bridie, your no-nonsense friendship and careful input into parts of this book both terrify and sustain me. For the rest of the Jabour family, especially Chris who loaned me his riverside home and desk with frog statue for some writing inspiration, I love you all. And Philomena, thank you for allowing me to furiously type at your gorgeous place as well. Grafton is my second home, as you know. Poor Matt deserves some form of national recognition.

There is Candice, with whom I once plotted a publishing empire based on the as-yet unrealised *Wish You Were Queer* series, I adore you and your dad-joke ministry. And Mon, for how happy she makes you. To the rest of our crew: style icon Georgia Waters, mood icon Sabina Husic, Russian icon Nick Martin. How lucky I am.

My band of Lost Boys – Perry, Tom and Mick – have made the process of this book a dream from start to finish. Fate has a habit of intervening for the best, sometimes. Perry, I am glad it sent us both to a strange by-election for Barnaby Joyce in Tamworth for it was there that I found your friendship. And to your sister, Liv, I long to be as bright and joyous. To Tom, I'm glad Perth spat you out. Thank you for persevering through my bi-weekly meltdowns and your mastery of the meme. And Mick, for making my own coping mechanisms look elegant in comparison. We love you.

There are scores of others, of course. A whole flotilla of extraordinary people who keep me afloat. Dan Nolan and Emily Mulligan, Sam Leckie, Michael Roddan, Anthony Galloway and Christine and Miles. Those included here are as likely to lift me up as they are to absolutely ruin me with a devastating putdown, but that is the bargain we have all struck in such close friendship.

Eric George, my brilliant and amusing buddy, thank you for being a sounding board on all manner of things ridiculous, serious or frequently both at the same time. Shannon Molloy, your star continues to shine.

Mitchell Bingemann, for featuring in the intellectual and comical development of my life, I am indebted. I also have two of your books still and a dead succulent.

My pal Sammy Cochrange has done it again; hanging in there for another year on the Rick train of anxiety and self-deprecation. I don't know how you do it, though I am glad that you do.

Emily Ritchie, for finishing the dinner when the phone rang. And for your bright-eyed candour. For Matthew Shaw, thank you. Your services in access to research have made this project infinitely easier.

To the Stained Daisies, my Kilby crew and all who have joined the ever-growing crowd of those sensations, what an honour to be among it. To Ben Caruso, for encouraging me down to Melbourne on a whim, you are a treasure. My colleagues at the *Saturday Paper* who put up with me while juggling this book and my work commitments are to be commended, especially during the final weeks of 2020 when all the disparate threads of the year became knotted.

And to the charming team at the Story Tree Cafe in Boonah, where I (finally) finished writing and editing this book. Your coffee and warmth kept me going.

There would bc no book without the encouragement and insight of my publisher, Catherine Milne, who first asked me to explain the concept while I was slightly tipsy at Byron Bay. I didn't know then how committed you would become, or how soothing, when I experienced my five or so crises of confidence. To James, for backing Catherine in when the acquisition became a contest, and Alice Wood who has already done so much to champion this project. I'm excited for what comes next.

To my agent, Jeanne Ryckmans, for accomplishing what I thought to be impossible and making me feel sick with wonder at the same time. Your know-how has changed my life. And, with emphasis, gratitude for my editors Maddy James and Lu Sierra. I have been rescued from myself by editors countless times throughout my career. There are no good writers without editors. No point in writing without them. Thank you, so much, for taking the poor soil of this manuscript and turning it into a garden. Maddy, especially, will be long remembered for a sadly now deleted intervention regarding the origins and meaning of the song 'Who Let The Dogs Out'.

Through this whole project I have learned only slightly more about myself as I have about that song and I would not have it any other way.

To the HarperCollins design team for the gorgeous cover of this work, I have been unable to stop staring at it. It's perfect.

My life has been sprinkled with the saving grace of amazing teachers, mentors and friends who have helped shape and form me through adversity. The list is long and growing still, but to each of them who I met at the precise right moments, a truly felt thank you. I hesitate to imagine where I would have ended were it not for your presence at a thousand points of potentially critical failure.

To all of the readers who have been with me since *One Hundred Years of Dirt* for the incredible, enduring reaction to that personal book. In this I have seen, and been able to clarify in my own thinking, the yearning for freedom from pain and hurt that can come through vulnerability. It has been, for me, a turning point.

At last, to Hamish and now Cormac. The new generation, whose inquiring minds are surrounded with love, the way I wish it were for all children. You have both expanded my heart.

List of Sources

INTRODUCTION

Albert Camus, 'Nuptials at Tipasa', *Nipasa*, 1938

Henry Nicholls, 'Celebrity pet: the rediscovery of Charles Darwin's long-lost Galapagos tortoise', *The Guardian*, 12 February 2014

Dr Karl, 'Female hyenas have last laugh', *ABC online*, 15 December 2009

Nicola Davis, 'A huge mouth and no anus – this could be our earliest known ancestor', *The Guardian*, 31 January 2017

James Baldwin, *The Fire Next Time*, Dial Press, 1963

Ludwig Wittgenstein, *Logico-Tractatus Philosophicus*, 1921

Tim Lomas, *Positive Lexicography*, drtimlomas.com/lexicography/cm4mi

TOUCH

Jamie Morgan MD, 'Womb with a view: sensory development in utero', UTSouthwestern Medical Center, 1 August 2017

Margaret Atwood, *The Blind Assassin*, McClelland and Stewart, 2000

Jane Perlez, 'Romania's Communist legacy: "Abortion Culture"', *New York Times*, 21 November 1996

Kate Silver, 'Romania's lost generation: Inside the Iron Curtain's orphanages', *All in the Mind*, ABC, 23 June 2014

Denisa-Adriana Oprea, 'Between the heroine mother and the absent woman: Motherhood and womanhood in the communist magazine *Femeia*', *European Journal of Women's Studies*, 2016

Janice Tomlin, 'Shame of a nation: the story of genocide by neglect', ABC News *20/20*, 1990

Vlad Odobescu, 'Half a million kids survived Romania's "slaughterhouses of souls". Now they want justice', *The World*, Public Radio International, 28 December 2015

Charles Nelson, Nathan Fox and Charles Zeanah, *Romania's abandoned children: Deprivation, brain development and the struggle for recovery*, Harvard University Press, 2014
Coroner's Court of Western Australia, 'Inquest into the death of Peta Susan Doig', 26 February 2015
Divinyls, 'I Touch Myself', song, Virgin Records, 1990
Federal Court of Australia, National Disability Insurance Agency v WRMF, FCAFC 79, 12 May 2020
Rick Morton, 'Exclusive: The seven-year plot to undermine the NDIS', *Saturday Paper*, 5 December 2020
Andrew Griffiths, 'How Paro the robot seal is being used to help UK dementia patients', *The Guardian*, 8 July 2014
Lauren Smiley, '27 days in Tokyo Bay: what happened on the *Diamond Princess*', *Wired*, 30 April 2020
Lillian Hung, Cindy Liu et al, 'The benefits of and barriers to using a social robot PARO in care settings: a scoping review', *BMC Geriatrics*, 23 August 2019
Harry Harlow and Stephen Suomi, 'Social recovery by isolation-reared monkeys', *PNAS*, Vol 68, 1 July 1971
Charles Collingwood, *Mother Love*, CBS Television Network, Carousel Films, 1960
Harry Harlow, 'The nature of love', *American Psychologist*, 1958
David Linden, 'The science of touching and feeling', TED Talk, 2016
Alvin Powell, '"Breathtakingly awful"', *The Harvard Gazette*, 5 October 2010
Franz Wright, *Walking to Martha's Vineyard*, Knopf, 2003

THE SELF

Meera Atkinson, *Traumata*, UQP, 2018
Rick Morton, 'Mental health cost of welfare', *Saturday Paper*, 9 November 2019
Mohan Pabba, 'Evolutionary development of the amygdaloid complex', *Frontiers in Neuroanatomy*, 28 August 2013
Hengameh Marzbani, Hamid Marateb and Marjan Mansourian, 'Neurofeedback: A Comprehensive Review on System Design, Methodology and Clinical Applications', *Basic and Clinical Neuroscience*, April 2016
John Cottingham, Robert Stoothoff and Dugald Murdoch, 'The Philosophical Writings of Descartes', *Cambridge University Press*, 1985
René Descartes, *Discourse on Method*, 1637
Julia Gresky, Elena Batieva, AO Kitova et al., 'New cases of trepanations from the 5th to 3rd millennia BC in Southern Russia in the context of previous research: Possible evidence for a ritually motivated tradition of cranial surgery?', *American Journal of Physical Anthropology*, April 2016
David Chalmers, 'Facing up to the problem of consciousness', *Journal of Consciousness Studies*, 1995
Michael Gazzaniga, Joseph Bogen and Roger Sperry, 'Some functional effects of sectioning the cerebral commissures in man,' PNAS, 1962
George Feifer, 'An Interview with Vladimir Nabokov', *Saturday Review*, 27 November 1976
Michelle Redinbaugh, Jessica Phillips, Niranjan Kambi et al., 'Thalamus Modulates Consciousness via Layer-specific Control of Cortex', *Neurone*, 2020

Cormac McCarthy, 'The Kekulé Problem: Where did language come from?', *Nautilus*, 20 April 2017
Daniel Dennett, *From Bacteria to Bach and Back: The evolution of minds*, WW Norton & Company, 2017
Maggie Schauer, Frank Neuner and Thomas Elbert, *Narrative Exposure Therapy*, Hogrefe Publishing, 2011
Bede, *Ecclesiastical History of the English People*, c. 731
Daniel Dennett, *Consciousness explained*, Little, Brown & Co, 1991
The Matrix: Reloaded, film, Warner Bros. Pictures, 2003
Leo Tolstoy, *The Diaries of Leo Tolstoy*, translated by CJ Hogarth and A Sirnis, Dent, 1917
Baruch Spinoza, *Ethics*, 1677

FORGIVENESS

E. Alex Young, 'In Conversation: Thandie Newton', *Vulture*, 7 July 2020
Wei-May Su and Louise Stone, 'Adult survivors of childhood trauma: Complex trauma, complex needs', *Australian Journal of General Practice*, July 2020
David Whyte, *Consolations: The Solace, Nourishment and Underlying Meaning of Everyday Words*, 2014
Jean Piaget, *The Moral Judgment of the Child*, 1932
Antoine de Saint Exupéry, *The Little Prince*, Reynal & Hitchcock, 1943
Robert D. Enright et al. (the Human Development Study Group), 'The moral development of forgiveness', *Handbook of Moral Behavior and Development*, 1992
Robert D. Enright, 'Piaget on the moral development of forgiveness: Identity or reciprocity?', *Human Development*, January 1994
Robert D. Enright and Joanna North, *Exploring Forgiveness*, The University of Wisconsin Press, 1998
'What South Africa can teach the US about racial justice and reconciliation', *The World*, Public Radio International, 11 June 2020
Bonny Ibhawoh, 'Do truth and reconciliation commissions heal divided nations?', *The Conversation*, 24 January 2019
Luke Pearson, 'What is a Makarrata? The Yolngu word is more than a synonym for treaty', ABC Radio National online, 10 August 2017
Michael Bradley, *Coniston*, University of Western Australia Publishing, 2019
John Cribbin, *The Killing Times*, Fontana/Collins, 1984
Diaries of T.G.H. Strehlow, Centre for Indigenous Family History Studies, www.cifhs.com/ntrecords/ntgeneral/F126_8_1_Anningie.html 2007
Dick Kimber, Coniston Massacre Series, *Alice Springs News*, 2003–2004
The Board of Inquiry, Coniston massacre, January 1929
Bob Plasto and David Millikan, *A Shifting Dreaming*, film, Imago/Endeavour, 1982
'Around the Territory', *Northern Standard*, 14 April 1950, page 8
Short St Gallery, Broome, Western Australia, www.shortstgallery.com.au
Nyadol Nyuon, Twitter, 2020 (Account no longer exists)

ANIMALS

Sandra Baker, Stephen Ellwood, Vito Tagarielli and David Macdonald, 'Mechanical Performance of Rat, Mouse and Mole Spring Traps, and Possible Implications for Welfare Performance', *PLoS One*, 2012

Thomas Nagel, 'What is it like to be a bat?', *Philosophical Review* 83, October 1974
Ella Morton, 'Revisiting the Dystopian Outback World of *Mad Max*', *Slate*, 29 July 2014
Emilia Terzon, 'Alien-looking shrimp of the desert appear in Central Australia after flooding rains,' ABC Radio Darwin online, 13 January 2017
Anne Musser, 'Dinosaurs – Rhoetosaurus brownie', Australian Museum, November 2020
Sarah Hudson, 'Dinosaur fossil changes fortunes for Outback family,' *Weekly Times*, 7 October 2015
Brian Handwerk, 'How Accurate Is Alpha's Theory of Dog Domestication?', *Smithsonian Magazine*, 15 August 2018
Lee Alan Dugatkin, 'The silver fox domestication experiment', *Evolution: Education and Outreach*, 2018
Arrested Development, television series, Season 3, episode 2, 'For British eyes only', Imagine Television, 26 September 2005
Aristotle, *Historia Animalium*, translated by D'Arcy Wentworth Thompson, Clarendon Press, 1910
Claudius Aelianus, *On the Nature of Animals*, translated by A.F. Scolfield, 1958
Eduardo Sampaio, Martim Costa Seco, Rui Rosa and Simon Gingins, 'Octopuses punch fishes during collaborative interspecific hunting events', *Ecology*, 18 December 2020
Peter Dockrill, 'Octopuses observed punching fish, perhaps out of spite, scientists say', *Science Alert*, 21 December 2020
Ed Yong, 'Octopus cares for her eggs for 53 months, then dies', *National Geographic*, 30 July 2014
Katherine Harmon, 'Unusual Offshore Octopods: The weapon-wielding blanket octopus', *Scientific American*, 5 April 2013
Piero Amodio et al., 'Shell Loss in Cephalopods: Trigger for, or by-product of, the evolution of intelligence? A reply to Mollo *et al.*', *Trends in Ecology and Evolution*, 4 June 2019
Piero Amodio et al., 'Grow Smart and Die Young: Why did cephalopods evolve intelligence?', *Trends in Ecology and Evolution*, 13 November 2018
David Attenborough, *Blue Planet II*, film, BBC, 2017
Culum Brown, Martin Garwood and Jane Williamson, 'It Pays to Cheat: Tactical deception in a cephalopod social signalling system', *Biology Letters*, The Royal Society, 4 July 2012
Peter Godfrey-Smith, *Other Minds: The Octopus, the Sea and the Deep Origins of Consciousness*, Farrar, Straus and Giroux, 2016
Sy Montgomery, *The Soul of an Octopus*, Simon & Schuster UK, 2016
Justine Hausheer, 'Meet the magnificently weird Mola Mola', *Cool Green Science*, Nature, 27 November 2017
Amy Strauss, 'How Pistol Shrimp Kill With Bubbles, *That's Life [Science]*, 26 December 2016
Christie Wilcox, 'How a wasp turns cockroaches into zombies', *Scientific American*, 1 May 2017
Ethel Pedley, *Dot and the Kangaroo*, Angus and Robertson, 1899
Dot and the Bunny, film, Yoram Gross Films, 1983

Wislawa Szymborska, 'On Death, Without Exaggeration' from *The People on the Bridge*, translated by S. Baranczak & C. Cavanagh, 1986

Becky Oskin, 'Japan Earthquake and Tsunami of 2011: Facts and information', *Live Science*, 13 September 2017

Thisanka Siripala, 'Japan's 3/11 recovery stalled by Fukushima decommissioning delays', *The Diplomat*, 13 March 2020

'Fukushima Daiichi Accident', World Nuclear Association, updated May 2020, www.world-nuclear.org/information-library/safety-and-security/safety-of-plants/fukushima-daiichi-accident.aspx

Charles Digges, 'Eight years after Fukushima, Japan struggles to trust nuclear power', *Bellona*, 12 March 2019

Sarah Jacobs, '"It feels like we're in jail": Japan spent $12 billion on seawalls after the devastating 2011 tsunami — and now locals are feeling like prisoners', *Business Insider*, 13 March 2018

Ludwig Wittgenstein, *Philosophical Investigations*, translated by GEM Anscombe, 1953

BEAUTY

Iosif Khriplovich, 'The Eventful Life of Fritz Houtermans', *Physics Today*, 1 July 1992

Misha Shifman, *Standing together in troubled times: Unpublished letters by Pauli, Einstein, Franck and others*, World Scientific Publishing, 2017

Viktor Frankl, *Man's Search for Meaning*, 1946

John Williams, 'Theme from *Schindler's List*', performed by Itzhak Perlman and the Boston Symphony Orchestra, 1993

Stephen Dunn, 'Meaninglessness', *Poetry*, February 1996

Leslie Paul, *The Annihilation of Man*, Faber & Faber, 1944

Caleb Daniloff and Robin Berghaus, 'Williams surprises Spielberg', *BU Today*, May 2009

John Sloboda, 'Music Structure and Emotional Response: Some empirical findings', *Psychology of Music*, October 1991

Sergei Rachmaninoff, *Symphony No 2 in E Minor, Op 27*, 1906–07

Ludwig van Beethoven, *Fidelio*, 1805

David Hockney, *Portrait of an Artist (Pool with Two Figures)*, painting, 1972

Louis Leroy, 'The Exhibition of the Impressionists', *Le Charivari*, 25 April 1874

Plotinus, *The First Ennead*, 250 AD, translated by Stephen Mackenna and B.S. Page

Alexander Nehamas, *Only a Promise of Happiness: The place of beauty in a world of art*, Princeton University Press, 2007

Anthony Madrid, 'And Alexander Wept', *Paris Review*, 19 March 2020

Valerius Maximus, Book 8, Chapter 14, 'The Desire for Glory', 31 AD, *Foreign Stories: section 2*, translation by Henry John Walker, 2004

MASCULINITY

Christos Tsiolkas, *Damascus*, Allen & Unwin, 2019

Rob Picheta, 'Kleenex is rebranding its "mansize" tissues as "extra large" after complaints of sexism', CNN, 18 October 2018

Brad Tuttle, '12 products marketed to one gender for no good reason', *Money*, 9 June 2016

Elaine Watson, 'Beyond brogurt … Powerful raises $4m, plans more high-protein innovations', *Food Navigator USA*, 7 November 2017
'The world's first toothpaste just for men', press release, Unilever, 21 February 2014
Bomb Cosmetics, Man Grenade Blaster, bombcosmetics.co.uk/man-grenade-blaster-w-l 2019
Alex Santoso, 'Q-Tips: Men's ultimate multi-tool', *Neatorama*, 15 July 2014
Danielle Braff, 'Marc Cuban takes a chunk of Dudes' bathroom wipes on "Shark Tank"', *Chicago Tribune*, 17 October 2015
Marilyn La Jeunesse, 'Canned wine is marketed to men who need to "shut up and drink"', *Mashable*, 26 November 2015
Inga Korolkovaite, '115 pointlessly gendered products that we can't believe exist', *Bored Panda*, 2019
Ocean Vuong, *On Earth We're Briefly Gorgeous*, Penguin, 2019
Miller McPherson, Lynn Smith-Lovin and Matthew E. Brashears, 'Social Isolation in America: Changes in core discussion networks over two decades', *American Sociological Review*, June 2006
'Men's social connectedness', Beyond Blue, June 2014
Jacqueline Boyle, Rhonda Garad and Helena Teede, 'There's a fundamental need to reverse the "pink recession"', *Lens*, Monash University, 14 December 2020
John Steinbeck, *The Grapes of Wrath*, Viking Press-James Lloyd, 1939
Reiss Smith, 'A straight guy named Kevin had to clarify his sexuality in order to enjoy a sunset. Yes, really', *Pink News*, 16 September 2019
Zöe Quinn, *Crash Override: How Gamergate (nearly) destroyed my life, and how we can win the fight against online hate*, Public Affairs, 2017
Milo Yiannopoulos, 'Am I too old for video games?', *The Kernal*, 2013 (no longer available)
'Report by the majority staff of the House Committee on the judiciary, Materials in support of H. Res 24, *Impeaching Donald John Trump, President of the United States, For High Crimes and Misdemeanors*', 12 January 2021
Organization for Security and Co-operation in Europe, 'Understanding the Role of Gender in Preventing and Countering Violent Extremism and Radicalization That Lead to Terrorism: Good Practices for Law Enforcement', *OSCE*, 26 April 2019
Jess Hill, *See What You Made Me Do*, Black Inc, 2019
Melissa Blasius, 'Horned D.C. protester makes first court appearance, refuses to eat in detention', *ABC15*, 11 January 2021
David Deitcher, *Dear Friends: American photographs of men together 1840-1918*, Abrams, 2001
John Williams, *Stoner*, Viking Press, 1965

LONELINESS

Amy Novotney, 'The Risks of Social Isolation', *American Psychological Association*, May 2019
Sophia Coppola, *Lost in Translation*, film, Focus Features, 2003
Jill Ker Conway, *The Road from Coorain*, Penguin Random House, 1989
Kenichiro Takafuji, 'Japan's first soapland bathhouse for foreigners offers wet and wild fun,' *Tokyo Reporter*, 7 November 2017

Philip Brasor, 'In Japan no one wants to talk about sex education', *Japan Times*, 7 April 2018
Norimitsu Onishi. 'A Generation in Japan Faces a Lonely Death', *New York Times*, 30 November 2017
National Institute of Population and Social Security Research (Japan), 'National Survey on Social Security and People's Life', 2017
Carol Morley, 'Joyce Carol Vincent: How could this young woman lie dead and undiscovered for almost three years?', *The Guardian*, 9 October 2011
Leo Tolstoy, *Recollections & Essays*, Oxford University Press, 1937
Anne-Pascale Le Berre, 'Emotional Processing and Social Cognition in Alcohol Use Disorder', *Neuropsychology*, September 2019
Rick Morton, 'Loneliness ministry recognises toll on modern society', *The Australian*, 20 January 2018
John O'Donohue, *Eternal Echoes: Celtic reflections on our yearning to belong*, Harper Perennial 2000, first published 1998
Olivia Laing, *The Lonely City: Adventures in the art of being alone*, Picador, 2016
Alan Teo and Albert Gaw, 'Hikikomori, A Japanese Culture-Bound Syndrome of Social Withdrawal? A Proposal for DSM-V', *Journal of Nervous and Mental Disease*, June 2010
Takahiro Kato, Shigenobu Kanba and Alan Teo, 'Hikikomori: Experience in Japan and international relevance', *World Psychiatry*, February 2018
Takahiro Kato, Shigenobu Kanba and Alan Teo, 'Hikikomori: Multidimensional understanding, assessment, and future international perspectives', *Psychiatry and Clinical Neuroscience*, 2019
Michael Finkel, 'The Strange & Curious Tale of the Last True Hermit', *GQ Magazine*, 5 August 2015
Ethan Siegel, 'The Salmon Cannon is a Stroke of Scientific and Environmental Brilliance', *Forbes*, 26 August 2019
Douglas Adams, *The Hitchhiker's Guide to the Galaxy: Restaurant at the End of the Universe*, Pan Books, 1980
David Eagleman, *Sum: Forty tales from the afterlives*, Pantheon Books, 2009
Keziah Weir, 'Why Poetry is Having a Moment Amid the Global Quarantine', *Vanity Fair*, 30 April 2020
Libby Sander and Oliver Bauman, '5 Reasons Why Zoom Meetings Are So Exhausting', *The Conversation*, 6 May 2020

KINDNESS

Laia Abril, On Abortion: And the Repercussions of Lack of Access, exhibition, Museum of Sex, New York, February – October 2020
Joel Lovell, 'George Saunders's Advice to Graduates', *New York Times*, 31 July 2013
Andy Gardner, 'Price's equation made clear', *Philosophical Transactions of the Royal Society B*, 9 March 2020
Michael Regnier, 'How Discovering an Equation for Altruism Cost George Price Everything', *Nautilus*, 16 June 2017
Oren Harman, *The Price of Altruism: George Price and the search for the origins of kindness*, W.W. Norton & Company, 2011
Naomi Shihab Nye, 'Kindness' from *Words under words: selected poems*, The Eighth Mountain Press, 1994

John Steinbeck, *The Grapes of Wrath*, Viking Press-James Lloyd, 1939
Esmé Weijun Wang, tweet, 27 June 2020, twitter.com/esmewang/status/1276557187897151488
David Whyte, *Consolations: The solace, nourishment and underlying meaning of everyday words*, Many Rivers Press, 2014
Lee Rowland and Oliver Scott Curry, 'A Range of Kindness Activities Boost Happiness', *Journal of Social Psychology*, 2018
John Rennie, 'How Complex Wholes Emerge from Simple Parts', *Quanta Magazine*, 20 December 2018
Lazyboy, 'Underwear Goes Inside the Pants', song, Universal, 2004
Madeleine Baran, 'Minneapolis pastor discusses struggles with same-sex attraction, plans return to pulpit', MPR News, 3 August 2010
'Mississippi Mayor Greg Davis outed after spending city funds at Toronto gay sex store', Public Radio International online, 20 December 2011
Rhuaridh Marr, 'Former GOP rep. Aaron Schock allegedly had his hand down a man's pants at Coachella', *Metro Weekly*, 17 April 2019
Gwen Aviles, 'Former GOP representative Aaron Schock comes out', NBC News, 5 March 2020
Michael Majchrowicz, 'Conversion therapy leader for 2 decades, McKrae Game disavows movement he helped fuel, *Post and Courier*, 30 August 2019

DYSFUNCTION

Fyodor Dostoyevsky, *The Brothers Karamazov*, Farrar, Straus and Giroux, 2002
Rick Morton, 'How one mine ate a town', *Saturday Paper*, 30 May 2020
Bessel van der Kolk, 'How Trauma Lodges in the Body', interview with Krista Tippett, *On Being*, 11 July 2013
Angela Ebert and Murray J. Dyck, 'The experience of mental death: The core feature of complex posttraumatic stress disorder', *Clinical Psychology Review*, 2004
Stan Zammit, Catrin Lewis, Sarah Dawson et al., 'Undetected post-traumatic stress disorder in secondary-care mental health services: systematic review', British Journal of Psychiatry, 2018
'Forecasting Future Outcomes: Stronger Communities Investment Unit - 2018 Insights Report', New South Wales Government, 5 July 2019
Sebastian Smee, *Net Loss: The inner life in the digital age*, Quarterly Essay 72, 2018
Clementine Ford, 'Evans may be an inspirational athlete, but he's no hero', ABC online, 15 August 2011
Anna Freytag, Katharina Knop-Huelss, Adrian Meier et al. 'Permanently Online – Always Stressed Out? The Effects of Permanent Connectedness on Stress Experiences', *Human Communication Research*, 30 December 2020
Kurt Vonnegut, *The Sirens of Titan*, Delacorte, 1959

DOUBT

Robert J. Dufford, 'All the Ends of the Earth', hymn, Robert J. Dufford, SJ, and OCP Publications, 1981
Nathanael West, *Miss Lonelyhearts*, Horace Liveright, 1933
Anne Maree Jensen and Jeanne Ryckmans, *The Flying Nun: And the Women of the West*, Random House Australia, 1998

Jacqueline Lynch and Tyne Logan, 'Knickers the steer, one of the world's biggest steers, avoids the abattoir thanks to his size', ABC online, 30 October 2018
Richard P. Feynman, *The Pleasure of Finding Things Out: The best short works of Richard P. Feynman*, Perseus Books Group, 1999
John O'Donohue, *Eternal Echoes: Celtic reflections on our yearning to belong*, HarperCollins Publishers, 1998
Christos Tsiolkas, *Damascus*, Allen & Unwin, 2019
Shannon Jenkins, 'Major Victorian government department split in two, new secretary appointed', *The Mandarin*, 30 November 2020
Bill Moyers and Mary Gordon and Colin McGinn, 'Bill Moyers on Faith and Reason', PBS, 30 June 2006
Jeremy Finley, 'FBI agents investigating if 5G paranoia was behind Nashville bombing', Fox10 News, 26 December 2020
'Birth of Science', Francis Bacon Society, 2017, francisbaconsociety.co.uk/francis-bacon/birth-of-science/

NEXT
Ann Finkbeiner, 'Looking for Neutrinos, Nature's Ghost Particles', *Smithsonian Magazine*, November 2010
Kurt Vonnegut, *The Sirens of Titan*, Delacorte, 1959
Bertrand Russell, *The Conquest of Happiness*, Horace Liveright, 1930
Leah Crane, 'LIGO has spotted another gravitational wave just after turning back on', *New Scientist*, 9 April 2019
'Facts: LIGO's extreme engineering', LIGO Laboratory website, www.ligo.caltech.edu/LA/page/facts
Nena, '99 Luftballons', song, Epic, 1983
George Saunders, *Lincoln in the Bardo*, Random House, 2017

BEGINNINGS
Albert Camus, *Le mythe de Sisyphe*, Gallimard, 1942
Friedrich Nietzsche, *Twilight of the Idols*, originally published 1888, translated by Walter Kaufmann, Viking, 1954
Joshua C. Feblowitz, 'Confusing The Wind: The Burj Khalifa, Mother Nature, and the Modern Skyscraper', *Inquiries Journal*, 2010
Albert Camus, '*Nuptials at Tipasa*', *Nuptials*, 1938
Paolo Sorrentin, *The Young Pope*, television series, 2016